Identity and Modernity
in Latin America

To Mercedes and Carolina

Identity and Modernity
in Latin America

Jorge Larrain

Polity

The right of Jorge Larrain to be identified as author of this work has been asserted in accordance with the Copyright, Designs and Patents Act 1988.

First published in 2000 by Polity Press in association with Blackwell Publishers Ltd

Editorial office:
Polity Press
65 Bridge Street
Cambridge CB2 1UR, UK

Marketing and production:
Blackwell Publishers Ltd
108 Cowley Road
Oxford OX4 1JF, UK

Published in the USA by
Blackwell Publishers Inc.
350 Main Street
Malden, MA 02148, USA

ISBN 0-7456-2623-8
ISBN 0-7456-2624-6 (pbk)

A catalogue record for this book is available from the British Library.

Library of Congress Cataloging-in-Publication Data

Larraín, Jorge, 1942–
    Identity and modernity in Latin America / Jorge Larrain.
        p.   cm.
    Includes index.
    ISBN 0-7456-2623-8 (alk. paper) – ISBN 0-7456-2624-6 (pbk. : alk. paper)
    1. Latin America – Civilization – Philosophy.   2. Civilization, Modern – Philosophy.   3. Postmodernism.   4. Identity (Psychology) – Latin America.   5. Ethnicity – Latin America.   6. Social change – Latin America – History.   7. Economic development – Social aspects – Latin America.   I. Title.

    F1408.3 .L246 2000
    980 – dc21   00-040086

Typeset in 10½ on 12 pt Sabon
by Best-set Typesetter Ltd., Hong Kong
Printed in Great Britain by MPG Books, Bodmin, Cornwall

This book is printed on acid-free paper.

Contents

Acknowledgements   viii

Introduction   1

1 Modernity and Identity   12
   Dimensions of modernity   12
   Crises of modernity   17
   Historical trajectories to modernity   19
   The Latin American trajectory to modernity   22
   The three component parts of identity   24
   Personal and collective identities   30
   National identity and the two poles of culture   34
   Different theoretical conceptions of national identity   37
   Globalization and identity   39

2 The Colonial Stage, Modernity Denied: 1492–1810   43
   Cultural reasons for a defeat   43
   The socioeconomic consequences of the conquest   45
   The Spanish and Portuguese construction of the other   48
   The judgement of European philosophy and science   53
   The construction of a colonial identity   60
   The case against the idea of a 'baroque' modernity   66

3 Oligarchic Modernity: 1810–1900   70
   Beginnings and limits of modernization (1810–1850)   70
   The search for a new identity   74

Consolidation of the exporting economy (1850–1900)   78
The new cultural synthesis: positivism and racism   81
The romantic novel and modernism   86
Modernity against old identity   89

4   The End of Oligarchic Modernity: 1900–1950   92
The crisis of oligarchic modernity and populist
  modernization   92
The transition   93
Anti-imperialism and the realist novel   94
Indigenismo   98
The national populist stage   100
The 1930s essayists and the Latin American character   104
Hispanism   108

5   Postwar Expansion: 1950–1970   114
Economic development and modernization   114
The new theories of development and modernization   117
The thought of the Economic Commission for Latin
  America   121
Theories of dependency   123
The problem of national culture and identity   125
The Latin American novel 'boom'   129

6   Dictatorships and the Lost Decade: 1970–1990   133
The crisis of the 1970s and 1980s   133
The ambivalence of Latin American modernity   136
Identity crisis   141
The search for a 'true' identity   142
Neo-Indigenismo   144
Cultural *mestizaje*   148
Identity and popular religiosity   150
Towards a critique of essentialism   157

7   The Neoliberal Stage: 1990 onwards   166
General mechanisms and tendencies of late
  modernity   166
Modernization, identity and neoliberalism
  in the 1990s   171
The identity of Archilocus' hedgehog   176
The ambiguities of postmodernism   181
The power of media and new trends in literature   188

8 Key Elements of Latin American Modernity and Identity **191**

Clientelism, traditionalism and weak civil society 191

Politics, democracy and human rights 194

Authoritarianism, legalistic lack of principle and masked racism 195

Exclusion and solidarity 198

The religious factor 201

Conclusion 206

Notes 208

Glossary 239

Index 241

Acknowledgements

I would like to thank John Thompson, Lynn Dunlop and the editorial board of Polity Press for believing in this book against many odds. Their patience and commitment throughout encouraged me to make it a better book, although I am sure I have not always succeeded. I would also like to thank Ann Bone for her painstaking and impressive work in improving my English.

Some of the material in this book draws on work I have published elsewhere:
    Modernidad, Razón e Identidad en América Latina (Santiago: Editorial Andrés Bello, 1996). Winner of the 1997 Municipal Prize for Literature in the Essay Genre, Santiago, Chile.
    'La Trayectoria Latinoamericana a la Modernidad', *Revista de Estudios Públicos*, no. 66 (Autumn, 1997), pp. 313–33. (ISSN 076-1115)
    'Identidades religiosas, secularización y esencialismo católico en América Latina', in *América Latina: un espacio cultural en el mundo globalizado*, ed. Manuel Antonio Garretón (Bogota: Convenio Andrés Bello, 1999), pp. 220–48.
    'Modernity and Identity: Cultural Change in Latin America', in *Latin America Transformed: Globalization and Modernity*, ed. R. Gwynne and C. Kay (London: Arnold, 1999), pp. 182–202. (ISBN 0340691654)
    'The Concept of Identity', in *National Identities and Sociopolitical Changes in Latin America*, ed. F. Durán-Cogan and Antonio Gómez Moriana (New York and London: Garland Publishing, 2000).

Introduction

This book is about modernity and identity in Latin America, their trajectories and relationships. In themselves these concepts have well-established contents and meanings and are discussed in many currents of thought. This is why the first chapter will be devoted to a theoretical elucidation of these two concepts in a general way. But even mentioning these phenomena in relation to Latin America raises difficult questions. In what sense can anyone speak of a Latin American identity? Is one not assuming a common ground which does not exist among Latin American nations? Can one speak of modernity in Latin America? Is there a specific Latin American trajectory to modernity? What are the relationships between identity and modernity in Latin America? Is not modernity opposed to identity in Latin America?

In Latin America there has always existed a consciousness of Latin American identity, articulated alongside national identities. Much of this stems without doubt from a shared history during the three centuries of Spanish domination, the independence wars in which the criollos of several countries (descended from the Spanish conquerors) fought together, the language, religion and many other common social, economic and cultural factors. There are signs that consciousness about these common elements has been growing in Latin America in recent times. The existence of this Latin American consciousness is shown by four kinds of facts. First, most Latin American authors who have ever written about identity assume that there is a Latin American identity either by directly describing its characteristics or by analysing the identity of their own countries and

extending their affirmations to the rest of Latin America. It is a fact
that Latin American authors frequently and with some ease go from
the national to the Latin American, and conversely.

Second, this is not only true of social science essays that directly
address the issue of identity, but in a different manner is also true of
narrative, poetry, music and television's *telenovelas* or soap operas.
They have also made possible this general perception of a Latin
American identity. In the literary field, for instance, many poets
directly assume a Latin American perspective. Think for instance of
Neruda's *Canto General* and some of the poems of José Martí, Rubén
Darío and César Vallejo. Fernando Ainsa has also mentioned the
recurrence of archetypal towns in the contemporary Latin American
novel such as Rumí in Ciro Alegría's *El mundo es ancho y ajeno*,
Macondo in Gabriel García Márquez's *One Hundred Years of Solitude*, Comala in Juan Rulfo's *Pedro Páramo*, El Valle in all the work
of Adonias Filho, Santa María in the work of Juan Carlos Onetti, etc.
These towns, even though they are all local, have become universally
representative of the Latin American. They are mythical and telluric
places, autarchic island-towns where the demarcation line between
history and myth is diffuse, representing a golden age, a centre which
in its isolation provides stability and happiness, a sense of identity.[1]

Third, that this consciousness does not only belong to intellectuals and novelists but also to common people is shown by the
marked enjoyment of each other's music, novels, dance and soap
operas. Most Latin American cultural practices have an important
and widespread continental impact. Brazilian sambas, Colombian
cumbias, Mexican corridos, Argentinian tangos and Cuban salsa are
not only heard daily on the radio and danced in parties all over Latin
America but they are also expressions with which Latin American
people easily and spontaneously communicate. In television, the soap
operas from Brazil, Argentina, Mexico, Venezuela and Chile are
exported and watched with enormous interest and relish everywhere
in Latin America. This sense of a common identity was also shown
by reactions to football matches in the 1998 World Cup. Although
there was at first a fairly nationalistic frame of mind, as some Latin
American national teams were eliminated allegiances switched to
those which were still in competition. There was a spontaneous sense
of Latin American solidarity which went well beyond any sense of a
solidarity among Europeans. This is significant because more and
more in Latin America the popular consciousness of national identity is mediated by football.

Fourth, it is also true that this sense of regional identity has been
frequently imputed, whether we like it or not, from without, espe-

cially from Europe. From the sixteenth century onwards South America has been spoken of and discursively constructed in Europe as a more or less integrated whole, most of the time endowed with pejorative characteristics. This is true as much of European 'scientific' discourse[2] as of the European popular imaginary. Thus a sense of the Latin American identity also emerges out of the elements shared by the Latin American nations as recognized and imputed to them by the European other. The access to these versions of identity and their internalization by the Latin American people was secured by three centuries of colonial domination.

I have come across only one Latin American author, Mario Sambarino,[3] who puts forward the idea that there is no common cultural ethos between Latin American nations. For him there is no such thing as a Latin American being. The question of a 'Latin American being' – or a 'national being' for that matter – is a false problem because these are historically and culturally generated modes of living, which do not have and cannot have an ontological reality, a kind of immobile legality. Clearly Sambarino's anti-essentialist conception of identity, which is to be praised because it is so rare in Latin America, leads him mistakenly to deny the possibility of a Latin American, or even a national, 'imagined community'. It may be inadequate to look for a Latin American or national essence, but if there is a national, or a Latin American, historically variable and relatively common way of living, then one can speak of a national identity or a Latin American identity as a historically changing 'cultural identity'.

It goes almost without saying that in Latin America there are also very strong national identities, which are mainly defined in relation to Latin American 'others', especially neighbouring countries. In this case differences are stressed more than similarities. Each national identity in Latin America has thus a Latin American common component and a specific one of its own. It is also possible to group some countries within Latin America as sharing more common features with one another than with the rest of the area, due to certain historical conditions, to their geographical location or to similar social factors. A good example would be the case of Argentina and Uruguay. Another one would be Peru and Bolivia. In this way it is possible to distinguish three or four groupings with different characteristics. For instance, Darcy Ribeiro has proposed a classification between 'witness peoples' (Mexico, Central America, Bolivia, Peru and Ecuador), 'new peoples' (Brazil, Venezuela, Colombia, Caribbean nations, Chile and Paraguay) and 'transplanted peoples' (Uruguay and Argentina).[4] Sambarino adopts a classification taken from Elman Service, which is similar to Darcy Ribeiro's: 'Indigenous America'

(Bolivia, Peru, Guatemala, Mexico), '"Mestiza" America' (Paraguay, Brazil, Chile, Colombia, Venezuela) and 'European America' (Uruguay, Argentina).[5]

In chapters 2 to 8, I shall mostly analyse the character and evolution of cultural elements common to all Latin America, along with a few relevant differences between some groups of countries. I shall do this by distinguishing certain historical stages. I shall not be able to study the peculiarities and differences of any national identity in particular, important as they are. Yet it should be borne in mind that in Latin America national identities and the regional Latin American identity, apart from each being a separate kind of collective 'cultural identity', are also closely linked. This is why in studying identity processes in Latin America, it is impossible to avoid a reference to this interplay between national identities and Latin American identity.

The theme of modernity in Latin America is full of historical paradoxes. Latin America was 'discovered' and colonized at the beginning of European modernity and thus became the 'other' of European modern identity. But Latin America was deliberately kept apart from the main processes of modernity by the colonial power. With the process of independence from Spain, Latin America enthusiastically embraced the Enlightenment's ideas, but more in their formal, cultural and discursive horizon than in their political and economic institutional practice, where for a long time traditional and excluding structures were kept in place. When finally political and economic modernity began to be implemented in practice during the twentieth century, cultural doubts began to emerge as to whether Latin America could adequately modernize, or whether it was good to modernize by following European and North American patterns. While in practice modernizing processes were widened, disquieting questions arose as to whether they could be carried out in an authentic manner. Hence, it could be said that Latin America was born in modern times without being allowed to become modern; when it could become modern, it became so only in the realm of programmatic discourse; and when it began to be modern in practice, then doubts emerged as to whether this conspired against its identity.

This book will try to show how from the beginning of the nineteenth century modernity has been presented in Latin America as an alternative to identity, as much by those who have been suspicious of enlightened modernity as by those who badly wanted it at all cost. Examples of the latter are plentiful. Nineteenth-century Latin American positivism, for instance, believed that 'order and progress' could be provided by the Enlightenment's ideas, and precisely because of this, it strongly opposed the prevalent Indo-Iberian cultural identity. In the same way, the optimistic North American theories of modernization in the 1950s believed in an ineluctable transition to modernity through a series of stages, which would eventually overcome the traditional cultural pattern. In many contemporary neoliberal positions in Latin America the idea is implicit that the application of appropriate economic policies is a sufficient condition for an accelerated development which will lead Latin America to a modernity similar to the European or North American one.

But at the same time those who oppose enlightened modernity in the twentieth century do it because of what they see as Latin America's true religious, Hispanic or Indian identity. For indigenistas, the true Latin American identity that modernity has destroyed has lain in the forgotten and oppressed Indian traditions since the conquest. For Hispanists, Latin America's true identity can be found in the Spanish medieval cultural values that have been forgotten by the modernization processes since independence. For religious currents that emphasize the Christian or even Catholic nature of the Latin American ethos, the true identity has not been recognized by the enlightened Latin American elite, but can still be found in popular religiosity. All of them believe that Latin American identity was formed in the past once and for all, and that it was subsequently lost in the alienated pursuit of modernity. All of them believe that as long as modernity takes courses of action which go against the true Latin American identity, it cannot succeed and will lead to failure. Hence they propose that the only way out of this dilemma is to recover the lost essence of Latin America by going back to the Indian cultural matrix or to the values of medieval Hispanic culture or to Christian religion.

Between these two extremes are those like Octavio Paz, Carlos Fuentes and Claudio Véliz who, despite adhering to modernity, try to show how difficult the process of Latin American modernization has been because of the Spanish baroque legacy. For Fuentes 'we are a continent in desperate search of its modernity';[6] for Paz, since the beginnings of the twentieth century we have been 'totally installed in pseudo-modernity',[7] that is to say, for Paz Latin American modernity has never become really genuine. More recently Claudio Véliz has argued in a similar vein that Latin America's stubborn baroque identity has been a major obstacle to its modernization and that only in the 1990s, bombarded by all sorts of consumer artefacts, did it begin to crumble and give way to an Anglo-Saxon kind of modernity.[8]

Somehow the Latin American identity would have delayed the search for modernity, or would have allowed only a semblance of modernity to be reached.

It is interesting to verify that in spite of the many differences among these authors and currents of thought, and their favourable or unfavourable positions with respect to modernity, in all of them modernity is conceived as an eminently European phenomenon which can only be understood from the perspective of European experience and self-consciousness. Which means that it is supposed to be totally alien to Latin America and can only exist in the region in conflict with its true identity. Some oppose it for this reason and others want to impose it in spite of this reason, but both recognize the existence of a conflict that has to be resolved in favour of one or the other. Modernity and identity are polarized as phenomena with opposite roots.

Contrary to these absolutist theories which present modernity and identity in Latin America as mutually excluding phenomena, I would like to show their continuity and interconnection. The same historical process of identity construction is, from independence onwards, a process of the construction of modernity. It is true that modernity was born in Europe, but Europe does not monopolize its entire trajectory. Precisely because it is a globalizing phenomenon, modernity is actively and not passively incorporated, adapted and put in context in Latin America in most institutional and value dimensions. That there are important differences with Europe in these institutional and value processes there is no doubt. Latin America has a specific way of being in modernity. Latin American modernity is not exactly the same as European modernity; it is a mixture, a hybrid, a product of a process of mediation which has its own trajectory; it is neither purely endogenous nor entirely imposed from without, and some call it subordinate or peripheral.[9]

The objective of this book is to show historically how, within the context of some distinct stages, Latin America has been simultaneously constructing its cultural identity and modernizing, and the way in which these two phenomena, in spite of being intimately interconnected, are frequently perceived as opposite alternatives. It will also try to show historically in what respects the Latin American trajectory to modernity differs from or converges with other trajectories, in order finally to arrive at an idea of the specific elements of Latin America's present modernity. In exploring historically the way in which identity and modernity have interacted in Latin America, I will also seek to explain why it is that, in spite of the fact that they are not mutually excluding phenomena, there has been such a marked tendency to consider modernity as something external and opposed to Latin American identity.

At the root of this mistaken perception is the obvious fact that Latin American identity began to be constructed as long ago as 1492, three centuries prior to the first steps towards modernity, which started in earnest with the independence process at the beginning of the nineteenth century. This displacement of modernity with respect to identity could not but promote the idea either that modernity is a late and unwelcome graft on to an already constituted identity, or that identity is an obsolete and traditional obstacle to an indispensable modernization. Corresponding with these two positions, there are inadequate conceptions of both identity and modernity. Oversimplified conceptions of modernity totally conflate its different trajectories into a single European or North American model that has to be repeated. Essentialist conceptions of cultural identity freeze its contents and do not consider real cultural change. The former tend to hold that modernity requires getting rid of an identity that presents many obstacles to its progress. The latter tend to hold that identity must prevail against the encroachments of a foreign modernizing model.

My reading of Latin American cultural history is that an emphasis on oversimplified theories of modernity has alternated with an emphasis on essentialist conceptions of identity, loosely following the alternation of stages of economic expansion and stagnation or recession. Theories of modernization are more widely accepted at times of accelerated development and economic expansion. Theories of identity have emerged with greater force in periods of crisis or stagnation when rates of economic growth and general welfare stall or go down.

My idea is that in Latin America's history there have been 'roughly speaking' six alternating stages, dealt with in chapters 2 to 7:

1 From 1492 to 1810, the colonial stage in which modernity was kept out.
2 From independence to 1900, the age of oligarchic modernity with important economic expansion.
3 From 1900 to 1950, the crisis of oligarchic modernity and beginnings of populist modernization. This is a long and difficult period with many crises and difficulties: two world wars, the Russian revolution and the major depression of the 1930s.
4 From 1950 to 1970, the postwar expansion.
5 From 1970 to 1990, the time of dictatorships, huge international debt and the 'lost decade' with negative growth.

6   From 1990 onwards, neoliberal modernization and economic
    expansion.

   Now, the alternation between identity and modernity in Latin
American history already suggests that questions about identity have
not always had the same relevance. In fact questions about identity
seem to disappear in situations of relative prosperity and stability.
This is not only an empirical fact but there are also good reasons for
this to be so. For identity to become an issue, a period of instability
and crisis, a threat to old-established ways, seems to be required. As
Kobena Mercer has put it, 'identity only becomes an issue when it is
in crisis, when something assumed to be fixed, coherent and stable is
displaced by the experience of doubt and uncertainty.'[10] This does not
mean that in times of stability identity stops being constructed; it only
means that at such times very few people are consciously concerned
with problems of identity – identity tends to be taken for granted.
   Within the six stages that I have delineated there are four moments
or periods of crisis when the issue of identity has acquired importance. Both the Indians and the Spanish undoubtedly raised the first
questions about identity during the critical years of conquest and
colonization. A second important moment when questions about
identity re-emerged was the crisis of independence and the period of
the constitution of the national states. A third critical period emerged
in Latin America between 1914 and the 1930s: in the wake of the
First World War and in the context of a huge international depression in the world capitalist system, the oligarchic rule of the Latin
American landowners began to crumble and the newly mobilized
middles classes and working classes came to challenge the old system.
A fourth crucial period can be detected around the 1970s: the exhaustion of populist regimes, progressive industrial stagnation and the
radicalism of the working classes led to a series of military coups in
many countries. I shall explore cultural production at these moments
with particular attention in order to ascertain the way in which the
Latin American identity was constructed.
   Most Latin American societies are not culturally unified and
despite some central forms of integration and synthesis, which
undoubtedly exist, cultural differences are still very important. These
are more accentuated in countries with an important Indian and
black ethnic component like Peru, Bolivia, Mexico,[11] Venezuela,
Brazil and Central America in general. In these plural societies there
exists an enormous cultural diversity. But such cultural differences
also exist, although to a lesser degree, in more homogeneous coun-

tries like Chile, Argentina and Uruguay. After independence, the new republics and their ruling classes tried very hard to construct not only a national state and a viable economy but also a sense of national identity. This national identity would respond to a national culture which had still to be constructed and which, it was hoped, would integrate the best elements and traditions of the existing ethnic cultures. But this, of course, was not a natural, spontaneous or ideologically neutral process. It was a very selective and excluding process, conducted from above, in which it was decided what to keep and what to ignore. This started with the adoption of Spanish as the national language (which means that many hundred Indian languages were condemned to second place or to extinction), but went on to cover many other cultural aspects including religion, art, etc.

Because of the original and persistent cultural heterogeneity, it can be argued that in most Latin American countries the state had to play a crucial role in the construction of national identities. It fell to the recently created Latin American states to create a sense of national unity and a national culture, in countries that after the independence wars were barely integrated. Hence to speak of national identities in Latin America is to speak of power relations, of ruling classes, which used the centralizing powers of the state and selectively decided what was going to count as national culture and what not. The history of Latin American national identities is closely interwoven with the interests of its ruling classes in their relationship with the state.

Any book on a collective identity, especially one that covers more or less half a continent, has to face some big methodological difficulties and decisions. A first important problem has to do with the kind of source material to be used in the analysis and the limits of the enterprise. Ideally, a complete book on Latin American identity should take into account all aspects of culture, that is to say both the more rigorous theoretical, scientific and artistic expressions of culture and the people's whole range of modes of life, customs, values and forms of entertainment. There is no doubt that identity is influenced by and expressed through all aspects of life: art, film, economics, politics, media (television, radio, newspapers), popular religion, ways of life, novels, poetry, painting, popular art, etc. But obviously any single work cannot hope to be as comprehensive as that, not just because there will be fields in which the author will not have the necessary expertise, but also because to do justice to each domain would require more than the space available in a single book. In other words, it is inevitable that one has to make some choices and privilege what one hopes are the most representative areas.

There are, for instance, those who deal with Latin American cultural identity exclusively from the point of view of literature. Even more, one of them maintains that

> it can be said without exaggeration that for the most part the Iberoamerican cultural identity has been defined by its narrative ... Literary fiction has been able to go beyond any anthropology treatise or sociological study in the perception of reality. Statistical data and objective information are most of the time secondary in the face of what can be evoked by the power of images and the suggestions of a metaphor.[12]

This is a pretty widespread view in some intellectual quarters outside Latin America. Although it may be true that sometimes literature's images and metaphors teach one more about a country or region than many sociological essays, I do not agree that identity in the Latin American case has been for the most part defined by literature. Literature is only one expression among others, although it is perfectly legitimate for a book to choose this angle as a way to study Latin American identity.

I have chosen a different path, probably determined by the fact that I am a sociologist. Basically, what my book does is to reconstruct the way in which the social sciences have directly dealt with the problem of identity and modernity in Latin America. I do not mean to exhaust the issue of identity or culture in Latin America, but only to trace the evolution of the complex relationship between identity and modernity as it has been seen and discussed by the Latin American social sciences. I understand social science in a wide sense, including essays and works of a philosophical, historical, sociological, political, economic and anthropological character. Although I believe this is a legitimate option, limited, but valid in itself, I have sought to enrich this approach with some secondary references to literature, religion and the role of the media in the various stages of Latin American development in order to present a more complete picture which includes at least some cultural practices. In so far as religion is concerned I shall not be concerned with Umbanda or Santeria, important as they may be, but with the main tendencies: Catholicism and the Pentecostal challenge because these have direct relevance for the issues of modernity and modernization in the area. I am conscious of the limitations of this effort. Still, although the social sciences, literature, religion and the media do not exhaust the cultural complexity of Latin America, I hope that by focusing on them I shall provide an account which will be representative and expressive of such complexity.

A second important problem has to do with the heterogeneity of Latin America, which not only includes many different nations of the Hispanic tradition, from the Caribbean to the extreme south, but also a giant country, Brazil, which belongs to the Portuguese tradition. Although the Hispanic and Portuguese traditions are not absolutely dissimilar, it is true that many works on Latin America have concentrated on Hispanic America and have tended to ignore Brazil – which, after all, is practically half the continent (constituting the eighth biggest economy in the world) and has an enormous cultural richness of its own. I consider Brazil an important part of Latin America, but the problematic of Latin American identity and modernity cannot be reduced to any single country, important as it may be. Yet obviously Brazil's sheer weight and importance within Latin America warrants some kind of special treatment. I am no expert in Brazilian cultural and socioeconomic processes but I shall try to incorporate as much as possible and whenever possible some elements drawn from Brazilian literature and social sciences. This, I am sure, will not be enough, but is more than I shall do for any other specific country of the Hispanic tradition.

1
Modernity and Identity

Prior to studying the issues of modernity and identity in Latin America it is necessary to clarify, if only very briefly, some theoretical aspects related to these concepts in order for the reader to know what I shall understand by them and where I stand in relation to conflicting theoretical traditions.

Dimensions of modernity

Modernity is a complex and multidimensional phenomenon, which requires to be studied from a variety of angles. Although the first writings showing an awareness of modernity as something new appear fairly early in the work of Machiavelli, Bacon and Descartes, the idea of modernity was given a decisive formulation in the discourse of the Enlightenment in the eighteenth century. The emergence of modernity is thus associated with a particular time (the eighteenth century) and a particular geographical place (Europe). The philosophical discourse of the Enlightenment understood modernity on the basis of key ideas such as freedom, tolerance, science, progress and reason, and in opposition to metaphysics, superstition and religion.

The ideas of freedom and individual autonomy at all levels were particularly important. When Kant wanted to define what Enlightenment was about, he asserted that it was basically related to autonomy of thought, 'to use one's own understanding without the guidance of another'.[1] For Hegel, too, freedom and subjectivity were the very foundation of modernity and for this reason he could say, 'the principle of the modern world is the freedom of subjectivity.'[2] Freedom appears as the basic and inalienable human right. At the economic level it means the possibility of pursuing one's own interests within a free market; at the political level it means the possibility for each individual to participate with equal rights in the formation of the political will; in the private sphere it implies ethical autonomy and the possibility of self-realization.[3]

However, as Wagner warns, this emphasis on subjective freedom is accompanied and virtually constrained by the recognition that there are also collective ends, common objectives and values that exist prior to individuals, that should limit individual freedoms. This is the source of the ambiguity that surrounds modernity.[4] And this very ambiguity has sometimes allowed very unilateral interpretations of modernity. Touraine, for example, has argued that for a long time modernity was defined fundamentally as a function of instrumental reason, science and technology, and that this other dimension of subjectivity, freedom and creativity has been concealed and subordinated in spite of being half of a complete idea of modernity.[5] Hence the objective of his critique is to 'delink modernity from a historical tradition that has reduced it to rationalization, and introduce the theme of the personal subject and subjectivity'.[6]

The ideas of freedom, tolerance, science, progress and reason were also crucial to Marx, Weber and Durkheim, who contributed to the foundation of sociology in the late nineteenth century. Their theories could be said to be important attempts at understanding modernity. Each of them underlined a different angle of modernity. For Marx, what was at the basis of modernity was the emergence of capitalism and the revolutionary bourgeoisie, which led to an unprecedented expansion of productive forces and to the creation of the world market. Durkheim tackled modernity from a different angle by following the ideas of Saint-Simon about the industrial system. Although the starting point is the same as in Marx, feudal society, Durkheim emphasizes far less the rising of the bourgeoisie as a new revolutionary class and very seldom refers to capitalism as the new mode of production implemented by it. The fundamental impulse to modernity is rather industrialism accompanied by the new scientific forces. In the work of Max Weber, modernity is closely associated with the processes of rationalization and disenchantment of the world. These processes entail that

> there are no mysterious incalculable forces that come into play, but rather that one can, in principle, master all things by calculation. This

means that the world is disenchanted. One need no longer have recourse to magical means in order to master or implore the spirits, as did the savage, for whom such mysterious powers existed.[7]

Each one of these three sociological versions contributes an insight into crucial aspects of modernity, thus confirming its multidimensional character. But there is more. Modernity could also be understood as a form of self-consciousness, as a specific mode of life and as a vital experience. As a form of self-consciousness it expresses the consciousness of an epoch which considered itself new *vis-à-vis* an obscure and stagnant past. According to Habermas, Hegel was the first philosopher who developed a clear concept of modernity precisely because he spoke of it, in a historical context, as a new age.[8] Modernity does not respect its own past and regards itself as the result of a transition from the traditional to the new. Benjamin too defined modernity as 'the new in the context of what has always been there', as a discontinuity of experience which is related to the past.[9] This novelty is related to a powerful feeling of self-confidence and superiority in respect of both its past and other societies which are considered to be backward. According to Bauman, this faith in its own principles and in the superiority of its own mode of life has led the European intellectual elite to considering European modernity as the point of reference for the interpretation of history, as the measure of other forms of life which appear immature, incomplete, underdeveloped or inferior.[10]

This feeling of superiority in respect of backward societies is not merely the result of a casual or *ex post facto* comparison, but is connected with the way in which modernity itself was born. It is precisely when Europe 'discovers' America that it can affirm itself as the centre of world history. America was the first periphery of modern Europe. As Dussel has put it, 'modernity as such was "born" when Europe was in a position to pose itself against an other, when, in other words, Europe could constitute itself as a unified ego exploring, conquering, colonizing an alterity that gave back its image of itself.'[11] The discovery and conquest of America is therefore 'a part of the process of the constitution of modern subjectivity itself'.[12]

Yet modernity's self-consciousness was not acquired in one go and has evolved historically. Berman has distinguished three phases in the history of modernity.[13] From the beginning of the sixteenth century to the end of the eighteenth century the levels of consciousness are low. The first writings which show some consciousness about modernity are still struggling to find the appropriate language to express the new reality, which they do not fully understand. The second

phase, starting with the revolutionary wave of the end of the eighteenth century, spans the whole of the nineteenth century. In this
period the European public shares the experience of living in a new
and revolutionary epoch. The very idea of modernity receives its
definitive formulation with the enlightened discourse of the eighteenth century, which highlights the new ideas of science, progress
and reason.[14] The third phase, in the twentieth century, witnesses
the expansion of the modernizing processes all over the world, with
the consequent development of a universal consciousness about
modernity.

Another dimension of modernity has been explored by Giddens,
who has argued that 'modernity refers to modes of social life or
organisation which emerged in Europe from about the seventeenth
century onwards and which subsequently became more or less worldwide in their influence.'[15] These modes of life combine democracy
with industrialism, general education with a mass culture, world
markets with big bureaucratic organizations. They are characterized
by their accelerated pace of change, by their globalizing tendencies,
by their reflexivity and by their new institutions. Giddens argues that
modernity is separated from the past by three main discontinuities:
first, the accelerated pace of change which characterizes modern societies; second, the wide scope of change processes which become
global; and third, the intrinsic nature of modern institutions which
cannot be found in the past.[16]

To these three discontinuities mentioned by Giddens I would add
a more fundamental philosophical one: modernity made the human
being the centre of the world, the measure of all things, as against
the old theocentric worldview which prevailed in medieval times. The
human being becomes 'the subject': the basis of all knowledge, the
master of all things, the necessary point of reference for all that goes
on. The world ceases to be an order created by God and becomes
'nature', with its own autonomous logic which the subject must know
in order to use it.

I think it is important to understand that all these areas of discontinuity manifested in new and specific modern institutions and
social practices were not created overnight and established in a
sweeping general process on all fronts at once. Wagner has quite
appropriately distinguished between the project of modernity as
expressed in the organized discourse of philosophers, which constructs a true imaginary of modernity, and the social practices and
modern institutions which each society has really managed to implement and develop. The discourse of modernity has always been more
advanced and complete than the actual social practice and institu-

tionalization of modernity in concrete societies. As Wagner puts it, ' "modernity", so to speak, had very few citizens by 1800, not many by 1900, and still today it is hardly the right word to characterize many current practices.'[17]

Modernity is also a vital experience. This aspect has been highlighted in contemporary times by Marshall Berman, David Frisby and David Harvey,[18] but its origins can be traced back both to Baudelaire and Simmel. In his famous essay of 1863, 'The Painter of Modern Life', Baudelaire stated that 'by "modernity" I mean the ephemeral, the fugitive, the contingent, the half of art whose other half is the eternal and the immutable.'[19] Simmel, in his turn, very much insisted on the idea of modernity as a vital experience that privileged the inner feelings of individuals in the face of a complex and changing world. This is why Simmel could define the essence of modernity as 'psychologism, the experiencing and interpretation of the world in terms of the reactions of our inner life, and indeed as an inner world'.[20] But this new kind of subjectivism is not purely positive; it is also a kind of retreat from the tensions that characterize modern life. In analysing two of the most important sites of modernity – the advanced money economy and the metropolis – he detects 'the increase in nervousness and the preponderance of an inner world as a retreat from excessive external stimuli'.[21]

The emergence of modernity is thus associated with an experience of mobility and social change, with a sense of dynamism; it expresses an overwhelming sense of ephemerality, fragmentation, contingency and chaotic change.[22] Modernity not only breaks abruptly with the past but is also characterized by a permanent process of internal ruptures and fragmentation. On the other hand, modernity nevertheless finds in reason and science a sense of the universal and necessary.[23] The simultaneous emphasis on change and science is manifested in what García Canclini calls the renovating project of modernity: 'the pursuit of incessant innovation and improvement typical of a relation with nature and society which is free from all sacred prescription as to how the world should be'.[24]

The vital experience of ephemerality and contingency becomes acute in times of more accelerated change and crisis, to such an extent that reality may be experienced as chaotic and feelings of disorientation and fragmentation can overwhelm individuals. These feelings, fruits of the exacerbation and radicalization of the vital experience of modernity, have led some contemporary authors to put forward the idea that modernity is at an end and is being replaced by postmodernity. At first, though, they merely contributed to a more critical appraisal of the process of change without sight being lost of its positive aspects. This was clearly so in the cases of Marx, Weber, Durkheim and Freud, for whom the vision of modernity as fundamentally dynamic and progressive had to be balanced by a more complex and critical analysis.

In effect, for Marx the positive experience of change and constant development is complemented by the negative experience of the reiterated destruction of many developmental achievements in the increasingly frequent and profound crises of capitalism. Weber, who described so well the process of the rationalization and disenchantment of the world in the West, also warned that the triumph of instrumental rationality did not lead to a realization of freedom but rather to an 'iron cage' of bureaucratic rationality from which there was hardly any escape. Durkheim, in his turn, although very clear about the advantages of industrialism, was aware that the rapidity with which industrialization had occurred could make society deviate from its natural course to organic solidarity, thus producing anomie, inequality and inadequate organization. Freud, too, while basically trusting science and reason, radically challenged the modern belief in a conscious subject fully in command of nature and of the self, by showing the role of the unconscious and instinctive forces that the subject cannot always control.

Little by little, though, the critiques of modernity became more radical and unilateral. Nietzsche, for instance, treated reason, truth and science as mere expressions of the will to power that is there for the enhancement of life. Influenced by him, Adorno and Horkheimer carried out a profound critique of the Enlightenment: its attempts at dominating nature had ended up subjecting human beings themselves to the domination of things. This idea was later developed by Marcuse in his critique of the consumer society and of one-dimensional man: technological reason had ceased to be in contradiction with domination and had increasingly become its new source of legitimacy. While the Marxist, Weberian and Freudian critiques maintained their faith in the unfulfilled promises of modernity, the Nietzschean current that reaches up to postmodernism today via the Frankfurt School questions the project of modernity itself.

Crises of modernity

I have already mentioned the fact that the progress of modernity has been uneven and that the impact of modern ideas did not always achieve the immediate implementation of modern social practices and institutions. The problem arises partly because of the utopian nature of many of the liberal ideas that unilaterally stressed the idea of freedom and autonomy. As Wagner has put it, 'the socially danger- ous openness of modernity was well recognized. As a consequence, the foundations of such society were only very incompletely elabo- rated in practice, and means were developed to contain the modern project.'[25] The exclusion of women from public life and the treatment of the working classes as 'dangerous classes' having to be controlled can be explained in this way.

The discourse of modernity was clear about individual rights, democracy, freedom and universal suffrage. Yet for a long time the vote was limited to bourgeois tax-paying white men. The incor- poration of women and the working class to the political system was the result of hard struggles and not a gratuitous concession of liberal modernity. It was this initial contrast between the promises of the modern discourse and the excluding tendencies of capitalist European societies that led to the emergence of important critiques of modernity.

The ambiguities of the modernization process, with its discursive promises and practical exclusions, the increasingly contradictory character of the capitalist economy which underpinned it, plus the very critiques which these inconsistencies brought about, led to what Wagner has called the first crisis of modernity. From the beginning of the twentieth century a process of the revision of modernity started in which the 'social question' increasingly assumed a fundamental importance. The first legislation protecting, enfranchising and regu- lating labour was introduced under the pressure of the increasingly organized working class. Liberal principles were subjected to critical scrutiny, especially after the slump of the 1930s. It was now increas- ingly thought that the state had a direct responsibility for education, health and social security, and a strong full-employment economy which could support them. This crisis led after the Second World War to what Wagner has called 'organized modernity', the golden epoch of capitalism from 1945 to 1973. During this period, dominated from an economic perspective by Keynesian thought, the population was well integrated into trade unions and parties, well protected by an increasingly complex welfare state, and all this was based on a mass consumption economy sustained by large-scale technological systems.[26]

As is well known, this stage of stability, economic growth and con- solidation of organized modernity nevertheless came to a halt soon after the beginning of the 1970s, and modernity plunged once more into a crisis. At the root of this second crisis of modernity was an accumulation problem. The weight of state expenditure on welfare became difficult to sustain, the rate of profit declined, investment diminished and unemployment not only went up but also became a chronic problem. The many regulations that conditioned the trade unions and industrial concerns began to be questioned as anachronistic and interfering. New, more flexible regimes of accumulation, employment and production began to prevail. Some authors even speak of the emergence of a new stage: 'disorganized capitalism'.[27] However, I agree with Wagner that the thesis of disorganized capitalism may be interesting in so far as it shows the break-up of an organized regime, but that it is rather poor in trying to offer an understanding of the new practices and emergent structures, because 'the alleged disorganization is in fact accompanied by strong reorganization attempts and, indeed, elements of the emergence of a new global order.'[28]

Is this second crisis a terminal crisis of modernity? This is the question that is hotly debated these days. The postmodernist theses certainly interpret the crisis in this sense, and argue that the new stage being opened up before us is a postmodern one in which reality has become fragmented or even, in certain extreme positions, dissolved. Others, like Giddens and Wagner, with whom I agree, argue against this position and accuse postmodernism of not seriously considering the actual situation of the human beings who must act in real social contexts.[29]

Historical trajectories to modernity

From the point of view of its historical evolution, modernity is a complex process that follows various routes.[30] It is frequently believed that modernity is an essentially Western European phenomenon and it is forgotten that its very globalizing tendency makes it expand all over the world, thus forcing it to connect with different realities and to acquire different configurations and trajectories. No doubt, modernity was born in Europe and Europe became a necessary point of reference for the processes of modernization in the rest of the world, but modernity has followed different routes in Japan and South East Asia; in North America and Australia; in Africa; and in Latin America.[31] Thus at least five routes to modernity can be distinguished which diverge, especially at the beginning, but which, as globalization expands, start to converge. To make a full analysis of these five trajectories is beyond the scope of this book. That is why,

after mentioning in a very brief and general manner some characteristics which distinguish the North American, Japanese, African and
European trajectories, I shall concentrate on the Latin American
route.

The North American trajectory to modernity is historically the
closest to the European one and is the result of a veritable cultural
transplant to another land.[32] But it differs from the European route
in that its initial progress was hindered by the English colonial power
until independence. Once independence was achieved, the process of
constructing modernity continued to be different from the European
one because the United States began without the burden of the 'old
regime'. Therefore, it did not have the same restrictions on political
participation and the 'social question' of welfare and social legislation for the working class arose only in a very attenuated way.[33]

The African trajectory to modernity has been very different
because it began with a colonial imposition of capitalism before the
end of the nineteenth century. The expansion of the British Empire
destroyed by force the traditional modes of production and tribal
modes of life. While Latin American modernity commenced with
independence at the beginning of the nineteenth century, African
modernity started with Africa's colonization and developed under the
colonial powers until the second half of the twentieth century. It
suffers therefore from all the traumas and instabilities which stem
from a very close colonial situation. An important problem of African
modernity has been that many local countries are artificial creations,
a result of the colonial powers demarcating territories for their own
convenience without taking into account the important tribal and
cultural divisions which still subsist.

Japan has also had a special trajectory to modernity which was
pushed forward by its own traditional dominant class as a way of
avoiding the colonizing designs of the West. The process started
well into the nineteenth century with the Meiji restoration of 1868.
This new elite wanted to keep a traditional mode of life but to construct a modern economy and state. The Meiji elite considered the
transition from a semifeudal system to a modern economy a necessity for national survival. Without modernization the Europeans
would end up conquering the country and creating a new colony, as
it was happening elsewhere in Asia. The former isolationist policy of
the Tokugawa regime had been successful for a while, but by the
middle of the nineteenth century European countries were already
aggressively 'opening up' the whole of Asia to international trade
and had forced Japan to sign a number of treaties which conceded

commercial privileges to foreigners. The Meiji reaction was to try to oppose foreign penetration by adopting the same foreign methods and instruments.

European modernity began incipiently out of endogenous processes around the sixteenth century and was consolidated with the Enlightenment in the eighteenth century. It could be said that the European trajectory to modernity evolved in five stages. From the beginning of the sixteenth century to the end of the eighteenth century one finds a founding stage where modernity existed more in the ideas of some philosophers, and where material and political progress as well as levels of general consciousness were low. The second phase, starting from the end of the eighteenth century revolutionary wave, covered most of the nineteenth century. On the economic front it was characterized by the industrial revolution and it was this process and the organized struggles of the working class that led to the political opening up of the system. In this period the Enlightenment ideas configured more precisely the meaning of modernity. Political life began to democratize and a wider public shared the experience of living in a new and revolutionary epoch. However, the distance between the project of modernity as an organized discourse establishing a true imaginary of modernity, and the modern social practices and institutions which each society actually developed and implemented was still huge.[34]

It is partly for this reason that the third stage, from 1900 to 1945, was a phase of crisis and transition. The ambiguities of the modernizing process, with its rhetorical promises and practical exclusions, and the very criticisms that these inconsistencies attracted, led to a process of the renovation of modernity in which the 'social question' assumed a fundamental importance.[35] Liberal principles were subjected to critique and the creation of a welfare state for all citizens was brought on to the agenda. These ideas were consolidated in practice in a fourth stage, which runs from 1945 to 1973. This was what Wagner has called 'organized modernity', the golden epoch of capitalism.[36] Nevertheless, this phase of stability and economic growth finished towards the end of the decade of the 1960s, and modernity once more entered a period of crisis. At the root of this second crisis of modernity was an economic problem of declining accumulation and excessive state expenditure. In the 1990s, the contours of a new, neoliberal stage began to appear in which a post-Fordist[37] regime of accumulation was entrenched. Universal state-supported welfare and full employment were no longer considered to be fully achievable goals and were partly abandoned.

The Latin American trajectory to modernity

As I anticipated in the Introduction, I am going to distinguish five stages in the Latin American trajectory to modernity, briefly describing them here and more fully exploring them in chapters 3–7 of this book.

(1) *From independence to 1900: oligarchic modernity* Latin American processes of modernization start later than the European and North American ones, at the beginning of the nineteenth century, with the process of independence – Spain and Portugal, the colonial powers, having prevented their expansion for at least three centuries. The ideas of the Enlightenment exercise an important influence on these modernization processes but they have to confront the resistance of the Indo-Iberian cultural pole, which has been consolidated during the three centuries of colonial life. Although the new ideas bring about the beginnings of many changes in politics and culture, the social order remains basically untouched. This is why the first stage of modernization during the nineteenth century may be called oligarchic.

(2) *From 1900 to 1950: the crisis of oligarchic modernity and populist modernization* The second stage during the first half of the twentieth century is connected with and reflects the first crisis of European modernity. But the consequences of the crisis are specific to Latin America: the oligarchic power begins to crumble, the so-called 'social question' comes to the fore, new populist regimes emerge which widen the franchise and incorporate the middle classes into government, and processes of import-substituting industrialization are initiated. Thus, while in Europe a crisis of liberal industrialism is experienced, in Latin America it is the prevailing oligarchic and aristocratic export-oriented system that enters into its terminal phase, and incipient industrialization processes start with some success. Whereas in Europe bourgeois industrialism brought about the end of aristocratic rule, in Latin America the end of the oligarchic regime occurs before industrialization. This is connected with the emergence of populist regimes and the development of clientelistic political relations.

(3) *From postwar to 1970: industrial expansion* The third stage, from the end of the Second World War, consolidates democracies with wider participation and important processes of modernization of the

Latin American social and economic base. Among them industrialization and expanded patterns of consumption, education and urbanization should be mentioned. The expansion of the mass media
(including television) and of radical political movements seeking
profound structural reforms are also noteworthy.[38] Theories of
modernization and the thinking of the Economic Commission for
Latin America are recognized and applied everywhere. Most states
develop interventionist and protectionist policies that control most of
economic life, but also introduce some aspects of a welfare state in
health, social security and housing. In spite of all this, the benefits of
modernity continue to be highly concentrated and the people at large
continue to be excluded.

(4) *From 1970 to 1990: dictatorships and the lost decade*   By the
end of the 1960s a new crisis begins which coincides with the second
crisis of European modernity. The process of industrialization and
development loses its dynamism and social and labour agitation
become widespread. While in Europe right-wing governments are
elected which seek to limit trade union power and state expenditure,
in Latin America the challenge of the Chilean socialist experiment
and the exhaustion of other political experiments of the left precipi-
tate a wave of military dictatorships which do the same, only in a
more drastic and authoritarian way. This shows the precariousness
of Latin American modern political institutions compared with the
European ones. They are incapable of channelling and absorbing
political turmoil within a framework of stability.

(5) *From 1990 onwards: neoliberal modernization*   The stage
which opens up after the end of dictatorships continues with, and
accelerates, economic and political modernization under the influence
of an already consolidated neoliberal ideology. Free market and open
economy policies produce in the first instance a significant diminution of industrial production and industrial employment. Only
Mexico and Brazil, the biggest countries in the area, manage, after a
while, to expand their industrial exports, thus compensating for the
flood of imports from foreign manufacturers. This is in sharp contrast to the trajectory in Asia, where the state was from the beginning very keen on promoting leading technologies and industrial
exports.

These economic processes occur now in a new political context
that revalues democracy, participation and respect for human rights.
Dictatorships all but disappear from the Latin American horizon in

the 1990s. In this way it can be appreciated that the Latin American trajectory to modernity is different from other models, in spite of sharing many features. It can also be seen that with the acceleration of globalization different trajectories begin to converge, so much so that in general terms they have the most recent stages in common, even though within them there are specific repercussions and consequences.

The three component parts of identity

Arising from modern philosophical thought a confusion has existed between two notions of identity, one referring to individual sameness and the other referring to qualitative identity.[39] The former stems from the Aristotelian and scholastic metaphysical traditions, which conceived of identity as one of the fundamental first principles of being and as a logical law of thought: every being is identical with itself and two contradictory propositions cannot be true or false at the same time. Qualitative identity seems to be a more appropriate conception for sociology inasmuch as it refers to a quality or conjunction of qualities with which a person or group sees themselves intimately connected. Yet it is possible to distinguish two different versions of it. First, there is a subjectivist position that conceives of identity as emerging from personal dispositions and which neglects the role of the social environment.[40] Second, from Marx onwards many sociologists and social psychologists have developed a conception whereby the social expectations of others play a crucial role in identification with some qualities.

If identity is not a given innate essence but a social process of construction we need to identify the constitutive elements from which it is constructed. I propose the idea that these elements are three. First, individuals define themselves, or identify themselves with some qualities, in terms of some shared social categories. In forming their personal identities most individuals share certain group allegiances or characteristics – such as religion, profession, gender, class, ethnicity, sexuality, nationality – which are culturally determined and contribute to specifying the subject and its sense of identity. In this sense it can be affirmed that culture is one of the determinants of personal identity. All personal identities are rooted in collective contexts culturally determined. This is how the idea of cultural identities emerges. Each of these shared categories is a cultural identity. In modern times the cultural identities which have had the most important influence on the formation of subjects are class, professional and national identities.

Second, there is the material element that in William James's seminal idea includes the body and other possessions capable of providing the subject with vital elements of self-recognition. In his words:

> It is clear that between what a man calls *me* and what he simply calls *mine* the line is difficult to draw . . . In the widest possible sense . . . a man's self is the sum total of all that he can call his, not only his body, and his psychic powers, but his clothes and his house, his wife and his children, his ancestors and friends, his reputation and works, his land and horses and yacht and bank account.[41]

The idea is that in producing, possessing, acquiring or shaping material things, human beings project their self, their own qualities into them; they see themselves in them and see them according to their own image. As Simmel said,

> All property means an extension of personality; my property is that which obeys my will, that is to say, that in which my self expresses and realizes itself externally. And this occurs before and more completely than anywhere else, in our own body, which, for that reason, constitutes our first and indisputable property.[42]

If this is so, then objects can influence human personality. The extent of this influence was clearly appreciated by Simmel, both in the case of artistic creation of material things and in the case of exchange. In respect of the former he said that 'the unity of the object which we create and its absence influences the corresponding configuration of our personality.'[43] In respect of the latter he said that the self is in such solidarity with its concrete possessions that even 'the giving away of values, whether it is in exchange or as a gift, may heighten the feeling of personal relation to the possession.'[44]

It is through this material aspect that identity can be related to consumption and to both traditional and cultural industries. These industries produce commodities, consumption goods which people acquire in the market, be they material objects or forms of entertainment and art. Each purchase or consumption of these commodities is both an act whereby people satisfy necessities and a cultural act in so far as it is a culturally determined manner of purchasing and consuming commodities. Thus, for instance, I can buy a ticket to the opera because I love opera and it gives me pleasure. But I can also buy a ticket to the opera in order to be seen in the company of certain people I deem to be important or of high status. I can buy a special car because it is nice and I need mobility, but I can also buy it in order to belong to a particular group or circle which is identifiable by using that particular kind of car. In other words, access to certain material goods, the consumption of certain commodities, may also become a means of access to an imagined group represented by those goods; it may become a form of looking for recognition. Material things make one belong or, rather, give one the feeling of belonging to a desired community. To this extent they contribute to shaping personal identities by symbolizing a collective or cultural identity.

In the third place, the construction of the self necessarily involves the existence of 'others' in a double sense. The others are those whose opinions about us we internalize. But they are also those against whom the self acquires its distinctiveness and specificity. The first sense entails that 'our total self-image involves our relations to other persons and their appraisal of us.'[45] The subject internalizes the expectations or attitudes of the others in respect of him or her, and these expectations of the others are transformed into his or her own self-expectations. Hence the subject defines himself or herself in terms of how the others see him or her. However, only the evaluations of others that are in some way significant to the subject really count for the construction and maintenance of that self-image. Early on, parents are the most significant others, but later a variety of others begin to operate (friends, relatives, peers, teachers, etc.).

The socially constructed self is thus immensely complex and variable, but at the same time it is expected to integrate its various aspects more or less successfully to become coherent and consistent in its tendencies and activities. The self-image of an adult, although dependent in various ways on others' evaluations, normally tends to be strong enough to exist with relative autonomy in relation to the opinions of any particular other. That is to say, the adult has to a certain extent already constructed its self on the basis of a long sequence of previous assessments occurring in the past. Indeed, if the self-image did not have a certain autonomy and the adult totally depended on what particular others thought of him or her at specific times, that person would be considered to be inadequate or lacking in character. The self-image that anyone has at a particular time is a reflection of others' evaluations, but only in so far as the previously developed self modifies them.[46] It is still true, though, that no individual identity can survive a total lack of recognition from all quarters.

Therefore, identity, in a personal sense, is something that the individual presents to others and that others present to him or her. The self presupposes the prior existence of the group and an evaluation of it. The meaning of identity responds not so much to the question 'who am I?' or 'what would I like to be?' as to the question 'who am I in the eyes of the others?'[47] or 'what would I like to be, considering the judgement significant others have of me?' Erikson expresses this idea by saying that in the process of identification 'the individual judges himself in the light of what he perceives to be the way in which others judge him.'[48] According to Erikson this aspect of identity is not well understood by the traditional psychoanalytic method because 'it has not developed terms to conceptualize the environment.'[49] The important thing to understand about this environment, which is expressed in German by the word *Umwelt*, is that it does not only surround us, but is also within us. In this sense, it could be said that identities come from without in so far as they are the manner in which others recognize us, but come from within in so far as our self-recognition is a function of the recognition of others, which we have internalized.

According to Honneth, the self-recognition that makes identity possible takes three forms: self-confidence, self-respect and self-esteem.[50] But, as I have already argued, the development of these forms of relation with the self depends fundamentally on the subject experiencing the recognition of others, whom she or he also recognizes. In other words, the construction of identity is an intersubjective process of mutual recognition. This is equivalent to what Taylor has called the fundamentally dialogical character of human life.[51] For Honneth self-confidence arises in the child only in so far as the expression of his or her needs is met by a positive answer of love and concern on the part of the others in charge of him or her. Equally, self-respect depends on others respecting the subject's human dignity and, consequently, the rights that accompany that dignity. Lastly, self-esteem can only exist if others recognize the contribution of a subject as valuable. In sum, a well-integrated identity depends on three forms of recognition: love or concern for the subject, respect for his or her rights and esteem for his or her contribution.

Simultaneously, Honneth argues that there are three forms of disrespect, which coexist with the three forms of recognition, and which could contribute to the creation of social conflicts and to a 'struggle for recognition' on the part of social sectors deprived of these forms of respect. The first form of disrespect is physical abuse or threats to the physical integrity of a person, which affects the subject's self-confidence. The second form is the systematic and structural exclusion of a person from having certain rights, which damages their self-respect. The third form is the cultural devaluation of certain modes of life or beliefs which are considered to be inferior or deficient, which prevents the subject from giving social value or esteem to his or her abilities and contributions.[52] The negative emotional reaction (rage, indignation) which accompanies the experience of disrespect represents for Honneth the motivational basis of the struggle for recognition: 'for it is only by regaining the possibility of active conduct that individuals can dispel the state of emotional tension into which they are forced as a result of humiliation.'[53]

Then, for Honneth the experience of disrespect would be the source of collective forms of resistance and social struggle. But these are not the automatic result of individual emotional responses. Only if the means for an intersubjective articulation of such negative emotions into a social movement exist will collective forms of struggle arise. Honneth uses Mead's distinction between the 'me' and the 'I' to found the idea of a struggle for recognition. While the 'me' reflects the expectations and images which others have of me, the 'I' actively seeks a wider recognition of my rights as part of a future ideal community.[54] People are always struggling to expand the range of their rights, for the recognition of greater spaces of autonomy and respect. This is the basis for the development of society, a continuous process in which the forms of recognition are broadened to new forms of freedom as much as to new groups of individuals. Individual identity, therefore, presupposes group expectations, not only as past expectations, but also as future possibilities.

The importance of Honneth's thought and of his interpretation of Mead is that it allows us to understand identity, not as a merely passive construction, but as a veritable interaction in which the subject's identity is built not just as an expression of the others' free recognition, but also as a result of a struggle to be recognized by the others. This struggle responds to the experience of disrespect which is lived as indignation and rage and which the 'I' does not accept. This struggle, at least in the case of the last two forms of recognition of rights and esteem, has the potential to become collective in so far as its goals could generalize themselves beyond individual intentions. At this point personal and collective identities meet.

The search for personal recognition can manifest itself and look for satisfaction in the struggle of the collective movement. But it can also manifest itself as a personal projection in consumer things, which have become symbols of the imagined community one wants to be a part of or respected by. By contrast to the collective struggle for recognition, the struggle for recognition based on consumption is highly individualized and atomized. It substitutes the vicarious aura of representative things for the real achievements of group struggle, and to this extent it changes nothing in reality, but constitutes an alternative that disarms and detracts from collective struggle. Consumption can substitute for collective action but it can hardly change the attitudes of others to make them recognize you. So, although things are inevitably a part of anyone's identity, they may also become a devious way of struggling for recognition.

Identity also presupposes the existence of others who have different modes of life, different values, customs and ideas. In order to define oneself the differences with others are accentuated. The definition of self always involves a distinction from the values, characteristics and modes of life of others: some groups, values and customs are presented as belonging outside the community. Thus the idea of 'us' as different from 'them' emerges. Sometimes, in order to define what is considered to be one's own, differences from what is someone else's are exaggerated. In these cases the normal process of differentiation is transformed into a process of opposition and hostility against the other. The process of differentiation from others is indispensable for the construction of one's own identity; the hostile opposition to others is not, and constitutes a danger of all identity construction processes.

This process of differentiation has always existed in all processes of identity construction and is also culturally determined. The ancient Greek world divided human beings into Greeks and barbarians. *Bárbaroi* were those who spoke other languages and could not speak Greek; they became the 'others' of Greek identity. However, as García-Gual has noted, from the principle of language differentiation a form of contempt very soon evolved: those who did not speak Greek were regarded as backward, rude, rebellious and intellectually inferior. The Greek language itself facilitated this transition from difference to contempt: the word *logos* had the double meaning of spoken word and reason, that is to say it meant both intelligible language and the realization of order. Thus the barbarians, who could not speak Greek, were also easily exposed to the judgement that they were irrational, lacking in order and logic. The Greek language became the vehicle of reason *par excellence*. Thus one can understand how Aristotle, Euripides and Isocrates came to justify slavery as the result of the natural superiority of the Greek and the natural inferiority of barbarians.[55]

There is also evidence that these mechanisms of identification existed in pre-Columbian America among the various indigenous peoples. Sahagun's chronicles tell us how the Nahuas in Central America considered Otomies as lazy and lascivious fools. So much so that among the Nahuas it was customary to use the word *otomi* to describe somebody who was stupid and could not understand things quickly. Equally, they considered Huaxtecas to be drunkards and impudent because they did not wear a loincloth. Nahuas also believed, like the Greeks, that their Nahuatl language was more refined and sophisticated than the unintelligible and rude languages of their neighbouring peoples.[56]

There are also numerous historical examples of identification in which opposition to the other is exaggerated to the point of promoting exclusion in varying degrees: from marking a difference one can go to distrust, from distrust one can go to open hostility and from there to aggression. This process of increasing exclusion is not of itself necessary, but it has happened too many times in history to be ignored as a remote possibility. By following Raul Hilberg, Bauman describes the sequence of logic which ended up in the Holocaust: 'it starts with the definition of the stranger. Once it has been defined, it can be separated. Once it has been separated, it can be deported. Once it has been deported, physical extermination could be the conclusion.'[57] This is the same logic that has more recently operated between Hutus and Tutsis in Rwanda, or between Bosnian Muslims and Serbs in the old Yugoslavia.

Personal and collective identities

What is the relationship between personal and collective identities? This is an important question that has to be answered before one can explore national or regional identities, which are the topic of this book. The first thing to be said about this distinction is that personal and collective identities are mutually necessary and interrelated. There cannot be personal identities without collective identities and vice versa. Which means that although there is certainly an analytical distinction between the two, they cannot be conceived apart and substantialized as entities to stand on their own without a reference to one another. This is because individuals cannot be conceived as isolated entities and opposed to the social world conceived as an external reality. Individuals are defined in their social relations and society reproduces itself and changes through individual actions. Personal identities are shaped by culturally defined collective identities, but these cannot exist separately from individuals.

I have already established above that in constructing their personal identities, individuals share some group allegiances or characteristics that are culturally determined. Implicit in this is the idea of collective identities such as nationality, gender, sexuality, ethnicity, class, etc.

Following Stuart Hall I have called these 'cultural identities'. They are collective forms of identity because they refer to some culturally defined characteristics that are shared by many individuals. Thus being Chilean or British makes us belong to a collective, it makes us part of a group that could be identified by some specific features. But in themselves, Britishness and Chileanness mean very little without a reference to concrete individual members who recreate them by means of their practices. Collective identities should not be hypostasized as if they had an independent existence and belonged to a fully integrated collective individual. As Giddens would put it, collective identities are continually recreated by individuals through the same means by which they express themselves as actors with an identity, but, at the same time, collective identities make such activities possible. Thus, by paraphrasing Giddens, it could be said that a collective identity is the means and the result of the individual identity it recursively organizes.[58]

This close relationship must not conceal the differences between these two forms of identity and, in particular, must avoid transposing the psychological elements of personal identities on to cultural identities. Whereas it may be possible to speak of a personal identity in terms of an individual's 'character' or 'psychic structure', it is not adequate to speak of a collective identity in terms of an 'ethnic character' or a collective psychic structure which would be shared by all the members of the collective. A collective identity has no character or psychic structure in the sense of a number of defined psychological traits. It cannot be said that a collective character manifests itself in the conjunction of individual characters, for instance that Chileans share a Chilean character structure which is different from the British character structure.

In anthropology, the American culturalist school including Margaret Mead, Ruth Benedict, Ralph Linton and Clyde Kluckhohn, among others, tended to work with this idea that individuals from a particular society have a common character structure, a cultural pattern, which can be described in terms of a series of psychological traits. Kluckhohn, for instance, described the Russian character as 'warm and human, tremendously dependent upon secure social affiliations, unstable, irrational, strong but undisciplined, thereby needing to be subjected to some kind of authority'.[59] Renato Ortiz has described how during the Second World War a series of anthropological studies about the national character of some foreign peoples appeared in the United States, financed by governmental agencies with a view to ascertaining the possible pattern of behaviour of enemy nations.[60] But the influence of this trend went beyond this narrow objective and in many other countries studies about national character have flourished until quite recently.

Latin America is no exception and has had its share of studies on national character. Some titles are suggestive: *The Chilean Character*; *The Brazilian National Character*; *Ideology, Alienation and National Identity: A Psycho-social Approximation to the Venezuelan Being*. Maritza Montero describes the Venezuelan character in terms of three positive traits, egalitarianism, courage and generosity, and seven negative features, laziness, passivity, emotiveness, authoritarianism, violence, pessimism, and lack of historical sense.[61] Leite does the same with the Brazilians, who appear as indolent, prejudiced, inapt for work, malicious, sensual, Dionysian.[62] Hernán Godoy, in his turn, concludes his description of the Chilean character by highlighting the following traits: will to face challenges, serenity in the face of adversity, habit of work and effort, sobriety, seriousness and prudence, lack of solemnity, inclination to order and discipline, sense of humour, great sensitivity to what appears ridiculous, patriotism, hospitality, openness to the world, interest in travel, critical spirit, but also obsequiousness, cruelty, improvidence, inhibition, pessimism, sadness, alcoholism, lack of imagination – and many more.[63]

These listings of psychological features supposedly belonging to a national character show their own inadequacy inasmuch as the features are patently not shared by everyone in those societies. It would be rash even to say that they are shared by a majority of a nation. They are abstract overgeneralizations which cannot be predicated of a nation as a whole. Besides, with such a degree of generality it is impossible to establish any sort of real distinction between different cultures. What does it mean to say that courage belongs to the Chilean national character, when exactly the same is said of the Venezuelan character, the British character, the North American character, the German character and so on? One suspects that in particular circumstances and given some specific conditions the people of any nation could show themselves to be courageous. Optimism, sadness, sensitiveness, courage, indolence, sensuality and so on cannot be deemed to be essential characteristics of the 'psychic structure' of any one people. It is a mistake to ontologize for a collective what are individual psychological traits.

In itself, a collective identity is purely a cultural artefact, a kind of 'imagined community', as Anderson puts it in the case of the nation.[64] What Anderson says of the nation is also partly applicable, I think, to other cultural identities like sexuality, ethnicity, class, gender, etc. In all these cases, the members of these imagined communities are limited but 'will never know most of their fellow-members, meet them, or even hear them, yet in the minds of each lives the image of their communion'.[65] Still, it is clear that one cannot entirely assimilate these cultural identities to one other and that each has its own history and individual resonance. Many millions have died or killed for their nations since modernity started. Up to now, by contrast, being heterosexual has not been something that has inspired a great sense of fraternity, and certainly very few, if any, have died for it. Being a homosexual has not involved nearly as much imagined fraternity as being Chilean or British, and yet it has increasingly entailed degrees of involvement and personal commitment on the part of many individuals which are greater than those of heterosexuals.

This means that each cultural identity demands a different amount of commitment from each individual member, or involves a different degree of imagined fraternity, and that this can change historically. There is nothing static about cultural identities. Class, nationality and sexuality hardly had a presence as cultural identities before modernity arrived and hence they could not count in the construction of personal identities. There are signs that class and national identities are beginning to decline in late modernity. Early modernity brought about and spread nation-states everywhere; late modernity and accelerated globalization have begun to erode their autonomy. Collective identities, therefore, historically begin, develop and can decline or disappear.

Cultural identities can overlap and are not mutually exclusive. In the construction of personal identities a number of them always concur in varying degrees. But not all of them are strictly necessary in the same way. For instance, it is very difficult to escape from the determinations of nationality and gender, but there is little problem in not being a supporter of some football club or not having a particular religion. Some cultural identities can also subsume or be a part of other cultural identities. For instance, I am Chilean and simultaneously Latin American in the same way as any British person is also European. Further subclassifications may become significant in some specific contexts. Thus, for instance, Western Europe could be contrasted with Eastern or Southern Europe and South America with Central or North America. All these divisions are culturally made and the communities they refer to are imagined in different ways. It may be hypothesized, for instance, that Latin Americanness means more to Chileans or Venezuelans than Europeanness means to British subjects, and this would be the consequence of having shared the same conquerors, the same language and many other cultural values.

Cultural identities work by producing meanings and stories with which individuals can identify. The more important the role of a collective identity for the construction of personal identities, the greater the appeal of meanings and narratives which are created to interpellate individuals so that they identify with them. The nation is a very special case in this respect because it has demanded and achieved a degree of commitment on the part of its members which is unparalleled by other cultural identities. Anderson has tried to explain the strength of this form of identity by drawing on its cultural origins, which suggest an affinity and continuity with religion: both are concerned with death and immortality, and with the ebbing of religious belief the nation represents a new way to continuity and immortality.[66]

Hall has shown various ways in which the discourse of the nation interpellates individuals so that they identify with it.[67] For instance, by telling and retelling the narrative of the nation which is present in national histories, in the literature, in the media and popular culture. Here one finds glorious historical events, images, symbols, landscapes and rituals, but also 'invented traditions' which, purporting to be very old, try to express in a symbolic way the continuity with a great past.[68] Another way is the emphasis on the timelessness of origins and traditions. This is almost always connected with a foundational myth in which reference is made to a pure, original people from which all virtues come.

National identity and the two poles of culture

It is very important to realize that national identities exist at two different poles of culture.[69] At one end, they exist in the public sphere as articulated discourses, highly selective and constructed from above by a variety of cultural agents and institutions (such as intellectuals, universities, media, research centres, etc.). At the other end, they exist in the social base as a form of personal and group subjectivity which expresses a variety of practices, modes of life and feelings which become representative of a nation's identity and which sometimes are not well represented in public versions of identity.[70] Whereas public versions tend to be more coherent and rigorous forms of consciousness elaborated by intellectuals, private versions are developed by people in more restricted and local spaces in the multiple conversations and exchanges of daily life and therefore tend to be less articulated and have a more concrete, contradictory and commonsense character. In order to understand these two dimensions better one could resort to Giddens's distinction between discursive consciousness and practical consciousness. The former consists in what social actors can say about the existent social and cultural conditions in the form of an articulate and elaborate discourse. Practical consciousness on the contrary consists in what actors know about their own reality but which they cannot express discursively.[71]

Public versions frequently want us to believe that there is only one true, naturally evolved version of national identity, able to determine with precision what belongs to it and what does not, and more or less shared by everyone in society. In fact the selective and excluding character of the symbolic construction process shows that there is nothing natural or spontaneous about it and that many other versions could equally be constructed around different selections and exclusions. A national identity is always, therefore, a terrain of conflict. The idea of a national identity is normally constructed around the interests and worldviews of dominant classes or groups in society through a variety of cultural institutions such as the media, educational, religious and military institutions, state apparatuses, etc. The criteria for defining it are always narrower and more selective than the increasingly complex and diversified cultural habits and practices of the people. In the public versions of national identity diversity gets carefully concealed behind a supposed uniformity.

This narrowing process in the discursive construction of a cultural identity is achieved through certain mechanisms.[72] Thus one can typically find a process of selection whereby only some features, symbols and group experiences are taken into account and others are excluded. There is also a process of evaluation whereby the values of certain classes, institutions or groups are presented as national values and those of others are excluded. So a moral community with supposedly shared values is constructed which leaves out other values. A process of opposition is also frequently resorted to whereby some groups, ways of life and ideas are presented as outside the national community. Cultural identity is defined as against these other groups: thus the idea of 'us' as opposed to 'them'. Differences are exaggerated in order to highlight the profile of one's own identity. Finally, one finds processes of naturalization whereby certain cultural features are presented as naturally given in the national character.

The distinction between public and private versions of identity does not mean that they constitute entirely separate worlds. Public versions of identity are constructed by selecting features from the modes of life of the common people, and, in their turn, they influence the way in which people see themselves. But this influence is not mechanical or automatic: many ethnic groups, regions or sections of society do not feel well represented by the dominant versions and do not share that sense of identity. Richard Johnson has represented this as a clockwise circular process, which entails four moments starting at the base of the circle.[73]

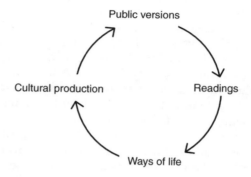

At the basis there is a complex society with an increasingly diversified culture and a huge variety of ways of life. From this big complex reservoir, cultural institutions such as the media, churches and educational and political apparatuses produce public versions of identity which select only some features that are considered to be representative, and exclude others. These public versions in their turn influence the way in which people see themselves and the way they act through an active and critical process of reading or reception, thus closing the circle. In this way local and private cultures constitute as much the beginning as the end of the circuit. Public versions are constructed from ways of life but also constitute sites of struggle, shaping the plurality of ways of life. In order to do this, though, they require an effective relationship with the common sense of the people, and a capacity to produce meanings, symbols and images that capture the popular imaginary.[74] This ability to shape everyday life is never simple and direct. Individuals and groups actively transform, reject, appropriate and reinterpret such discourses in their daily life.

I have underlined the role of cultural institutions in the construction of different discursive versions of national identity, but there is little doubt that there is one political institution, the state, which has enormous weight in articulating national identity discourses. It does this not only through its own cultural and educational institutions, and not only through the discourses of other state institutions such as the army and a variety of mass media under its control, but also, apart from these obvious sources, through the provision or creation of much of the content of identity discourses: traditions, ceremonies, celebrations, national days, remembrance days, military parades, etc.

State ceremonial, the flag, the national anthem, national anniversaries are all state-created symbols which seek to enhance a sense of common identity by uniting and enacting the imagined community which is the nation.

Different theoretical conceptions of national identity

There are at least three theoretical traditions within which national identity can be understood. Richard Johnson has analysed two theoretical traditions, constructivism and essentialism.[75] Constructivism emphasizes the discursively constructed character of identity and therefore its openness to any change. Essentialism underlines the fixed character, and closedness to any change, of identity. To these I should add a third, intermediate position, which for lack of a better name I call historical-structural. This approach stresses the fact that identity is constructed not solely by discourse but also by the solidified practices of a people and therefore it can change but in a materially conditioned manner. Constructivist theories derive from poststructuralist positions,[76] which assign crucial importance to discourse as the central element around which social life is organized. In this intellectual tradition, subjects and actors, as much as social-political movements, are constituted by a variety of discourses. It is not the subject that creates discourses; it is the discourse that creates the subjects or the 'subject positions' which can be filled by a variety of individuals.[77]

In the terrain of national identity, a constructivist version underlines the capacity of a discourse to construct the nation, its ability to interpellate individuals and constitute them as national subjects within a conception of the nation articulated by discourse. Constructivism overestimates the power of discourse to construct the nation, in contrast to essentialist visions which consider the national fundament as something given and not arbitrarily constructed by a discourse. In privileging the foundational role of highly articulated and coherent discourses, constructivism necessarily conceives of national identity as constructed 'from above', in the public sphere, and neglects private and popular forms.[78] The overrating of public versions excessively simplifies the study of identity and ignores the complexity of the problem by assuming that there is a total correspondence between public discourse and the feelings of people in general. But this correspondence cannot be simply assumed.

The essentialist conception, at the other extreme, conceives of national identity as an already established set of common experiences and shared fundamental values, constituted in the past, as an essence, once and for all. In the words of Hall, it is 'a sort of collective "one true self", hiding inside the many other, more superficial or artificially imposed "selves", which people with a shared history and ancestry hold in common'.[79] According to this definition each people or nation has an essence, some shared experience of 'oneness' which provides a stable set of meanings, codes and frames of reference underlying the more superficial differences and historical changes of the people. A process of dehistoricization is employed whereby 'an original history . . . is frozen as heritage, as tradition.'[80] What was an original historical moment is converted into patrimony, into a legacy which is received from the past and which cannot be questioned. As García Canclini puts it, for essentialism 'the ultimate end of culture is to convert itself into nature. Be natural as a given.'[81]

This essence can be temporarily lost, and it could even be abandoned or disregarded by sectors of the people, but it cannot totally disappear: it will survive and can be restored, rediscovered, excavated from some privileged reservoir which might be a language, a religion, an ethnic group, etc. The price of neglecting or disregarding such an essence is alienation and failure. No nation can indefinitely and with impunity go against its own true inner being. This conception of identity is not only selective and evaluative in the sense that only some features and values are taken into account while others are excluded, but it is also usually set in opposition to some features. That is to say, it is defined against some values, ways of life and ideas that are presented as outside the national community. Cultural differences are thus not only exaggerated but fixed forever. Above all, essentialism does not allow for any cultural identity to change or receive new contributions; it is trapped in a rigid distinction between what is considered to be its own patrimony and what is supposed to be alien.

The historical-structural conception, which I favour, seeks to establish a balance between the two extreme positions just outlined. On the one hand it conceives of cultural identity as something which is continuously constructed and reconstructed within new historical contexts and situations, as something in respect of which it can never be said that is finally resolved or definitively constituted as a fixed set of values and common experiences. On the other hand, it does not conceive of the construction of identity as a mere process of public discourse, but considers also the practices and meanings accumulated in the daily life of people. The historical-structural version conceives of identity as a dynamic interrelation of the public and private poles, the two necessary moments of a circular process of mutual interaction. As Hall has put it, in a historical conception, identity is a matter of 'becoming' as well as of 'being'. It belongs to the future as much as to the past. It is not something which already exists, transcending place, time, history and culture. Cultural identities come from somewhere, have histories. But like everything which is historical, they undergo constant transformation. Far from being eternally fixed in some essentialized past, they are subject to the continuous 'play' of history, culture and power.[82]

It is important to underline that this conception does not only look at the past as the privileged reservoir of identity but also looks at the future and conceives of identity as a project. The question about identity is therefore not just 'who are we?' but also 'who do we want to be?' As Habermas proposes, 'identity is not something pre-given, but also, and simultaneously, our own project.'[83] This has to be understood as much at the level of public discourse as at the level of individuals and group experiences. It is clear that no project articulated by a specific discourse could pretend to have a monopoly of identity construction without considering the popular forms, meanings and traditions accumulated in daily life by longstanding practices. But it is also true that in the construction of the future according to a project, not all historical traditions have the same value. Habermas insists on the profound ambivalence of national traditions: not everything that constitutes a national tradition is necessarily good and acceptable for the future. It may be true that a nation cannot freely choose its traditions, but at least it can politically decide whether or not to continue with some of them.[84]

Globalization and identity

The process of globalization occurring in late modernity has an important effect on cultural identities for three main reasons. First, because in the formation or construction of any cultural identity the idea of the 'other' is crucial, and globalization puts individuals, groups and nations in contact with a series of new 'others' in relation to whom they can define themselves. This can only happen through the media. As Thompson has noted, 'the process of self-formation is increasingly nourished by mediated symbolic materials.'[85] The construction of personal identities has become more complex and open-ended because the media increasingly mediate it. The globalization of communications by means of electronic signals has allowed the separation of social relations from the local contexts of interaction.

This means not only that in relation to each person the number of 'significant others' has substantially increased, but also that such others come to be known not by means of their physical presence but through the media, especially through televised images. This loosens, 'without destroying – the connection between self-formation and shared locale'.[86] The impact of relationships with absent 'others' for the construction of identity is not to be underrated. Recent statistics tell us that almost throughout the world, children spend annually more hours in front of a TV set than at school. This means that the media have increasingly mediated the construction of personal identities. As Kellner maintains, 'television and other cultural forms mediated by the media play a crucial role in the structuration of contemporary identities.'[87]

But the way in which television influences the construction of identities should not be simplified. On the one hand, television puts people in contact with the reality of faraway worlds and shows other cultures and ways of living. In this sense it contributes to the break-down of national barriers. Language is no obstacle since TV penetrates more through images, fantasies and emotions; it attracts people as an entertaining spectacle rather than through logical argument. People learn from it in a way that is totally different from schooling. And this leads to some kind of cultural homogenization in the world. But this influence is always actively reinterpreted in local contexts and sometimes with different purposes. Thus, for instance, research has shown that until recently the most popular soap opera watched by young people of Asian origin in Southall, London, was *Neighbours*, but that it was used by the parents to reinforce traditional values and by the youngsters to challenge those values.[88]

Television may also try to help in the creation and recreation of national traditions. Thus for instance the Welsh language soap opera *Pobol y Cwm* seemed to perform that role in Wales, just as the game show *She and He* was adapted in Slovenia to reinvent and support family national traditions.[89] National identities in late modernity are increasingly dependent on the media creation of imaginary links among the members of a nation.[90] Television, in particular, is very good at creating the fiction of intimacy and close interaction with the audience, and nationalistic interests have exploited this quality. The power of an entertaining spectacle transmitted through images is very useful to create and maintain traditions that boost national feelings. However, as Thompson has shown, the media can also have negative consequences for self-formation: the intrusion of ideological messages, increasing dependency of the self on the media, inability to assimilate the increasing number of messages (symbolic overload) and obsessive attachment to media-transmitted symbolic materials.[91]

Second, globalization has affected the construction of identities in so far as it has quickened the pace of change in all sorts of relations and this makes it more difficult for the subject to make sense of what is going on, to see the continuity between past and present, and therefore to form a unitary view of herself and to know how to act. Furthermore, the general explosion of communications, images and simulacra makes it more difficult to conceive of a single reality both at the social and individual level. This makes the construction of personal identities a more complex and difficult process, subject to many leaps and changes. But identities have not been entirely dissolved or decentred, as postmodernists maintain; they are rather reconstructed and redefined in new cultural contexts. The difficulties produced by rapid change and time-space compression justify the emergence of these new feelings of ephemerality, contingency and lack of unity in individuals. But they do not necessarily justify the idea of a totally dislocated subject.

The third reason why globalization is important for identity formation is that the major transformations brought about by globalization tend to uproot widely shared cultural identities and, as a consequence, also affect the construction of personal identities. Processes of disarticulation and dislocation occur whereby many people cease to see themselves in terms of traditional collective contexts which once provided a sense of identity.[92] In early modernity the cultural identities which had a dominant influence on the formation of subjects were class and national identities. It is precisely these two cultural identities that are beginning to be affected by accelerated globalization. National identity, while still very strong, has nevertheless lost some of its appeal because of the erosion of the autonomy of the nation-state in the face of an increasingly internationalized economy, and because of the growing importance of supranational organizations.

But it would be a mistake to believe that there is simply a tendency to dissolve nationalisms, localisms and regionalisms. The more profound the universalizing tendencies are, the more particular peoples, ethnic groups or sections of society seek to reaffirm their difference and the more they become attached to their locality.[93] One has only to look at the dissolution of the Soviet Union and of Yugoslavia to realize that nationalism is not dead. National identities were strengthened as a form of resistance to the monolithic central power which used to rule those countries. But from another point of view it is also true that the homogenization implicit in the globalization of culture and the internationalization of the economy are eroding national identities, and this trend can be clearly seen in the European Community. In Latin America, a weakening of all sorts of nationalistic trends can also be observed.

Nevertheless, as some social categories decline, so new social contexts appear or become articulated as the most accepted providers of a sense of identity. Thus the decline of class and national identities is accompanied by the rise of other relevant collective contexts which are connected with the emergence of new social movements: ethnic identities (anti-racist movements), gender identities (feminist movements), sexual identities (homosexual movements) and many others. Personal identity does not disappear in total fragmentation and dispersion, as postmodernists imagine; it is reconstructed and redefined in other terms. It is true that globalization brings about a greater consciousness about one's own identity, a greater opportunity for self-definition, the idea that identities are constructed and can be modified within the boundaries of certain social relations. But this does not mean that we are entirely free to adopt any identity we want.

2

The Colonial Stage, Modernity Denied

1492–1810

Cultural reasons for a defeat

America is supposed to have been 'discovered' in 1492. The word 'Indian' given to the New World's inhabitants itself entails a mistake: Columbus believed that he had arrived in India. As Gissi has argued, the very word 'discovery' is equivocal because America's inhabitants had discovered it many centuries before the arrival of Columbus.[1] This is why Enrique Dussel has argued that instead of a 'discovery' of America, we are in the presence of 'the invention of America's Asiatic being'.[2] Dussel is critically following here the work of Edmundo O'Gorman, who in 1958 was the first to propose the idea that America was not 'discovered' but rather invented 'as a result of a complex ideological process which ended up, through a series of trials and hypotheses, by conceding (to these lands) a peculiar sense of their own, a sense, in effect, of being the "fourth part" of the world.'[3] But it took years for this to happen. Columbus was 'on the verge of starting his second journey, and yet still no America had been discovered. Why? Simply because America still did not exist.'[4]

The Indian cultures the Spanish encountered were variegated and rather isolated from one another,[5] which explains the fact that they could be separately picked on and defeated by the conquerors one after the other. Fernando Ainsa has argued that, contrary to what common sense may suggest, cultures subjected to external influence and exchange could be more resilient than cultures solidly structured but isolated. Indigenous cultures in Latin America, living in almost total autonomy, were not prepared for exchange and crumbled before the presence of the unknown.[6] Hernan Cortés's ability to exploit the internal struggles between various Mexican peoples was certainly crucial to his victory. He defeated Moctezuma with the help of other Indian nations which the Aztecs had subjected and enslaved. Another reason was the Spanish superiority in weapons and technology. In spite of being a sophisticated culture from many points of view, the Indians did not know how to work metals, nor were they very advanced in a technological sense. They did not know the wheel and did not possess an advanced sailing technique.[7] Still, as Wachtel has argued, technological factors were of limited importance.[8]

The most important reason for the Indians' relatively easy defeat has to be found elsewhere, in their own culture. Through their poems and mythologies it is possible to conclude that the Indians regarded history as destiny and catastrophe.[9] Everything was for them predetermined and preordained. They could not grasp the Spanish conquerors within the oral cultural categories they worked with. Initially they thought the Spaniards were gods. This was bound to disarm them. In particular the old myth of the return of Quetzalcóatl[10] seemed to have been applied by Moctezuma to Cortés and this would partly explain his lack of resistance to the advancing Spanish. But the mythical status of gods did not survive for long. More important was the Indians' ritualistic conception of war whereby the aim was not to kill the enemy but to take prisoners in order to sacrifice them later to the gods.[11] Equally important was the fatalistic conception of history: such a conception paralyses any effective response because it gives the impression that things cannot be otherwise, that the course of events is set and cannot be altered by any action. This gave the Spanish a tremendous initial advantage.

The idea of progress was totally foreign to the Indian cultures. Their world was turned to and controlled by the past. Life was continual warfare and sacrifice but was not going towards an open and unknown future; it was dominated by tradition. Time was conceived as cyclical and repetitive. Everything had been preordained; whatever happened was the realization of a predetermined destiny. The strong feeling of inexorable fate helped the native cultures to accept pain with stoicism and resignation. This was expressed in poems and songs of great sadness and melancholy. So they could not respond adequately to the Spanish invasion, which totally surprised them. Their world was a ritual world and so they desperately sought to reduce the startling event of conquest to the old categories and prophecies. They could not deal with it as a new event in the face of which they had to improvise. Their culture did not allow that. Todorov has made the point that, ultimately, the Spanish superiority consisted in the fact that the Spanish conquerors understood the Indian world much better than the Indians understood the Spanish world. And yet this superior understanding was the very instrument that allowed the Spanish to destroy the Indian civilization.[12]

For the Indians, defeat was a trauma and psychological shock of unimaginable proportions; it meant the end of their world, the end of their civilization and ancient traditions. At a very early stage they understood that their whole universe had been shattered and annihilated. In Mexico as much as in Peru, defeat was experienced as the collapse of the world, as the total loss of power of their gods, in sum, as 'a catastrophe of cosmic proportions' which they experienced with 'an inconsolable sense of loss'.[13] So powerful was the trauma that, according to Wachtel, it remained imprinted in the mental structures of the twentieth century's Indians, to be seen in their present-day folklore.[14]

Olivia Harris has argued, on the contrary, that many Indians 'seem to have expressed indifference or at least evinced very little surprise at the arrival of the Europeans', and that the supposed god-like status of the Spanish as well as the Indian sense of catastrophe were part of a European mythologization of events, rather than a part of Indian culture.[15] Although some of Harris's anthropological criticisms are useful because they remind us that stories told from the perspective of Europeans may have an interest in presenting them as cunning and forceful and the Indians as disconcerted and lost, the proof of these arguments is not as convincing as the data presented by Todorov and Wachtel.

The socioeconomic consequences of the conquest

Wars, massacres, hard labour, ill-treatment, and contagious diseases brought from Europe against which the Indians had no defence, decimated the original Indian population. Research by historical demographers from the University of California at Berkeley has shown the extent of the demographic collapse.[16] They estimate that by 1500, at the beginning of the conquest, some 80 million natives lived in the Americas. By 1550 there were only 10 million left. In the particular case of Mexico, the first Indian empire to be conquered, figures are even harsher: the population was reduced from 25 million to 1 million during the first century of domination.[17] It is only in the twentieth century that Mexico manages to get back to the level of population existing before the arrival of the Spanish. In Peru the population was reduced from about 8 million in 1530 to about 1.3 million in 1590.[18] In the Chilean case something similar but less dramatic occurred: the original 1 million Indians were almost wiped out during the first century and by the end of the colonial times, three centuries later, they reached 400,000.[19]

These figures have led many authors to argue that the Spanish conquest of America amounted to a blatant case of genocide, belittling any other case of systematic killing in the twentieth century.[20] The truth is that the dramatic fall in the number of Indians was not always due to massacres. On the one hand, many Indians were integrated into Hispanic society as 'mestizos' or concubines and therefore were not counted as Indians.[21] On the other hand, disease produced the majority of deaths, direct killings a minority, and ill-treatments at work a few more. But high mortality rates were compounded by such appalling conditions for the survivors that the normal reproductive processes were also affected.[22] The total disruption of the social fabric produced by the killings, enslavement and exhaustion due to hard labour and poor food brought about a drastic fall in the birthrate.

The conquerors brought with them to Latin America semi-feudal and slave institutions. Contrary to André Gunder Frank's theory,[23] the colonization of Latin America did not mean the direct introduction of the capitalist mode of production even though production was exported to a world capitalist market. It could hardly have been otherwise since Spain and Portugal were still feudal countries during the sixteenth and seventeenth centuries. Violence was used in order to introduce forced labour and servile relations of production such as the encomienda[24] and the latifundia or hacienda system. These Latin American predominantly precapitalist modes of production were externally oriented and diverted outwards by the colonial power, but this integration into the international market did not make them capitalist. The situation of North America, Africa, India and the Caribbean is very different because their capitalism was directly imposed by British colonial rule.

In the encounter between the Iberian conquerors and the Indians various situations emerged. In some areas like the Caribbean the natives disappeared very quickly, decimated by illness, war or forced labour. Along the Brazilian, Guyanan and Venezuelan coast many Indians ran away into the jungle. In both cases they were replaced by black slaves brought from Africa. In other cases the Indians were subjected to the servile encomienda mode of production. This was the situation of the Quechuas in Peru and Bolivia, Aztecs in Mexico and some tribes in central Chile. Some Indians such as the Mapuches in southern Chile did not entirely submit, and were suppressed every time they rebelled in a process of practical extermination that took centuries. Other more fortunate Indians managed to survive unscathed, especially if they lived in faraway, self-sufficient communities. However, they were discriminated against in terms of their language, culture and colour; they had no political rights, lived in segregated communities and generally depended on the colonial power for all juridical and economic matters.

The encomienda system gave rise to the first set of class relations between colonial masters and Indian serfs. Unlike other colonial nations, the Spanish mixed themselves with the Indians, partly because of the scarcity of white women[25] and partly because many Indian peoples offered their daughters in matrimony to the Spanish in order to set the seal on political alliances. In this way many polygamous relationships were established.[26] This is how a new important subordinate social category emerged: the mestizo who is a mixture of Spanish and Indian.[27] Simultaneously, where the Indians were wiped out, a new labour force was required and hence black Africans were imported and the slave mode of production introduced. It is calculated that about 10 million black Africans were forcibly brought to America (3.5 million alone to Brazil). There were basically two types of slaves: the plantation slave and the family slave.[28]

Thus two essential precapitalist modes of production were widely established throughout Latin American: black slavery and Indian serfdom. It is true that some Indians too were made slaves. The law authorized the enslavement of Indians who took arms against the Spanish. However both the crown and the church were adamant that apart from that exceptional case, Indians were not normally to be enslaved. Neither the church nor the crown had any misgivings about black slavery though. (Even the best defender and supporter of the Indians' rights, Bishop Bartolomé de las Casas, had a family slave.) Hence, we have the constitution of a precapitalist class system which operated along racial lines: black slaves, Indian serfs, mestizos and white masters (owners of the land and the mines).

The disintegration of the Aztec and Inca empires in Mexico and Peru did not mean that all indigenous political structures disappeared. In fact the power of 'caciques', 'curacas' and other intermediate chiefs was maintained and sometimes increased as they renegotiated their position within the colonial structures. They mediated between Indian communities and the Spanish authorities and on many occasions they succeeded in getting favourable legislation and practical protection for such communities. Where such communities were large (Mexico, Peru, Bolivia), the process of *mestizaje* (the mixing of Indian and Spanish, from which the mestizos come) was wider and more successful. In these cases the Spanish religious influence covered but did not fully transform Indian cultural forms, which continued under different appearances as a form of resistance. In fact, as Brading has argued, a distinction should be drawn between the Indian elite and the Indian peasantry. The latter mostly took the path of stoic resignation and dissimulation. The former in many cases 'desperately sought both to assimilate the Spanish language and religion and also to maintain certain strands of their own culture . . . it was through a positive avowal of Christianity that they encountered the concepts which enabled them to frame an acceptable defence of their social identity.'[29]

The Spanish and Portuguese construction of the other

The year 1492 is not only significant because of the 'discovery' of America, but also because in a double movement Spain got rid of its internal 'others' (Moors and Jews) and discovered its new external 'others' (the natives) of the new world. There are good reasons to believe that the former affected the latter because the harsh process of excluding Moors and Jews could not but predispose them to intolerance of the new others. The Iberian culture in 1492 was far from being rationalistic and modern: rather it was permeated by religion, absolute moral values and intolerance to anything different. Spain was still a semifeudal country. Since the Spanish culture of the time was narrow and intolerant, it is no wonder that the conquerors could only see the Indians through their cultural prism. The first example of this is Columbus calling the natives 'Indians' – the name that they are still quite inappropriately given – because he thought that he had arrived in India.

Columbus's first impressions of the natives were somehow positive if patronizing: the Indians were a physically beautiful, peaceful and generous people, but were also naked and primitive, cowardly and deprived of all culture. The early fascination with the Indians was accompanied by a good dose of paternalism: they had to be converted to the true religion and civilized. As the conquest progressed and the Indians put up some forms of resistance, it was necessary to subject them by force of arms, and in the course of this process first impressions about the Indians soon changed. The description of the first chroniclers is quite different from the early Columbus: the Indians were cannibals, inclined to homosexuality, keen on keeping their nakedness, eaters of lice, rather antagonistic to the Catholic faith and, at least in the case of the Aztecs, given to human sacrifices.[30] All this made them inferior beings in the eyes of the Spanish. In Brazil they were called bugres (buggers) and seen as cannibals and primitives without civilization. The fact that they had 'no law, no king, and no faith was proof of their deficiencies'.[31]

The identity of the colonists partly depended on their not being like the Indians, their new 'others'. This process of opposition was a powerful mechanism in the construction of the Spanish and Portuguese identities. As Schwartz puts it, 'as elsewhere in the Americas, in Brazil the Indians provided an example of what the colonists were not and what they should not be. Indian barbarism and paganism were continually contrasted to Portuguese civility and Catholicism.'[32] The catalogue of defects found in the Indians was large: irrationality, homosexuality, profligacy, primitivism, cannibalism, rebelliousness, laziness, barbarism, passivity, etc. Some of them really mattered in practice because they could justify the legal enslavement of the Indians in spite of the general opposition of the Spanish and Portuguese crowns to, and legislation against, Indian slavery. In Spanish America rebelliousness was good enough a legal reason to enslave Indians. In Brazil cannibalism and buggery justified the same treatment.

The Spanish and Portuguese conquerors wanted not only fame and glory but also gold, silver, land, servants and slaves. In fact the search for gold is a dominant factor in their writings. Bitterli, an independent Swiss historian, maintains that 'this immoderate greed for riches took precedence over all the other objectives of their voyage, such as the desire for geographical knowledge or the aim of making Christian converts.'[33] But they also tried to conceal their greedy motives. Evangelizing and civilizing were two good and superior missions that could serve as an ideological[34] screen for their true motives. The civilizing mission made it necessary to construct the idea of uncivilized and barbarous Indians. The religious mission also proceeded in the same ideological way. Exploiting the Indians by means of hard work could be justified by expressing the wish to convert them to the true religion and thus saving their souls.

Religious justifications were always invoked to dominate and enslave the Indians. Before attacking and enslaving them, the Spaniards went so far as to draw up a document, the Requirement, which stated a series of Christian principles and the fact that America had been given to the Spanish monarchs by the Pope. Every conquistador was supposed to read the Requirement to the Indians, and this was sometimes done in Spanish, which they could not understand. The Requirement concluded thus: 'If you do not acknowledge this by promptly obeying the Pope and his majesty the King of Castile, and becoming his vassals, or if you maliciously delay in doing so, I declare unto you that with God's help I shall advance upon you with fire and sword and I shall make war upon you everywhere and in every way I can.'[35] Needless to say, immediately after the reading the Indians were made prisoners, or massacred if they resisted.

Even if those directly killed by the Spanish were a minority, it is horrifying to read the numerous and well-documented accounts of torture, indiscriminate killings and massacres of Indians for the flimsiest of reasons. As Jerónimo de San Miguel, a priest, writes to the king in 1550, 'they have burnt some Indians alive, to others they have with great cruelty cut off their hands, noses, tongues and other members, thrown the Indians to the dogs and cut off the breast of women . . .'[36] Two different positions have been taken in assessing this appalling conduct. Todorov argues that greed and power alone cannot explain these cruelties, and that their logic presupposes the Spanish construction of the Indians as inferior beings, halfway between human beings and animals.[37] Bitterli, on the other hand, argues that the European conquistadors 'knew full well that the members of archaic cultures were human beings' and that, therefore, 'it is impossible to absolve them of the charge that they subsequently treated these people worse than animals.'[38]

It may well be that these two positions are not as irreconcilable as they seem. The Europeans did in fact construct the Indians as less than human in their accounts, but they cannot be excused for doing that. We are not dealing here with a genuine mistake committed in good faith, but rather with a wilful blindness to the truth. It was in their interest to conceive of the Indians as less than human. Thus one might say that the Spanish refused to recognize the Indians as equal subjects in order to take advantage of them, but they still needed ideological justifications to proceed and assuage their conscience. Yet it is also true to say that they also wanted to impose their culture, their religion and their morality in their own right. This kind of ethnocentrism had strong support in the predominant theological views of the Catholic Counter-Reformation, for which error could not have the same rights as truth and, therefore, pagan errors had to be forcibly rooted out and Christian truth imposed at all cost.

In spite of the general trends followed by the conquest there were among churchmen and conquerors different positions in relation to the treatment of the Indians. As early as 1511, Antonio de Montesinos raised his voice to condemn the extermination of the Tainos in Hispaniola. Bishop Bartolomé de las Casas was also from the beginning a staunch defender of the Indians. In his books he described in detail all the horrors caused by the Spanish. He entered into all sorts of polemics against those who considered the Indians to be inferior. Famous is the controversy he pursued with Juan Ginés de Sepúlveda who thought the wars against the Indians were just. Ginés de Sepúlveda believed in the Aristotelian idea that barbarous peoples are natural slaves, and further justified his position by saying that it was legitimate to abolish the abominable custom of eating human flesh, to save innocent Indians from human sacrifices, and to propagate the Christian religion.

Las Casas on the contrary argued that even if cannibalism and human sacrifices were evils, it did not follow that war against their practitioners was a sensible remedy. Even in the pagan practices of the Indians Las Casas discovered elements of Christianity. He upheld the principle that the Indians were born free and should have the same rights as the Spanish. He rejected all violence against them and personally attempted to colonize some regions by using priests rather than soldiers. For half a century Bishop Las Casas devoted his life to defending the Indians against the rapaciousness and cruelty of the Spanish. And he did influence the Spanish court, as can be seen from the laws about the Indians passed by Philip II in 1573. However, it is still true that for Las Casas, following the widespread beliefs of the time, Christianity was the only true religion and the only conceivable ideal for the Indians to aspire to.

This shows that in the construction of the other, the attitudes of the Spanish were far from being monolithic. On the one hand there were those who emphasized difference to the point that Indians became less than human beings and could be killed and enslaved without any problem. On the other hand there were those who emphasized equality before God to the point that all cultural differences had to give way to the assimilation of the Indians to the true religion. Although the latter is a more enlightened approach because it respects the Indians as human subjects, it too forms part of a colonization project which does not respect cultural differences and leads to assimilation. As Todorov has convincingly argued, there are two elemental forms in the experience of the other within a colonization process: one starts from difference which is soon translated in terms of superiority/inferiority, the other starts from equality which is soon translated into identity and assimilation. Both attitudes rest on egocentrism, on the identification of the values of the colonial power with universal values, which must prevail.[39]

So, even if some theologians and missionaries, particularly Bishop Las Casas, were highly critical of the forced conversion of Indians,

and accepted only persuasion as the means of evangelization, ultimately nobody recognized at the time the right of Indians to keep
their own religion and moral norms. We are back then to the basic
problem of ethnocentrism: the Spanish did not recognize the Indians
as equal subjects entitled to be different and to keep their own
culture. In the best of cases, when the Indians were considered as
equal subjects and not as half animals, they were supposed to
abandon their beliefs and be assimilated to the true religion. Generally speaking the Indians did not want a new religion or a new
culture. The paradox is that even if compassionate missionaries
wanted to save the Indians from ill-treatment, they were prepared to
destroy their culture.

Gruzinski has argued with good reason that the conquest of Latin
America resulted in a process of Europeanization which cannot be
reduced to the imposition of the colonial system and Christianity
alone: it was also a true process of colonization of the Indian imaginary[40] whereby radical and dramatic changes occurred in the representation of the human being and human relations, in modes of
expression, in conceptions of history and modes of fixing the past, in
the perception of the real and the imaginary, in the Indian relationship to time and space, life and death.[41] Which in a way means, as
Wachtel has pointed out, that the violence of the initial conquest was
maintained throughout the colonial period on the terrain of culture,
systematically destructuring the Indian world.[42]

Yet it was not only the Indians who were despised and treated as
inferior beings. Mestizos too suffered from the same fate and were
rejected by the white conquerors in spite of having half their blood.
It was as if having Indian blood irredeemably contaminated their
good half. This was partly because the peninsular whites wanted to
define their identity in opposition to the mixed bloods. In Brazil mestizos (called 'mamelucos') were excluded from religious orders and
public office.[43] But in addition to this discrimination, mestizos were
also scorned by the Indians.[44] So their position was socially very difficult. Still, it is also true that in Spanish America many mestizos,
especially those born in wedlock, were categorized as Spaniards,
which eventually led to most criollo families having some Indian
blood in them. Even worse was the situation of the castas, a combination of mulattos, pardos and other mixes, who were the result of
unions between blacks, Indians and whites. Some sixteen different
racial variations came to be distinguished during colonial times, all
of them placed in a racial hierarchy in which the lowest place was
disputed between Indians and blacks.

Pagden has shown an interesting evolution in the evaluation of the Indians by the Spaniards. If at the beginning the images of the Indians as a whole were consistently derogatory and contemptuous, in time 'there developed in the Spanish mind a clear distinction between the living Indian and his ancestors. Like the old conquistadors themselves, the Inca and the ancient Mexica . . . with whom they had fought their legendary battles became rapidly mythologized.'[45] This procedure was in part necessary for the Spanish to enhance their own military and heroic profile. They themselves grew in stature if their defeated enemy assumed heroic proportions. So, while the living Indian was still considered a backward, uncivilized human being, full of vices, the old Indians who resisted the Spanish were elevated to a mythical status. Good examples of this procedure are Sigüenza y Góngora's *Theatro de virtudes políticas* in Mexico and Alonso de Ercilla's *La Araucana* in Chile.

As a new class of native-born landowners and criollos began to emerge, Spanish and Portuguese-born rulers developed a contemptuous attitude towards them too. As Pagden notes, Peninsulars 'sought for, and inevitably discovered, similarities in behaviour between the criollos and the very wild Indians'.[46] In this they were supported by prevalent European theories emphasizing the importance of the climate and the physical environment in the determination of people's mental disposition. Thus native-born criollos, being affected by the same environment, had to share the same deformations and character weaknesses as the Indians. Hence the Duke of Linares could say of them, 'lying is their common style, giving false testimony a general custom and envy and emulation common practice.'[47] Yet, on the other hand, the European 'scientific' descriptions of the natural inferiority of animals and humans in the New World must have come from the early reports they received from the first conquerors themselves. It is therefore worthwhile to explore these views.

The judgement of European philosophy and science

The experiences of the first colonists in America, North and South, the way in which they constructed the native Indians as uncivilized, sometimes half-human beings, and their accounts of them were determinant of the way in which European philosophy and science conceived of them and of the American environment. These theories in their turn reinforced such prejudices by providing them with a scientific and philosophical prestige and certainly by infiltrating the minds of the new waves of colonists, who continued to flow into the New World. One of the main and earliest ideas was that certain kinds of climate had a crucial but pernicious influence on human beings, animals and the physical environment, which justified the vision of a degenerate world. For instance, as early as 1756, in his essay on national characters, Hume proposed the idea that the inhabitants of tropical and Polar Regions were inferior to the rest of the human species.[48] Through these analyses a particular way of constructing the 'other' can be detected which could only reinforce the prejudices acquired by direct experience.

Natural sciences were particularly instrumental in the creation of stereotypes by describing the natural world of South America as inferior to the European. Buffon, a natural scientist of the Enlightenment, who is credited with having created the modern approach of the natural sciences, maintained by the mid-eighteenth century that all animal species in South America were inferior to and weaker than their European counterparts. Even domestic animals brought from Europe had difficulties in settling in, were reduced to small sizes and lacked the strength and virtues of the European prototypes. The reason for this was the existence of a hostile and humid nature, full of unhealthy air. The only animals that could develop well in these circumstances were reptiles and insects, which are humid and cold creatures. This hostile nature was also bound to affect the human species:

> the reproductive organs of the savages are weak and small; they have no hair in their bodies or beards, nor are they attracted to females. Although lighter than the European, due to his habit of running more, is nevertheless much less strong in his body: and also is much less sensitive and yet much more fearful and cowardly; he lacks vivacity, and he has no life in his soul; the activity of his body is less an exercise or willing movement than an automatic reaction to his needs; deprive him of hunger and thirst, and the active cause of all his movements will be destroyed at the same time; he will remain stupidly standing or lying during days.[49]

It is somehow paradoxical that the work of Buffon, celebrated by Cassirer as the producer of 'a new type of natural science', recommended, from the point of view of its method, as similar to Newton's *Principia Mathematica*,[50] should be capable of putting forward, in all seriousness, such incredible arguments. Buffon wanted to be guided only by experience and wanted to widen the capacity for observation of natural reality in order to generalize from verified facts, thus combining them into conclusions. The extreme empiricism of Buffon led him to mistrust the categories imposed by reason on reality, for instance the notions of class and species. These notions could be useful while the research was going on, in order to introduce some order into the observed things, but would almost inevitably lead to confusing mental categories with what happens in reality, the signs with the signified things.

Buffon's nominalism, therefore, led him to accept the existence only of individuals and to reject the categories of species and gender. Buffon finds the confirmation of this idea precisely in studying the American continent, where the animals are not the same as in Europe, and where if one thought that the same classes or species could be found, they are so changed that they could scarcely be recognized.[51] This idea, which according to Cassirer opens up the evolutionary perspectives which Darwin was to use later on, is nevertheless simultaneously responsible for judging the whole of American nature as inferior: which goes to show that even an empirical science based on observations could be influenced by preconceptions, prejudices and stereotypes.

The idea of beardless, weird men surrounded by a cold and hostile climate appears repeatedly in the literature of the Enlightenment. Voltaire spoke of the inhabitants of the American continent as 'a new species of man without beard'. According to him experience had demonstrated 'the European superiority over the Americans, who, easily defeated everywhere, never dared to try a revolution even if they were a thousand to one'.[52] The American continent was scarcely populated precisely because of natural causes: excessive cold, humidity and flooding, very high mountains and violent and durable poisons; last but not least, 'the human species' stupidity in a part of this hemisphere must have had much influence upon depopulation.'[53] Voltaire repeats Buffon's ideas about smaller animals, lions without manes and a pestilent and humid nature.

Montesquieu also asserts a relationship between tropical climates and fearfulness and weak character:

> it is not surprising that the cowardice of the peoples of hot climates has almost always made them slaves and that the courage of the peoples of cold climates has kept them free. This is an effect which derives from its natural cause. This has also been found true in America; the despotic empires of Mexico and Peru were close to the Equator, and all free and small peoples were and still are closer to the poles.[54]

Montesquieu's prejudice against sugar-producing black slaves in America is as marked as the poverty of his argument. He says that if he had to defend black slavery he would say that sugar would be too expensive if its production were not made by slaves:

> those involved are black from top to bottom, and have such flat noses which is almost impossible to feel compassion for them . . . a proof that Negroes have no common sense is that they appreciate more a glass necklace than one of gold . . . it is impossible for us to assume that those people are men for if we assumed that they are men, one would begin to believe that we ourselves are not Christians.[55]

The crudeness and poverty of the argument are quite shocking in today's eyes, but, in the context of the day, hardly amazing.

Cornelius de Pauw, one of Buffon's followers and a great defender of reason and progress, radicalized the anti-American stereotypes by referring to the natives as little more than animals, degenerate beings surrounded by a decaying natural world. 'They have less sensitivity, less humanity, less taste and less instinct, less heart and less intelligence, in fact less of everything. They are like stupid children, incurably lazy and incapable of any mental progress.'[56] According to de Pauw, in America animals lose their tail, dogs do not bark, camels' genitalia do not work; iron is so weak that one cannot make nails with it. De Pauw concludes in consternation that 'it is without doubt a huge and terrible spectacle to see half of the globe so completely mistreated by Nature that everything in it is either degenerate or monstrous.'[57]

It is possible to find traces of Buffon's and de Pauw's thoughts in Kant. According to Cassirer the Kantian idea that there is a need for an 'archaeology of nature' derives from Buffon's thought.[58] Kant wrote in 1775 that the American natives were 'an under-race not well formed yet (or half degenerate)'. Their physical appearance as much as their 'frigid and insensitive temperament' prove the long residence of their ancestors in the glacial regions of the north: 'their vital force is almost extinguished and they are too weak for any agricultural labour.'[59] Elsewhere Kant argues that 'American peoples are incapable of civilisation. They lack the strength of motivation; because they lack passion and affection. They do not attract each other by love, and thus are also fruitless. They speak very little, never caress each other, they do not worry about anything, and are lazy.'[60]

In 1788 Kant considers the climate as responsible for the fact that the American race is 'too weak for hard work, too indifferent to pursue something with care, incapable of all culture, in fact lower still than the Negro.'[61] Late in the eighteenth century Kant continues to write, in the same vein as Buffon and de Pauw, that in America there are no lions, that birds, even though pretty and colourful, do not sing well, that men develop precociously in the tropics but never reach the perfection of men in the moderate zones, etc.[62] Once more we face the paradox of an author who put reason on the highest of pedestals, who understood by Enlightenment the human capacity to overcome immaturity and leave aside dogmas and formulae in order to think for himself,[63] and who, nevertheless, naively believed in Buffon's and de Pauw's extravagant descriptions about the congenital inferiority of nature and humanity in America.

Malthus concentrated on the differences between North and South American colonies. In the latter he accused Spain and Portugal of cruelty, violence, maladministration, etc.: 'Whatever may be the character of the Spanish inhabitants of Mexico and Peru at the present moment, we cannot read the accounts of these countries without feeling strongly that the race destroyed was, in moral worth as well as numbers, superior to the race of their destroyers.'[64] The English North-American colonies, on the contrary, 'far outstripped all the others in the progress of their population. To the quantity of rich land which they possessed in common with the Spanish and Portuguese colonies, they added a greater degree of liberty and equality.'[65] That Malthus's point was not so much to praise the moral value of the natives as to attack the character of the Spanish colonizers in contrast with the talents and tact of the British colonizers was shown by his multiple remarks about the indolence, ignorance and improvidence of the Indians. The natural richness and fertility of the soil in those countries foster these bad habits. The easier it was to make a living, the greater the tendency to leisure.[66]

In his *Lectures on the Philosophy of World History*, Hegel described South America as 'physically and spiritually impotent', a place where 'even the animals show the same inferiority as the human beings', who, in their turn, are considered to be 'obviously unintelligent individuals with little capacity for education'. 'Their inferiority in all respects, even in stature, can be seen in every particular' – for instance, in Paraguay 'a clergyman used to ring a bell at midnight to remind them to perform their matrimonial duties, for it would otherwise never have occurred to them to do so.' The natives are compared to 'unenlightened children, living from one day to the next, and untouched by higher thoughts or aspirations'; they inhabit a world where events 'are but an echo of the Old World and the expression of an alien life'.[67] The inferiority of animals in South America affects birds in a special way: they have colourful and brilliant feathers with which northern birds cannot compete, but they do not know how to sing! Hegel hopes nevertheless, that 'when the day comes in which the forests of Brazil do not resonate any more with the inarticulate tones of degenerate men, then many singing birds will produce more refined melodies.'[68]

Gerbi comments that from this one must deduce that the poor South American birds ruined their voices by hearing the awful noises emitted by the degenerate savages and making the mistake of trying to imitate them. If the aborigines were a weak, degenerate and disappearing race, the Latin American Creoles descended from the Spanish conquerors did not fare any better in Hegel's description. Their character was linked to that of the Spanish:

> Living far away from the mother country on which they depended, they had more scope to indulge their arbitrary inclinations ... The noble and magnanimous aspects of the Spanish character did not accompany them to America. The Creoles, who are descended from the Spanish immigrants, lived on in the presumptuous ways they had inherited, and behaved in an arrogant manner towards the natives.[69]

Hegel distinguished between world-historical peoples, who were culturally developed and capable of building a strong state, thus contributing to the progress of world history; and peoples without history, who were spiritually weak and unable to build a strong state, thus having no civilizing mission to carry out in history. The latter had to submit to the former. Thus, for instance, China represented for Hegel a stationary nation which did not contribute to the progress of world history. His description of South America clearly shows that for him it had no autonomous role to play in the development of the human spirit either; and that, on the contrary, it constituted a world where events were a mere expression of the Old World.

By following Hegel, Schelling argued that the human race was divided into two large groups and that only the smaller one possessed a human aspect. The largest mass of human beings was outside history, unable to contribute to the development of the human spirit, foreign to all art that goes beyond instinctive ability.[70] All this was especially true of African and South American natives, but the latter were weaker and more docile and therefore were in danger of disappearing, unable to bear the hard labour imposed on them by the Spanish. As a consequence, Schelling justified black slavery in South America as the only means to protect the natives. He resorts to the authority of Bishop Bartolomé de las Casas, the great defender of South American Indians, in order to depict black slavery as a merciful operation destined to save both the Indians and the black soul:

It is not due to an evil mind or to contempt for men that Las Casas conceived of and carried out the project of replacing the weak American race by the robust African race in the exploitation of the silver and gold mines, a project that, certainly, has not had as a consequence commerce with black slaves (because these unfortunate people had already been victims of such commerce, and under its most evil form), but the exportation of blacks, which a merciful spirit could consider as the only way to save from eternal death this human race abandoned to terrible barbarism, and these lost souls almost without hope.[71]

Although Schelling recognizes in a footnote that Las Casas was not the first to conceive the idea of replacing Indians by black slaves in the mines, he insists that Las Casas wrote about this idea in 1517 and that the trade of black slaves was organized from that moment onwards. That Las Casas did have such an idea is historically true, but it is not accurate to say that the slave trade was organized as a consequence of Las Casas's words. The slave trade had already started when Las Casas wrote about this topic. It is also disingenuous not to clarify that later on Las Casas greatly lamented having proposed such an idea and openly criticized the Portuguese slave trade and the ill-treatment of black slaves on sugar plantations.

What is it within modernity that allows such constructions of the other as the ones I have shown above? It seems to me that this phenomenon could be explained in two ways. On the one hand, it is possible to think of the rise of instrumental reason in connection with the first modern philosophies. Horkheimer provides the basic argument here with his distinction between subjective and objective reason.[72] Religious and metaphysical systems were based on objective reason: a principle inherent in reality which is concerned with the goodness, hierarchy and desirability of ends and purposes. Modern philosophers attacked objective reason because of its dogmatic and authoritarian character. Subjective reason is no longer concerned with ends or the desirability of purposes; it is only concerned with means. This brings about tolerance and respect for different positions, whose validity and desirability cannot be decided by science.

However, the idea of tolerance is ambivalent. On the one hand, it means freedom from dogmatic authority; on the other, 'it furthers an attitude of neutrality towards all spiritual content, which is thus surrendered to relativism.'[73] The domination of subjective reason means the domination of self-interest; it also means that crucial principles such as tolerance, freedom and equality can no longer be justified by principles of objective reason and therefore lose their intellectual foundation. Subjective reason or science cannot decide that a value is better than its opposite. Once the philosophical grounding of values on objective reason has disappeared, any party or group can argue that certain values are good for them but not for others, and nobody can oppose an argument on the basis of reason. The more the concept of reason becomes instrumental and separated from the idea of a principle inherent in reality, the more it will lend itself to the most blatant lies.[74] It is because subjective reason conforms to anything that it may justify racism and slavery. Subjective reason is unable to adjudicate in issues related to absolute principles, values or morals.

On the other hand, the problem cannot be reduced to the primacy of instrumental reason alone. The theory of ideology can provide an additional kind of explanation by introducing the idea of the need to conceal the greedy and exploitative intentions of the European colonial expansion abroad. It was in the Europeans' interest to overlook – or wilfully misrepresent – the specific character of the cultures they encountered. It can be argued that the shameful exploitation of indigenous peoples for economic gain necessitated the ideological concealment and justification of its worst excesses by stressing time and again that Indians were inferior and full of vices and by pretending that their enslavement and hard labour would make them better and would save their souls. Very few authors would have dared openly to justify slavery by admitting that otherwise sugar would be too expensive, as Montesquieu did in a rare display of honesty.

The construction of a colonial identity

From the original encounter between the Spanish culture and the Indian cultures a pattern emerged, heavily influenced by the Catholic religion, closely related to political authoritarianism and not very open to scientific reason. It easily coexisted with slavery, racism, the Inquisition, and religious monopoly. This is not surprising if one realizes that Spain had become the last European fortress of a world destined to disappear: Christendom. From the middle of the sixteenth century Spain assumed with vigour and dedication the leadership of the Counter-Reformation, the defence of Christendom and the struggle against the Protestant heresy which invaded the rest of Europe.[75] The conquerors who arrived to America were then the representatives of an almost extinct world who came to impose a model that was fundamentally anti-modern. This could not but have enormous repercussions for the colonies being born. As Zea has put it, 'Spain, being unable to reconquer Europe for the Catholic cause, will close its cultural frontiers and within them the America which fate has given it for colonization is locked.'[76]

The church quickly became a very powerful and wealthy institution in Latin America. After the first hundred years, the church had 70,000 churches, chapels and oratories, 200 convents[77] and in many areas it owned close to half the available land. The church did allow the servitude of Indians under the encomienda system (as a convenient compensation for teaching them the true religion), but it never condoned their slavery or the excesses of the encomenderos. However, it did not apply the same principles to the black people brought from Africa as slaves. Most religious orders themselves, especially the Jesuits, had black slaves and tried to justify it. It is not therefore very surprising that in all the Latin American colonial societies maintained by servile work, manual labour was regarded with disdain.

The Spanish Inquisition forbade practically all the available scientific books and only allowed scholastic philosophy to be taught at the newly created universities.[78] The new experimental and natural sciences were deliberately excluded.[79] This is what Zea has called the double enclosure: 'Spain imposes on America a political and social enclosure and the Catholic church a mental enclosure.'[80] These two enclosures connected political authoritarianism with religious obedience to God and left a profound and long-lasting mark on the cultural ethos of Latin America. As de Imaz has maintained, 'for three centuries there was a very clear relationship between political authoritarianism and the legitimating role of the Inquisition.'[81] Flores Galindo has documented well how in the seventeenth century the persistent struggles of religious congregations against idolatry in the central sierra of Peru had a connotation of political control: 'the relative precariousness of the military system forced an apparent hypertrophy of religious mechanisms, so that, in that way, through fervour or more frequently fear, control over men could be secured.'[82]

What kind of Catholicism was thus transmitted? In the first place the Spanish and Portuguese brought with them a Catholicism steeped in the idea of Christendom, for which there were no sharp distinctions between the evangelizing mission and its commercial and economic interests. As Sepúlveda puts it,

> the religious dimension appeared in the self-consciousness of the crown's emissaries as the defining element of the identity of the whole of 'New Spain'. Therefore, the defence of the 'true religion', of the cultural identity and of the political and commercial interests of New

Spain were all the same thing. It was therefore normal that that which
was perceived as a threat to this cultural identity, was also perceived
as a threat to the 'true religion'.[83]

In other words, the Catholicism brought by the peninsulars was the
central element of the cultural identity of the region, the central
nucleus of all aspects of life. Second, Catholicism was forced upon
the Indians. They were asked to accept without discussion the authority of the church and the king. If they failed to agree, or if their productivity was low, corporal punishment was applied. True, not all
aspects of Christianity had to be forced on them in the same way.
The Indians' own highly ritualized religions and sacrifices easily connected with Catholic liturgy. They loved choral music, expressive religious imagery and the liturgical richness of the Catholic ceremonies.
Yet on the whole Catholicism was imposed.

As Indians could not oppose Catholicism without endangering
their lives, in many cases they formally accepted the new religion but
secretly maintained their own beliefs. Their spontaneous liking of
religious ritual was particularly appropriate for this secret form of
resistance because they could easily cover up their own religious
beliefs under a veneer of Catholic religion acceptable to the Spanish:
the external practice of the rituals. That the Spanish suspected that
the Indians' own beliefs were alive is shown by the great campaigns
to 'extirpate' idolatry at the beginning of the seventeenth century.
This is why some commentators have observed that evangelization
remained superficial and that the Catholicism which was spread was
rather nominal, external and cultic and did not entail a deep conversion – a feature which is supposed to have survived until now.[84]
As Bengoa has put it,

> the ritual evangelization of the old indigenous structures did not
> change the societal and religious matrix of the pre-Hispanic cultures.
> These had – and still have – enough strength to express themselves
> through rites which have been redefined and which in time have
> become their own form of expression and in many cases of resistance.[85]

Darcy Ribeiro has argued that Indians, mestizos and even the elites
formed during the colonial period were forced to internalize a vision
of the world and of themselves which was alien to them and which
underpinned European domination. According to him even the most
lucid layers of the emerging mestizo peoples became used to seeing
themselves and their peoples as a very low section of humankind,
inferior to Europeans, and destined to play a subaltern role in history.
The cultural conceptions of Indian and black were compulsorily eradi-

cated in order to give way to a new self-conception which reproduced the ideas and values of the invaders and which described them as inferior and grotesque creatures incapable of progress. This adoption of the other's attitude determines the spurious and alienating character of the newly emerging cultures: they are full of exogenous and uprooting values.[86] Although I agree that the self-image of these new peoples was low (it could not be otherwise given the invaders' dominant attitudes and expectations), it is a different matter altogether to accept that the newly emerging cultures were necessarily inauthentic and alienating.

Ribeiro takes his idea of authentic cultures from Sapir, who defines them as those cultures which are inherently harmonious and balanced and which give their bearers a sense of inner satisfaction because they are internally produced.[87] According to this view an inauthentic or alienating culture would be one which comes from the outside to impose itself on a people. If a culture is inauthentic or alienating because it is not internally produced, then it is not inauthentic *per se*, but only in relation to those who did not develop it. Yet unless one conceives the internally produced culture of a colonized country as a close, incommensurable essence, it is possible that it may fully incorporate elements of the dominant culture and, to that extent, the syncretic result may become 'authentic' by the internal adoption of foreign values. Alternatively, it is also possible that a culture which is internally produced, that is to say 'authentic', may produce dissatisfaction in many of its bearers, who would prefer new ways. Are the old ways necessarily more 'authentic' than the new ones? I do not think so.

The fact that some cultural features and values are internally produced is no guarantee that they are worth keeping, nor are alien values necessarily bad for another culture. If authenticity applies only to those autochthonous cultures produced by a people without any contact with others, then there is hardly any authentic culture left in the world today and even the indigenous cultures in pre-Columbian America were not authentic either. This is the reason why authenticity and inauthenticity are not adequate concepts to deal with the problems stemming from the encounter between cultures (unless one has an essentialist concept of culture). In Latin America the Indian cultures were indeed all but destroyed by the Iberian conquerors, but this did not necessarily make the newly emerging syncretic cultures inauthentic. All the same, it is true that the conflict of cultures did create a problem of identity for the newly emerging peoples.

The emergence of a colonial identity, that is to say, the emergence of an identity different from the Spanish or Portuguese metropolitan identities, was a slow and complicated process which took place in different sectors of society at different times and with different rhythms. There is little doubt that for a long time the European-born colonists in South America identified themselves with Spain and Portugal. Yet from the very beginning there was also a notion of the singularity and distinctiveness of the situation in South America. As Uslar Pietri has put it, even 'the very Spanish who established themselves in the New World, when they returned to the Peninsula, were inevitably seen as different. The early figure of the Indiano, in the language as much as in the popular consciousness, proves it.'[88] On the other hand, as Schwartz has argued in the case of Brazil, 'a feeling of distinctiveness, a lack of identification with Europe, and a profound realization of the colonial reality existed precociously among the *mestiço* and mulatto populations.'[89] This can be clearly extended to Spanish America and can be justified on the grounds that mestizos, mulattos and people of other racial mixes born in America could not have a particular attachment to Spain or Portugal, which they did not know.

Although this can be surmised as most probable, it is more difficult to show, given the character of 'practical consciousness'[90] which such feelings have. As we saw in chapter 1, identity exists not only at the level of public discourse, but also as a form of personal and group subjectivity which expresses a variety of practices, modes of life and feelings developed by common people in more restricted and local spaces in the multiple conversations and exchanges of daily life. Nevertheless, the blatant discrimination these lower classes suffered at the hands of the European-born administrators and landowners must have powerfully contributed to the early construction of a separate identity. In the long run even the native-born agrarian class which assumed the role of local nobility also developed a separate identity in opposition to the European-born administrators and commercial bourgeoisie. According to David Brading this began to happen in the early seventeenth century when they realized that, in spite of being descendants of the conquerors, they were excluded from official governing posts by those coming directly from the Peninsula.[91] By the close of the eighteenth century there was intense animosity between the American-born elite and the Spanish and Portuguese.

To the accusations of the Peninsulars that criollos were tainted with the same Indian vices and faults, the criollos responded by developing a distinct identity in which at least two features stood out. As Pagden has shown, there was first of all an attempt 'to create, at least among the white community, a model Christian society', observant of its duties and overzealous in its worshipping of God. The other feature was conspicuous expenditure, as much in clothes as in coaches, churches, fiestas, public ceremonies and private residences. It was as if the authority and self-image of the criollo elite depended on its ability to show off its wealth to the others.[92]

But not all aspects of the colonial identity were shared in the same way by all the regions in South America. Darcy Ribeiro has introduced a useful classification of three distinct situations which emerged out of the European expansion. He distinguishes between 'witness peoples', 'new peoples' and 'transplanted peoples'.[93] These categories can be used to describe different cultural situations arising out of the impact of the European conquest and giving rise to different identities. 'Witness peoples' are the survivors of the major autonomous civilizations of South America which were destroyed by the European advance. This is the case of Mexico, Central America and the Andean countries such as Bolivia, Peru and Ecuador. In these places a drastic process of deculturation (loss of own culture) took place and the Hispanic culture was acculturated. But the weight of the collapsed culture was such that the Spanish could not entirely uproot it and it has survived sometimes in a masked way. The identity of the 'witness peoples' is very much marked by the presence/ collapse of the original culture and by a sense of the catastrophic accompanied by a strong emotional charge.[94]

The 'new peoples' are the product of the fusion of European, indigenous and African ethnic groups. This mixing process created a new ethnic group with a new culture. These peoples are no longer strongly attached to an old, autonomous and powerful cultural tradition as the 'witness peoples' are. Their relatively weaker cultural strength made them lose their own identity in a more radical manner. Two subgroups can be distinguished, one with an African matrix (Brazilians, Venezuelans, Colombians and Caribbeans) and another with an indigenous matrix (Chileans, Paraguayans, Uruguayans and Argentinians). In these cases a new identity emerged in which the presence of the original cultures was far less marked.[95]

Finally, the 'transplanted peoples' are those created by European migrations of people who did not mix with the indigenous peoples (USA, Canada) and reconstituted a European way of life abroad. Argentina and Uruguay are special cases because, having been born as 'new peoples', they became 'transplanted peoples' after massive Italian and Spanish immigration. In this case the influence of the Indo-Iberian cultural legacy is almost lost, or at least greatly diminished, and is replaced at all levels by a European culture. In this case there is hardly any presence of the original cultures in the new national identity.[96]

But even within each of these groupings one can find further differences. For instance, among the 'witness peoples' the construction of a national identity by the creole aristocracy was not exactly the same in Peru as in Mexico. Whereas the Peruvian Creoles 'found it difficult to install the Inca empire as the foundation of their *patria* ... by contrast, in New Spain, creole patriots insisted on the continuity between Tenochtitlan and the viceregal capital that was built on its ruins.'[97] This difference was very important for the future development of a national identity and the way in which Indians were treated. In Mexico the tendency to integrate the Indians and their culture into the new nation continued after independence, even if this was not always very successful. In Peru, on the contrary, the integration of the Indians into the nation has been far more problematic and their cultural exclusion by the elite far more apparent.

The case against the idea of a 'baroque' modernity

My analysis so far has pointed in the direction of a colonial period in which modernity could not penetrate. It was excluded by the Spanish and Portuguese construction of a cultural identity in which traditional Catholicism played a central role and which tried to maintain and defend a situation of Christendom which was being challenged by the Reformation and by modernization processes in the rest of Europe.[98] There are some authors, however, who have argued that this religious identity was not necessarily anti-modern, but rather responded to a different kind of modernity. Thus Morandé and Cousiño maintain that there was a kind of modernity which existed prior to the Enlightenment and which therefore was not based on instrumental reason or science: baroque modernity.[99] According to them, this was not only the cradle in which the Latin American identity was born, but it could also show the way for a pattern of modernization in accordance with the religious substratum of Latin American identity.

Hence for Cousiño and Morandé, there is an opposition between enlightened modernity and baroque modernity, but both models have a modern character. Whereas the logic of the enlightened model rests on mercantile exchange and is marked by the importance of the written text, baroque modernity finds its foundation in ritual and dramatic representation, and is marked by the importance of oral transmission:

> Baroque society does not aspire to constituting a public of readers capable of generating a rationalized public opinion. The baroque public places are not cafés and clubs, but fundamentally the theatre and the fiestas, many of them taking place on occasions of religious celebrations.
>
> Nature and man appear as baroque topics in so far as they are the occasion for infinitude and transcendence. In marked opposition to enlightened rationalism, which seeks to find the laws that rule over the natural and the human, Baroque is not so much interested in the natural as in the marvellous that is expressed in nature.[100]

But this suggestion has serious problems. The principal one appears in the very definition of modernity. For Cousiño a project is modern when it seeks to resolve the crisis of medieval Christendom and tries to reconstitute an ecumenical principle which can account for diversity.[101] This to say that Cousiño understands modernity in purely formal terms and in a strict relationship to a religious problem. This is why the Catholic Counter-Reformation and the Council of Trent, which are at the basis of baroque culture, can appear as a form of modernity even earlier than Enlightened modernity.

It is undeniable that modernity in its origins is related to religious problems, in the sense that, to a great extent, it arises against the religious conception of life and world. This does not mean, though, that modernity inexorably leads to a total secularization of society. But neither can one derive an argument that gives a genuinely modern character to the traditional Catholicism involved in the Spanish Counter-Reformation and the Council of Trent. The content of modernity cannot be reduced to the reconstitution of an ecumenical principle or to a religious project. As we saw in chapter 1, modernity is about reason, progress, political democracy, science, commodity production, new conception of time and space and rapid change. These are its fundamental contents, and for this reason the Counter-Reformation and the Council of Trent do not seem modern but rather pawns in the defence of the old premodern regime.

In his classic work on baroque culture, Maravall maintains that it is a reaction designed to integrate a society threatened by crisis and social agitation. He describes it as a 'directed' and 'conservative' culture which aimed to 'achieve immobility or, at least, to impose a direction on the advancing forces which the Renaissance had set in motion', which was connected with 'a restored, agrarian-based seigneurial society' and which 'organizes its resources to maintain and strengthen the order of traditional society, based on a regime of privileges and crowned by a form of government related to estates and absolute monarchy.'[102] Following this line of argument Véliz affirms that 'the baroque is an assertion of stability, a refusal to give way, a glorification of obstinacy, an affirmation of belief, an indictment of change as an illusion, a reiteration of faith in things as they are, a rejection of the lure of things as they could be . . .'[103]

All these characteristics seem clearly anti-modern. It might be counter-argued that modernity is not necessarily defined by the features mentioned earlier, for such characteristics are only typical of a specific late modern project, the Enlightenment project of the eighteenth century, and that modernity started earlier than that and comprises other projects, of a very different nature. It is true that modernity started earlier than the Enlightenment, but this does not mean that its contents were totally different from or antagonistic to the Enlightenment; rather the latter represents its most refined form. The point is this: modernity is not just a historical time subsequent to the crisis of Christendom when all phenomena, including the Counter-Reformation and the Council of Trent, acquired a modern character because they were a response to that crisis.[104] Modernity is not simply what develops according to 'today's mode', as Parker has put it,[105] where everything that happens in contemporary times could be included.

Nor can modernity be defined in purely formal terms as an attempt to find a universal principle that accounts for diversity. A great variety of situations and different, even antagonistic, projects may fall under such a wide definition. Modernity has contents and principles which cannot accommodate just any historical project, even if it is a contemporary project. It is not possible to conceive of a modern project that appreciates reason and the market, and another equally modern project which appreciates dramatic representation and has contempt for reason and the market. Baroque culture developed during the modern epoch in Spain, but it is not of itself a modern project; indeed it is strictly speaking an anti-modern project.

Wagner has argued that modernity is an uneven historical process, in which, to be properly understood, one must distinguish between two aspects: the discourse of modernity, which constitutes a modern imaginary, and the modern practices and institutions themselves.[106] Modernity started as a discourse breaking with the theocentric medieval world and constitutes an imaginary of new ideas with meaning for the individual and society. But in the reality of specific social contexts, not all practices, orientations and institutions were based on that imaginary. At the beginning modernity could only count on a few intellectuals, and little by little it expanded its influence over social practices, which means that even today not all practices and orientations are fully modern. As Wagner puts it, 'a number of social practices can be truly better understood as a rejection – partial or radical – of modernity's imaginary significance, whose impact gave rise to its development.'[107] My point is precisely that what is called baroque culture must be understood as a rejection of the imaginary of modernity.[108]

The distinction between enlightened modernity and baroque modernity may entail a double simplification. First, it favours a unilateral understanding of European enlightened modernity as a process which inevitably, and to the exclusion of everything else, leads to an absolute predominance of instrumental reason. Second, it favours the idea that it is possible or plausible to think of a kind of modernity which excludes instrumental rationality. To these one must answer, first, that European enlightened modernity has gone much further than the mere production of technically useful knowledge, and has also engendered the rational bases themselves for the critique of instrumental reason. Second, that instrumental rationality, science and technology, in spite of their problems, are necessary for society to resolve its problems. European enlightened modernity can neither be reduced to the mere triumph of instrumental reason, nor can it be conceived without instrumental reason.

3
Oligarchic Modernity
1810–1900

Beginnings and limits of modernization
(1810–1850)

During the eighteenth century Spain began to lose profits in the colonial trade due to fraud and contraband. Its response by the end of the century was to introduce a series of administrative reforms to strengthen its control, and to pay for them it imposed high taxes. This provoked a series of uprisings in the colonies. Simultaneously the power and economic significance of Spain in the world systematically declined. Its naval power was destroyed in the war against Britain and this affected even further its ability to maintain the trade monopoly. The local producers and merchants in Latin America soon realized that colonial relations were an obstacle to a more direct, expanding and profitable trade with Great Britain and other European nations. The obstacles against free trade with Europe coupled with the political exclusion of the locally born criollos from administrative and governmental tasks were the two main motivations behind the independence process.

These motivations reflect how during the eighteenth century the local criollos had increasingly acquired self-consciousness as a group, and their distinct identity manifested itself in many struggles for recognition. Local elites made many petitions and complaints which indicated their increasing cohesion and a clear awareness of their interests. As Jocelyn-Holt has shown in the Chilean case, this increased self-consciousness manifested itself not only as class cohesion, but also as a regional or local identity, as a sense of the 'Chilean'.[1] This was also the case elsewhere in Latin America. The Napoleonic invasion of Spain finally provided the opportunity for the criollos to rise. At the beginning this was a peaceful process which did not even question the legitimacy of the Spanish monarchy in Latin America. As the monarchy in Spain had been toppled, in 1810 the local councils, called cabildos, laid claim to the exercise of power until the monarchy was restored. Inevitably, though, this led to a clash with the Iberian administrators and the wars of independence started.

In general the war against the Iberian-led forces was directed by the criollo urban elites. But it was compounded by racial issues, especially in those countries with a high proportion of Indians like Peru. At first the Indians became allies of the Iberian forces simply because they were directly exploited by the criollos and they feared that independence would exacerbate their servitude. When the expeditionary force from Buenos Aires and Santiago tried to enlist the support of the Indians by freeing them from the payment of tribute and declaring them equal, the criollos switched to the Iberian side since what they feared the most was uprisings by the Indians and the loss of their free labour. In Mexico, too, the independence movement proclaimed the freedom and equality of the Indians and this led some criollo elites to side with Spain. In general, the hierarchy of the church and the slave-owners opposed the independence process, but many creole priests sided with the rebels. Indeed in Mexico they took the initiative, as shown by the leadership of Hidalgo and Morelos. By maintaining benevolent neutrality and providing some material help, Britain and the United States contributed to the success of the Latin American rebels, but they abstained from direct intervention. By 1825 the wars of independence were over and the process of independence from Spanish colonialism had been completed.

The legacy of fifteen years of independence wars was rather heavy in terms of disrupted economies, militarized societies, generalized violence and unstable political institutions. Additionally, the enlightened ideas of change which the elite wanted to implement had to confront the resistance of the Indo-Iberian cultural pole which had been consolidated during the three centuries of colonial rule. Yet these circumstances did not totally prevent Latin American societies from starting deep processes of change and modernization. But these modernization processes were marked by ambiguity. Tulio Halperin has shown, for instance, how the important social weight of the armed forces, 'which emerges at the very time that a process of limited but real democratization of Latin American social and political life is occurring, begins by being an aspect of such democratization, but very soon is transformed into a guarantee against the excessive extension of that process.'[2]

Religious and educational freedom was established in most countries, but education was restricted to a tiny segment of the population, and other religions did not have a real chance to expand in practice, as Catholicism remained the official state religion. The same ambiguity was shown in respect of slavery and the castas. Discrimination did not end overnight, but blacks, mestizos, mulattos and Indians acquired a new place in many countries, especially because they were needed as recruits in the army. Thus even without slavery being abolished, many blacks had had to be freed because of the war. In the long run these changes led the new republics to eliminate slavery, and prompted new forms of stratification not dependent on skin colour. However, this process was slower in plantation economies like Brazil, Puerto Rico and Cuba, which depended on slaves for manual work. In Brazil, for instance, which had the greatest concentration of black slaves, slavery was finally abolished only in 1888, in spite of the fact that the 1824 constitution incorporated an important part of the French Universal Declaration of Human Rights.[3] It is quite telling, for instance, that in 1887 the Bishop of Maranhao was still unable to convince the Carmelite monks in his diocese to free their slaves.[4]

For the Indian communities independence did not bring about significant progress. The Indians nominally became equal citizens of a country but continued to be oppressed as socially inferior communities by the triumphant criollos and mestizos. Independence also meant the division of the Indians between different nationalities. Thus the Mapuches were divided between Chile and Argentina, the Guaranies between Paraguay, Argentina and Brazil; the Quechuas were divided between Bolivia, Peru, Chile and Ecuador, etc. From 1822 onwards the Indians were doubly marginalized: first divided between foreign nations and then largely deprived of their lands by the triumphant criollos. However, quite a few Indian communities, poor Spanish and mestizos, did manage to keep small plots. The social marginality and oppression of the Indians after independence has led some authors to speak of the maintenance of a colonial relationship which, in order to be differentiated from the Spanish colonial system, is called internal colonialism.[5] However, little by little, class relationships began to erode the colonial relationship, especially through the expedient of depriving the Indians of their lands, forcing them to work for a salary in the haciendas.

The economic base of the new system of classes in the new republics was mainly the hacienda, which determined the existence of the landlord class and the semi-servile peasants (who take different names according to the country: 'inquilinos', 'campesinos', 'huasipungueros'). There was also a free peasant economy made up of some closed Indian communities, mestizos and poor Spanish but it was not as important socially or economically as the hacienda. In the haciendas the peasants or tenants had the obligation to work for the landlord at certain times but could keep a small plot for themselves and their family to provide their own food. They were hardly free. They were typically tied up with debts which could never be repaid, and they had to ask their landlords for practically everything, including the administration of justice.

Given all these characteristics, the first stage of modernization during the nineteenth century might be called oligarchic, in spite of the obvious contradiction in terms, because of its restricted character. Two features of this stage must be underlined. First, during this time liberal ideas were adopted, lay education was expanded, a free press was established, a republican state was built up and democratic forms of government were introduced, but all this with extraordinary restrictions *de facto* on the wide participation of the people. As Hale has argued, liberal ideas were applied in an environment which was 'resistant and hostile' 'in countries which were highly stratified, socially and racially, and economically underdeveloped and in which the tradition of centralized state authority ran deep.'[6] Perhaps for these very reasons, Latin Americans embraced liberalism very selectively, and not all 'liberal' ideas were equally acceptable to them.[7]

From the very beginning some of the heroes of independence and the founding fathers of the Latin American republics thought that fully fledged representative democracy was not the best form of government for the Latin American situation. Two important examples are Bolívar and Portales. Bolívar argued that experience had shown that 'perfectly representative institutions are not adequate to our character, customs and present perspective' and that, for instance, the most advanced American republic from the point of view of its political institutions, Venezuela, had been the 'clearest of examples of the inefficacy of the democratic and federal form for our nascent states'.[8] Bolívar's idea was to build an authoritarian republic with a president for life and a very reduced electorate. Thus he tried to organize the republics of Bolivia, Peru, Venezuela and Colombia along these lines.[9] Portales, in Chile, was also of the opinion that 'democracy, so much preached by dreamers, is an absurdity in countries like the American ones, full of vices and where citizens lack all virtue'; the republican system had to be adopted but including 'a strong, centralized government, whose functionaries should be true models of virtue and patriotism, thus guiding citizens into a path of order and virtue. When they have been moralized, then the completely liberal government may come, free and full of ideals, where all citizens play a part.'[10]

Yet in spite of these doubts about democracy, some important progress in this area must be also recognized. The duality of progress and restriction in the democratic process can be clearly seen, for instance, in the Chilean electoral processes of the nineteenth century. They excluded the great majority of the population,[11] including women, but at the same time, recent research has shown that the majority of the voters came from middle and low strata and the electoral campaigns deeply involved many more people, including women.[12]

Second, contrary to the European trajectory, industrialization was postponed and replaced by a system exporting raw materials which preserved the backwardness of the productive sectors, especially under the hacienda system. The achievement of political independence meant a redefinition of the Latin American export economy in respect of a new metropolis, Great Britain, and the consolidation of the landowners as the new rural-based political ruling class. They created and organized states and juridical orders that guaranteed their political power and the conditions for the continuation of export-oriented production. This task of creating new national states was not easy after a prolonged war, and it lasted, with many upheavals and disruptions, from 1825 to 1850. Some mining countries like Mexico, Peru and Bolivia were plunged into years of anarchy and war, which led to economic stagnation and almost permanent political instability. Other countries like Argentina and Chile prospered by exporting agricultural products, and in the case of Chile also silver and copper. In the latter, political stability was achieved earlier by means of alliances between the traditional landowners and the exporting and/or mining interests.

The search for a new identity

The process of independence at the beginning of the nineteenth century precipitated a crisis of the colonial cultural pattern. The eighteenth-century French Enlightenment and British liberalism played a very important ideological role in this process. Just as much as the criollos wanted freedom to trade with Britain and the rest of Europe, they also wanted cultural freedom from the tutelage of the church. Along with contraband goods, the criollos received banned books and arguments to support their growing subversion. The wars of independence were fought under the theoretical banner of the Enlightenment.

The process of independence marked the beginning of a sustained development of the press, both for and against independence. Newspapers had existed in colonial times, especially in the eighteenth century, but they were very limited in numbers and heavily controlled by the colonial power. With the new spaces of freedom provided by the collapse of the Spanish monarchy, numerous newspapers emerged in Mexico, Chile, Argentina and other countries, and they took on themselves the mission of spreading republican and liberal ideas. Most notable were Camilo Henríquez' *La Aurora de Chile* (1812–13) and José Joaquín Fernández de Lizardi's *El Pensador Mexicano* (1812–14). They were particularly important for the creation of a national consciousness. After independence was achieved, the press suffered the consequences of the anarchistic struggles for power and the political instability which ensued in many countries. It became very militant, partisan and ephemeral and was thereby repressed by the governments of the day.[13]

Fernández de Lizardi was also one of the first novelists of Latin America and certainly the most important literary figure of the independence period. His most important novels, *El Periquillo Sarmiento* (1816), *La Quijotita y su prima* (1819) and the posthumously published *Don Catrín de la Fachenda*, highlighted the new criollo values and criticized colonial institutions. By defending total religious freedom, equality of rights and women's emancipation, he represented the most liberal wing of independentist thought. In *La Quijotita y su prima* Fernández de Lizardi, very unusually for his time, exposed the unfortunate consequences of not properly educating women.[14] Another writer of the independence time, Mariano Melgar, a Peruvian mestizo and poet, is significant both because he fought and died for independence and because he criticized the oppression of the Indians. His poems adopted the form of the *yaravi*, a kind of Indian song. In one of them, entitled *El Cantero y el asno*, he compared the situation of the Indian with that of a donkey physically abused.[15]

With the process of independence, a crisis of identity which had been developing in Latin America since the end of the eighteenth century reached a culminating point. This identity crisis and the consequent struggle are well reflected in Bolívar's 'Letter from Jamaica' where he states that a 'reciprocal benevolence, a tender solicitude for the cradle and the glory of our fathers, in sum, all that formed our hope, came to us from Spain. From here a principle of adhesion was born which seemed eternal.' But the oppressive conduct of the Spaniards has altered all that and 'at present the contrary happens: we are threatened and fear death, dishonour and what is bad; we suffer everything from this denatured stepmother.'[16] But the crisis is not just a reaction against an unfair mother, it is deeper and touches the inner being: 'we are neither Indians nor Europeans, but a middle species between the legitimate owners of the country and the Spanish usurpers.'[17] In this text Bolívar shows how the distinct colonial identity resulting from *mestizaje* is no longer merely different from the metropolitan identity, but is prepared to rebel against it. A few years later he goes even further and minimizes the European contribution: 'let us bear in mind that we are a people who are not European, or North American, that more than emanating from Europe, we are rather a composite of Africa and America.'[18]

The second element of this identity crisis was a kind of uncertainty about the new identity that would emerge out of it. Many founding fathers dreamed of a united continent and privileged a collective Latin American identity over more regional allegiances. Thus Bolívar maintained that

> It is an ambitious idea to pretend to form in the whole of the New World only one nation with only one link that bonds its parts among themselves and with the whole. Since it has one origin, one language, one custom and one religion, it should therefore have only one government; but it is not possible because remote climates, diverse situations, opposite interests, dissimilar characters divide America.[19]

Other leaders and intellectuals throughout the nineteenth century such as Francisco de Miranda (Venezuela), Bernardo Monteagudo (Argentina), José Maria Samper (Colombia), Eugenio María de Hostos (Puerto Rico) and Francisco Bilbao (Chile) preached the same idea of Latin American unity. Many of them were increasingly conscious of the dangers which the growing power of the United States represented for Latin America and thought that Latin American unity, of the kind dreamed of by Bolívar, was the only possible answer to this challenge. Hostos, for instance, put forward the idea that the New Continent would give to humankind two great benefits: the discovery of the Pacific Ocean and the discovery of federation. America would become the centre of the world because of the fusion of its races in the same civilization and a union of all its nations.[20]

Bilbao too wanted to create a confederation of South American republics capable of defending its territorial integrity against Europeans and North Americans. In a paper read in Paris in 1856 to a Latin American audience, Bilbao says that 'the historical time has come for the unity of South America; the second campaign opens up that should add to the conquered independence the association of our peoples.'[21] Yet, as is well known, this and other initiatives never prospered, and little by little the more restricted identity of each country imposed itself. Which is not to say that the Latin American consciousness about a common identity does not exist; it does, but it has not been strong enough to underpin a successful search for political unity.

A third aspect of the identity crisis was the struggle for intellectual independence, or 'mental emancipation' as the Mexican Gabino Barreda called it.[22] Political independence did not suffice; it was also necessary to change old habits of thought, to renovate customs, to abandon colonial attitudes. Under the idea of 'mental emancipation' Barreda advocated three kinds of emancipation: scientific, religious and political. The Chilean Manuel de Salas exclaimed as early as 1811: 'they have kept us in darkness. The good thoughts which we read in the few useful writings which, by oversight, fell into our hands were labelled as fantasies and tales . . . I am sick and tired of hearing . . . "this is not adaptable".'[23] Bilbao was also one of the intellectuals committed to mental emancipation and even if he warned Latin Americans about the dangers of North American hegemony, he still insisted that the vital elements of its civilization, science, industry and art had to be incorporated into Latin American education.[24] He called for the de-Hispanicizing and de-Catholicizing of Chile and Latin America.[25] Less wary of North Americans, Lastarria maintained that *the emancipation of the spirit* is the great objective of the Hispano-American revolution', the opposite of the principle inspiring Spanish civilization. Hence he considered the Spanish tutelage as barren and exhorted Latin Americans to reconstruct social science as the Anglo-Americans had done.[26]

The problem with this kind of 'mental emancipation' is that in these authors it assumed the paradoxical connotation of freeing the mind from traditional Spanish culture in order to embrace French and English culture. Most of them did not realize that they were substituting one foreign cultural legacy for another foreign cultural legacy. Very few authors had the subtlety and balance to be open to what came from Europe without being too servile to it. Andrés Bello, a Venezuelan living in Chile, was a notable exception. He accepted what came from European culture, including Spain, but warned intellectuals 'not to imagine that we could find in it what is not, or cannot be, there'. That is to say, the specificity and peculiarity of each Latin American country should be the starting point for intellectuals. For Bello it was all right to use European ideas, but more than anything else it was necessary to imitate the European independence of mind.[27] In the field of literature, the Argentinian Esteban Echeverría is another good example. He maintained that it was absurd to be American in politics and Spanish in literature, and hence sought to incorporate the influence of Argentinian geography and climate in his work. In his narrative poem *La Cautiva* (1837) he tried to discover the way in which the pampa, with all its elements of isolation and roughness, conditioned the Argentinian situation.[28]

A fourth aspect in the search for a new identity was the crucial role played in it by the ruling oligarchy. Since independence it had been elaborating a sense of its own distinctiveness while, at the same time, by means of its control over the state, elaborating the first elements of a national identity.[29] Throughout the nineteenth century there was, on the one hand, a process of continuous construction of a separate class identity in which fashion, refinement, conspicuous consumption, lavish architecture and the privatization of public spaces became the main symbols that segregated the ruling elite from the rest.[30] But on the other hand, by using the state, and as wars and crises arose, the same elite created the first discursive versions of national identity which were capable of integrating wide sections of society into a sense of imagined community.

Consolidation of the exporting economy (1850–1900)

From the 1850s onwards, coinciding with the British abolition of the Corn Laws, practically all Latin American countries expanded and consolidated their exporting economies and their participation in international trade. Most governments followed free trade policies at the behest of the ruling groups exporting primary products. It goes without saying that these policies were also in the interest of the British industrial bourgeoisie, and the penetration of modern products from Britain contributed to the dismantling of local traditional industry and the delaying of modern industrialization.[31] Throughout Latin America there was a clear growth of imports and luxury consumption, which could be seen in the sophisticated dresses worn by the aristocracy and magnificent houses with precious woods and marbles imported from Europe. Santiago, Valparaiso, Buenos Aires, Lima, Rio de Janeiro became richer cities, with paved streets, new theatres and gas illumination.

It can be maintained that capitalism began to develop in Latin America well after the wars of independence, by the mid-nineteenth century, in a very slow process. As the demand for exports of agricultural products expanded, a double situation emerged. On the one hand, the exploitation of servile labour increased. Simultaneously, as Halperin has shown, throughout Latin America a new assault began on Indian lands, especially, but not only, to keep up with the expansion of the European export markets. On the other hand, the conditions for the emergence of capitalist agricultural enterprise were created. The scarcity of free labour was partly compensated for by the immigration of workers from Europe and China. New workers were also achieved by desertions from the haciendas and by depriving the Indians of their land. Thus the first forms of a rural proletariat were created. The new capitalist forms slowly eroded the hacienda system without any dramatic leaps.[32] At the same time, governments began to receive direct loans from European countries, especially Great Britain, and European capital also began to be invested in transport, railways and commercial and mining projects. All of this definitively confirmed Latin America as a raw material exporting area and an importer of European industrial goods.[33] As Cardoso and Faletto have put it:

> The Latin American countries were linked to the international market through a variety of products: the wheat and copper of Chile; the wool and livestock of the River Plate; the guano of Peru; the coffee of Venezuela, Brazil, Colombia, and Central America; and the sugar of the West Indies, Brazil, Mexico, and Peru. It is interesting to note that these products could still be developed with national capital and that there were sufficient local resources to finance diversified and large-scale undertakings.[34]

In some countries such as Brazil and Argentina national producers managed to keep the control of investment, labour and technology, even if marketing and international prices were beyond their control. But not all Latin American countries were able to keep national control of their main productive sectors and two types of foreign enclaves were formed: mining and plantation.[35] In the case of mining, national producers were displaced because of their inability 'to compete in the production of commodities requiring technology, marketing systems, and heavy capital investment'.[36] Thus towards the end of the nineteenth century Chile and Peru lost their control over the production of nitrates and guano respectively, and these began to be exploited by foreign companies. In the case of plantations, national producers for the international market were almost non-existent and the enclave was formed by the direct expansion of the major economies. Thus Central American republics had their economies, and most of their political life too, dominated by plantations controlled by big North American companies. In these enclaves the main process of capital accumulation was in the hands of a foreign company which controlled labour, technology, investment, and the international marketing of the produce. Local ruling groups had to withdraw from the international market and cater for the internal market.

The export economies of Latin America not only developed important financial and mercantile sectors, but also promoted the initial stages of an urban-industrial society. Groups such as the big landowners, agricultural capitalists, mine owners, merchants and bankers were all linked in varying ways to production for export. The diversification of the export economy during the last quarter of the nineteenth century led to the appearance of other classes, mainly the middle class, the industrial bourgeoisie and the working class. The growth of an industrial bourgeoisie accompanied by technically trained professionals, civil and military bureaucracies and white-collar workers depended on the way the export system was organized in each country. For instance, a stronger and more autonomous bourgeoisie and larger middle classes developed in those countries like Argentina and Uruguay where export production was kept under national control. These new classes were smaller and weaker in countries such as Chile and Peru where the main exports were controlled by foreign investment.

The new prosperity and the increasing prestige of liberalism nevertheless had their detractors. In particular the Catholic Church played a conservative role, opposing liberal reforms and defending privileges. This was also a reaction against the attempts by liberalism at constructing a secular state, free from religious tutelage.[37] During the process of independence the church had been debilitated by events, and the newly emerging countries had been rather isolated from Rome. Now, in the recently acquired stability of the mid-nineteenth century, the church, reconstituted with many foreign priests, became very vocal and combative in its advocacy of a social order retaining numerous elements of Christendom which secured it a privileged position. In this way it became the linchpin of the most conservatives forces in society. Yet, as Halperin has pointed out, 'cautiously in Argentina, more decidedly in Uruguay, Mexico,

Venezuela and Central America, the progress of liberalism had resulted in a struggle to limit the role of the church in Latin American life.'[38] Admittedly, in some cases pro-liberal and lay political forces had their greedy eyes on the church's lands and general wealth. In the end, though, the church learned to live within the new circumstances and coexisted with the new liberal regimes, which displaced the old conservative ones. Little by little the Catholic Church surrendered its privileges and followed a road which finally ended up in its ceasing to be the official state religion during the twentieth century.

For a long time then, Latin America lived through the paradox of having an aristocratic ruling class of agrarian origin which assumed a liberal ideology and constructed a democratic and republican state, but restricted political and economic participation to the members of the ruling alliance and kept semi-servile relations of production in its haciendas. The latter were even further exacerbated in mid-nineteenth century, with a bid rapidly to increase production for export. A substantial gap was created between the liberal principles proclaimed and the reality of the exclusion and semifeudal exploitation of the peasants. It is not, though, that the liberalism of the agrarian oligarchy was only a facade or an ideological screen to deceive. The incorporation of the new Latin American republics into the world market necessitated liberalism in its dimensions of free trade and openness to international markets. Besides, it was also necessary for the ruling class to create some institutions inspired by liberalism that could secure pacific competition and equality of opportunity for all the groups and sectors which participated in the ruling alliance.

The new cultural synthesis: positivism and racism

As I have shown, Latin American modernization during the nineteenth century was more successful in bringing about new political structures and new cultural ideas than social and political participation. Generally speaking, it was very restricted in that it did not reach the majority of the people. Yet in spite of these limitations, the modernization introduced went hand in hand with a reconstitution of cultural identity in which the values of freedom, democracy, racial equality, science and lay education made a considerable advance vis-à-vis the prevalent values of colonial times. By the second half of the nineteenth century the contours of a distinctive second pole of Latin American culture were thus emerging with some strength. The old values received from colonial society had been heavily influenced by the Catholic religion, closely related to political authoritarianism and not very open to scientific reason, thus justifying slavery, racism, the Inquisition and a religious monopoly. The new pole wanted to incorporate the European ideas of scientific reason and liberalism.

The positivism derived from Auguste Comte[39] was very influential. Not that the new Enlightenment values and practices of the new republics totally displaced the Indo-Iberian cultural pole, but they at least modified and transformed it in important ways. The scientific rationality of nineteenth-century Europe became quite important among the Latin American ruling classes and university academics. They thought it was the only hope for bringing about 'order and progress' in the newly emerging republics. This manifested itself especially in a wish to refashion higher education in order to form a new elite. New institutions were created to become centres of modern science: in Mexico the Escuela Nacional Preparatoria inspired by Barreda, in Argentina the Escuela Normal de Paraná formed by Sarmiento, in Chile the Instituto Pedagógico of the University of Chile created by Letelier, in Brazil the Escola Militar managed by Constant.[40] Positivism also influenced the emergence of a 'scientific politics' in Latin America which gave liberalism a more technocratic and managerial face. By following Comte's ideas, Sierra and Barreda in Mexico, and Lastarria in Chile advocated this new scientific form for politics.[41]

By the end of the nineteenth century the influence of positivism and other enlightened ideas was at its peak. Pro-modern thinkers of the time felt that modernity could only be achieved if the Indo-Iberian cultural pattern was totally replaced by a new one, but were not able to recognize how deeply influenced by the old racist prejudices they still were. At the same time, their vision of modernity was shaped by the naive wish to become a true image of the United States or Europe. Latin America was still to be civilized and its barbaric cultural features eradicated. So the essayists of the time tended to dismiss the Indo-Iberian cultural pattern bequeathed by three centuries of colonialism and hoped that European or North American solutions could be implemented to make up for what they saw as inherent Latin American deficiencies. In many cases the descriptions of those deficiencies had clearly racist overtones and were deeply influenced by the thought of Spencer, Gobineau, Taine and, above all, Gustave Le Bon. The nineteenth-century European vision of the world, which considered Latin American peoples as racially inferior because of their Indian and black components, is still present in Latin American upper classes. This is why backwardness is explained as a fatality derived from innate characteristics.

Domingo Faustino Sarmiento, the most important representative of this tradition, explicitly argued that the real struggle in Latin America was one between civilization and barbarism. Europe and the United States represented the former, racial inferiority the latter. In his major work, *Facundo*, he proposed the idea that in Argentina in 1810 'there were two different, incompatible and rival societies: two diverse civilizations: the one Spanish, European, civilized and the other barbarian, American, almost Indian . . .'[42] For Sarmiento civilized life is associated with commerce and urban life, which generate culture and progress. The Indian and the gaucho live in the pampa, isolated from all civilization and sociability. Facundo is precisely the true story of an uneducated gaucho, a brutal highwayman who lives a natural and rebellious life, managing to dominate La Rioja province until the dictator Rosas has him killed. Both men represent Argentinian barbarism.

According to Sarmiento, Latin Americans were born of a mixture of three races – Spanish, Indian and black – which by their very nature were opposed to the spirit which had made civilization possible. He argued that 'from the fusion of these three families a homogeneous whole has resulted which is distinguished by its love for idleness and industrial incapacity . . . The American races . . . show themselves to be incapable of devoting themselves, even through compulsion, to continuous and hard work.'[43] Consequently, even if he accepted that exterminating savages may have been unjust, he celebrated the fact that 'thanks to this injustice, America, instead of being abandoned to the savages, incapable of progress, is today occupied by the Caucasian race, the most perfect, the most intelligent, the most beautiful and the most progressive of all that populate the earth.'[44]

Juan Bautista Alberdi held similar ideas and argued that 'the American man suffers from a racial ineptitude for freedom and industry.'[45] For him 'Europe is the centre of the civilization of the centuries and of humanitarian progress.' 'When American intelligence has come to the same level as European intelligence, the sun of its complete emancipation will shine.'[46] By contrast, the Indian was not and could not be a real part of society: 'the Indian does justice to us; he calls us *Spanish* up until today. I do not know any distinguished person of our societies that has a pehuenche or araucano name . . . Who knows a gentleman among us that boasts to be an Indian through and through? Who would marry his sister or daughter to an Indian from Araucanía and not a thousand times rather to an English cobbler?'[47]

Sarmiento and Alberdi's vision was more or less shared by positivists like José Gil Fortoul (Venezuela), Javier Prado (Peru) and José Ingenieros (Argentina). Prado, speaking about obstacles to progress in Peru, maintained that 'the principal obstacle has come, necessarily, from what is the first social factor: *race* . . . I cannot but recognize the pernicious influence which inferior races have exercised on Peru.'[48] Gil Fortoul, in his turn, argued in similar vein that some races, like the European, have better aptitudes than others for civilization.[49] Thus in fashion and elegance the French spirit predominates, in letters and sciences the French, German and Italian one; in industry and commerce the English spirit.[50] True, both Gil Fortoul and Prado rejected Gustave Le Bon's idea that the *mestizaje* of Spaniard and Indian produced a bastard race, lacking in energy, morality and will. But, even if reluctantly, they accepted that the original races were inferior.

A similar line is taken by Ingenieros, who maintains that 'the superiority of the white race is a fact accepted even by those who deny the existence of race struggle.' By following Spencer's Social Darwinism, he goes on to argue that 'natural selection, in the long run inviolable for man as for the other species, tends to extinguish coloured races, when they find themselves facing the white one.'[51] Carlos Octavio Bunge, in Argentina, published in 1903 a 'social clinic treaty', modelled on Le Bon's ideas, which sought to study Latin American political organization through a psychological analysis of its three basic races.[52] He defended the white race of Spanish origin as individualist and superior. The Indian oscillated between passive fatalism and vengeance,[53] and at any rate tended to disappear as a result of the degeneration of the Indian race. Servilism and infatuation characterized the black.[54] Hence racial mixes could not be much better: mestizos lacked moral sense and psychic stability, mulattos were false, impulsive and petulant.[55] Equally, the Peruvian Francisco García Calderón argued in 1912 that race was the 'key to the incurable disorder that divides America'.[56] Similarly, in 1909 Alcides Arguedas, a Bolivian, addressed a devastating racial critique to the cholos (mestizos), but it was the infusion of Indian blood that seemed to be responsible for most of the defects of the Bolivian character.[57]

Yet it was in Brazil that the racist mentality derived from a combination of Comte's positivism, Spencer's evolutionism, Gobineau's works and in general Social Darwinism was at its peak. Sílvio Romero's *Historia da Literatura Brasileira*, Euclides da Cunha's *Os Sertões* and Nina Rodrigues' *As Raças Humanas e a Responsabilidade Penal no Brasil*, works by the most prominent authors of the end of the nineteenth century, put together the effects of the environment with those of racial factors to explain Brazil's backwardness. They all believed in the existence of superior and inferior races and asserted the supremacy of the white race. Because of the mix with inferior races, the mestizo, prevalent in the Brazilian people, was considered to have biologically inherited many defects and problems, especially apathy, improvidence and moral imbalance. These features combined with a variety of geographical regions were supposed to determine, for instance, 'the neurasthenia of the coastal mulatto', the 'rigidity of the mestizo from the interior' (Da Cunha) and 'the apathy of the mameluco from Amazonia' (Rodrigues).[58]

It is not therefore surprising that some of the policies these authors proposed to modernize Latin America consisted in improving its race by means of European immigration. Sarmiento proposed that Latin Americans should follow a policy of generalized acceptance of immigration from Europe, partly because it was an inevitable phenomenon and partly because it would be 'like the water which fertilizes by irrigation certain lands'.[59] For him it was absolutely clear that 'we need to mix ourselves with the population of countries more advanced than ours, so that they communicate to us their arts, their industries, their activity and their work attitude.'[60] Alberdi proclaimed 'let us open wide the doors! Let Europe penetrate us from all sides'; 'In America, to populate is to govern.'[61] Prado, evoking Alberdi, argued that

> it is *necessary to increase* the number of our population, and what is more, to *change its condition* in a sense advantageous to the cause of progress. *In America to govern is to populate*; and the population must be sought in the spontaneous immigration, attracted by the action of laws, governments and individuals, of superior and vigorous races which, by mixing with ours, bring practical ideas of freedom, work and industry. Let us not promote; let us oppose the immigration of inferior races.[62]

Arguedas too proposed 'selected' immigration, while García Calderón praised the blood cleansing which Italian and Basque immigrants were carrying out in Argentina. Ingenieros, in his turn, saw modernization more clearly in terms of the creation of an anti-feudal capitalist class, but white immigration still seemed to be crucial for that process. Thus he considered that the political future of Argentina had changed:

> because of the incorporation of a great mass of immigrants of the white race, its descendants, already enriched, are entering the capitalist class in formation and they will be rather hostile to the feudal oligarchies, aiming to take away their political power: it will be the struggle of the capitalist bourgeoisie against feudal privileges . . . From this point of view European immigration, after having contributed with their arms

to recovering the country's economic forces, will contribute with their
sons to the improvement of national politics.[63]

Even when the proposed solutions for modernizing Latin America
were not as radical as this, the authors influenced by the Enlightenment and positivism insisted that massive public education had to
compensate for the weaknesses of the race. Sarmiento rhetorically
asked what South America could do in order to achieve the prosperous destiny of North America – and he answered in the typical
enlightened manner: 'Instruction, education diffused through the
mass of the inhabitants', 'to level itself up; and it is already doing it
with the other European races, by making up for the Indian blood
with modern ideas, by finishing with the Middle Ages.'[64] In the same
vein Gil Fortoul argued that 'the intellectual and moral influence
of the more civilized peoples has begun to neutralize or modify the
primitive influences of the race.'[65] The importance of the United
States as the idealized example to follow in all this is paramount.
While Alberdi wanted to educate to form practical men, 'Yankees of
the South', Sarmiento pleaded 'let us be the United States of South
America.'

Any improvement of Latin America, therefore, depended on Latin
Americans being able to replace their colonial and racial heritage by
means of immigration and/or scientific education. As a good com-
plement to education Sarmiento also praised the role of the press,
which he considered a privileged medium to promote freedom and
progress. Sarmiento worked as a journalist throughout his life and
during his stay in Chile in 1840 he worked on *El Mercurio* of Valparaiso and later founded *El Nacional* in Santiago. He regarded the
press as a great help in educating the public, especially in countries,
like the Latin American ones, where the educational system faltered;
but it was also needed to create a public opinion which was conscious
of the public matters that needed reform.[66]

The romantic novel and modernism

The opposition between barbarism and civilization was not only
explicitly developed in critical essays, but was also an important
subtext of many romantic literary works of the time. Unlike European romanticism, which wanted to escape from civilization to find
refuge in nature, Latin American romanticism wanted to escape from
isolation and barbarism of nature. I have already mentioned Esteban
Echeverría's idea that Latin American literature had to draw its orig-

inality from local customs, forms of government and geographical factors, especially the pampa in the Argentinian case. But in his early narrative poem *La Cautiva* (1837) the pampa also represented the barbaric, a hostile and rough environment full of reptiles and dangerous animals from which the protagonists try, without success, to flee. María and her husband Brian, both prisoners of the Indians, represent civilization confronted by the brutality of natural forces, to which the Indians themselves belong. The poem describes scenes in which drunk Indians like vampires suck the blood from a horse which has had its throat cut. Once more there is the confrontation between the civilized white race and the cruel Indian race.[67]

José Mármol's novel *Amalia* (1851) is also set in the context of the opposition between civilization and barbarism. The protagonists, Eduardo, Daniel and Amalia, struggle against the tyrant Rosas but in the end succumb and are killed. Civilization is represented by a small number of intellectuals among whom the three protagonists are counted. But they are surrounded and confronted by the hostile pampa, gauchos, Indians and blacks. It is a gaucho who betrays Eduardo at the beginning of the novel. Blacks and mulattos appear as agents who have sold out to Rosas.

There are, nevertheless, various important literary pieces which express this opposition but in an inverted form: Lucio Mansilla's *Una excursión a los indios ranqueles* (1870) and José Hernández' famous poem *Martín Fierro* (1872). The former, written from a Christian perspective, presents the Indians as having many virtues, and often criticizes civilization. The latter praises the independence, strength, courage and self-confidence of the gaucho and constructs him as a mythical figure, a prototype of all the early Argentinian virtues, which are sadly about to disappear.[68] The Peruvian novelist Clorinda Matto de Turner in her novel *Aves sin Nido* (1889) depicts the barbarism of rural life, but she also denounces the injustices committed against the Indians. Her solution to the problem is education. Other novels which seek to rescue the image of the Indian are Alejandro Magariños Cervantes' *Caramurú* (1848), Juan León Mera's *Cumandá* (1871), Manuel de Jesus Galván's *Enriquillo* (1879) and José de Alençar's *Iracema* and *O Guarani* (1857).[69] Towards the end of the nineteenth century, then, an incipient trend that comes to the defence of the Indians manifests itself in novels, thus anticipating in time the emergence of Indigenismo.

There were also a few novels which came to the defence of black people: Gertrudis López de Avellaneda's *Sab* (1841), Anselmo Suárez y Romero's *Francisco* (1880) and Aluisio Azevedo's *O Mulato* (1881). Equally Euclides da Cunha, a journalist, published *Os Sertões* in 1903 on the famous uprising of Antonio Conselheiro in Brazil, where, in spite of being a part of the military expedition against the rebels, he takes their side. He also channelled his wish to help those people through education. Justo Sierra, in Mexico, also proposed the redemption of the Indians by means of education.[70]

Another very common literary expression of this time is the novel with a woman protagonist: *María* (1867) by the Colombian Jorge Isaacs, *Cecilia Valdés* (1892) by the Cuban Cirilo Villaverde, *Manuela* (1866) by the Colombian Eugenio Díaz, *Clemencia* (1869) by the Mexican Ignacio Altamirano, *Soledad* (1847) by the Argentinian Bartolomé Mitre, and *Cumandá* (1879) by the Ecuadorian Juan León Mera. They all have a common theme which has to do with love encumbered by class and racial obstacles. The protagonists are special women, mestizo like Manuela, or Jew like María, or criollo brought up by Indians like Cumandá, or mulatto like Cecilia. Their love affairs end up in tragedy because of prevailing discrimination.[71] Although most of these novels identify themselves with the downtrodden and oppressed, they portray interracial love as impossible. To this extent they still reflect, although in a special manner, the opposition between civilization and barbarism and the predominant racism.

By the end of the nineteenth century a new trend had appeared in poetry that was named modernism.[72] The movement was heavily influenced by French modernism and was characterized by the wish to innovate in the use of language, style and rhythm. It privileged form and art for art's sake; its concern was eminently aesthetic. This trend is well represented by the Nicaraguan poet Rubén Darío, who published his famous book of poems *Azul* in 1888 and *Prosas Profanas* in 1896. Modernists were no longer committed to any cause that was not art itself, and their revolutionary innovative character had to do with form rather than content. Hence many literary critics and essayists have subsequently accused them of shallowness, individualism, imitation, apoliticism and uprootedness. Still, it is difficult not to recognize the fact that, in spite of his subservient imitation of French fashion in poetry and his reactionary politics, Darío was a great Latin American poet, as many present-day literary figures acknowledge.

In effect, Alejo Carpentier, a Cuban novelist and critic, regrets the fact that Darío took presents 'from a petty Central American tyrant' and 'rubbed shoulders with half-witted politicians, reactionaries, tinpot generals, and found them agreeable and even interesting'.[73] Yet he accepts that he was a great poet. The Venezuelan essayist and novelist Arturo Uslar Pietri has maintained that Darío deceived himself into believing that he was influenced by French modern literary fashion whereas in fact he should have recognized that his great poetry was a product of *mestizaje*.[74] Octavio Paz, in his turn, has argued that the accusation of superficiality against Darío is a misunderstanding and that Latin American modernism responded to the wish to react against the spiritual vacuum left by positivism.[75] Be that as it may, from my point of view it is interesting to highlight the fact that modernism shares with positivism an outward-looking orientation and is still placed within the problematic of civilization versus barbarism. As Franco has put it, 'the modernist was therefore a mediator between European taste and Hispanic American barbarism.'[76] The movements in poetry and in social science are different, but both are turned towards the paradigm of European culture and are clearly bedazzled by Parisian fashion. In this respect they have something in common that was typical of the second half of the nineteenth century.

Modernity against old identity

For most nineteenth-century Latin American authors, then, of both fiction and non-fiction, there was clearly a need to achieve modernity by destroying the colonial cultural identity. But it was not easy to dismantle such an identity and they themselves unwittingly shared its racism and elitism. Still, their projects of modernization are also projects of a new cultural identity with characteristics opposite to the Indo-Iberian cultural pattern they detested. They wanted to construct it on the basis of the values of the Enlightenment: political and religious freedom, science and reason. We have seen how they adopted many of these values only in theory, and how the democratic progress they brought about was restricted to the ruling classes. Yet, in spite of that, there is no doubt that a major cultural change was being produced and that a renovated identity began to emerge – in which, nevertheless, many of the old values still remained.

A recurrent tension between the Indo-Iberian pole and the positivist pole has subsisted because the more recent rationalistic pattern never succeeded in totally replacing the original cultural matrix, just as this earlier model never succeeded either in totally eliminating ethnically based cultural diversity. That the colonial pattern and ethnic cultures were still very resilient and influential was shown by the fact that positivism itself became for many Latin American intellectuals a new kind of totalizing, dogmatic and secularized religion, and that, apart from some exceptions, it rarely led to successful scientific research.[77] It is quite striking to see how these autochthonous positivist versions of the Latin American situation coincided with some derogatory visions of Latin America coming from Europe itself. The nineteenth-century European impression of Latin America was that this continent was still dominated by irrational forces and constituted by peoples without history. Classical political economists, Hegel and Marx and Engels more or less coincided in underlining the inferior and irrational character of the Latin Americans, which made the European or North American tutelage over these independent republics still necessary and good.

It is important to insist, though, that not everybody's reception of European rationalism and empiricism had racist overtones. In many poets and novelists, too, the overcoming of barbarism was not necessarily tied up with any contempt for the 'lower' races; on the contrary, they praised the virtues of Indians and popular types like the gaucho. In many intellectual quarters, rationalism meant only the wish to modernize, an emphasis on the importance of science and a belief in education. This is partly the reason why, within Latin America itself, no significant challenge to the supremacy of the European rational-scientific pattern and to the Latin American ability to absorb it and use it emerged until the beginning of the twentieth century.

On the whole it is quite clear that the consumption of European values by enlightened Latin American intellectuals was rather uncritical, to the point that even the racist overtones of modern European theories were assimilated without protest. This total cultural surrender is well encapsulated in Alberdi's famous dictum: 'In America all that is not European is barbaric.'[78] Such theories can be clearly labelled 'ideological' in the classical Marxist sense: they conceal the real contradictions of the new republics by highlighting racial factors as the ones responsible for Latin American backwardness. But in addition, they also show some kind of cultural shallowness. Salazar Bondy has expressed this idea by saying that in Latin America there is a defect of culture, which is the result of an imitative consciousness.[79] Subercaseaux has put forward something similar when he talks of the existence of a 'deficit of cultural depth' in Chile in the nineteenth century.[80] This stems from the fact that in its very foundational moment, Latin American culture defined itself as pure opposition to the colonial past and to Spanish culture; as a result it was in the paradoxical situation of having to found a culture of its own on the basis of foreign elements taken from France and Britain, which could only interest a tiny elite and did not represent vast social sectors.

This does not necessarily mean, though, that a sense of national identity failed to be created during the nineteenth century. As we saw in chapter 1, the state plays a crucial role in the construction of national identities and, in the case of Latin America, this role was particularly enhanced by the need to overcome an enormous cultural diversity at the base of society. In this sense it can be argued that even if, during the nineteenth century, the culture of the elite in Latin America was quite distant from the real life of the people, nevertheless a sense of national identity did increasingly emerge, partly out of popular practices and partly articulated by the state: the latter, not only through its own daily activities, but also by taking advantage of difficulties, catastrophes, divisions and especially wars, could appeal through the written press to patriotism in order to build up a sense of community.[81] It has to be clear, though, that the elite controlled the state, and that by means of such control they decisively contributed to the construction of the official discourses that articulated every section of society.[82]

4

The End of
Oligarchic Modernity
1900–1950

The crisis of oligarchic modernity and populist modernization

Developments in Latin America during the first half of the twentieth century historically coincided with – and reflected – the first crisis of European modernity. Two major wars and recessions mark the period from 1914 to 1939. World markets were disorganized by the First World War and narrowed by the Russian revolution, thus disrupting international capitalism. The first symptoms of the crisis were already showing by the beginning of the twentieth century, in the acute competition to get new markets all over the world and the imperialist race to establish new colonies. It all ended in the First World War, the communist revolutionary upheavals in Central and Eastern Europe and the dissolution of the nineteenth-century world economy. Added to this there quickly followed the breakdown of the international gold standard in the 1930s and the Great Depression. This led directly to Fascism and Nazism, the Second World War and the end of the liberal state. Karl Polanyi has convincingly argued that 'the origins of the cataclysm lay in the utopian endeavour of economic liberalism to set up a self-regulating market system.'[1] In other words, the crisis was a crisis of nineteenth-century institutionalized liberalism.

In so far as Latin America is concerned, two stages can be distinguished in this long period. The first thirty years constituted a time of transition in which the middle classes made their appearance as political forces and the 'social question' became an important issue. This was also a time in which the unquestioned cultural supremacy of positivism began to be challenged and to give way to positions which reappraised the values of *mestizaje* and indigenous peoples. From 1930 onwards populist and nationalist regimes were consolidated which tried to initiate a policy of import-substituting industrialization, thus ending the outward-oriented period of development. They also organized the working class and provided the first elements of social legislation and of a welfare state. At this time, traditional intellectuals made their appearance, either voicing bitter disappointment about the Latin American character or opposing the new modernizing state policies in the name of Hispanic values.

The transition

Just as the dynamism of the Industrial Revolution in Europe had been determinant for the expansion of Latin American exports in the nineteenth century, so the successive crises of European capitalism during the first half of the twentieth century determined the end of that prosperous period. The landowning oligarchic power began to crumble as a consequence of the decline of the export economy, accelerated by the First World war and the Great Depression. The expansion and diversification of the export economy had led, towards the end of the nineteenth century, to the emergence of a middle class which was struggling for political rights, and it took advantage of the economic problems of the ruling landowning class to make its entry on to the political scene. Hence, while in Europe a crisis of liberal industrialism was occurring, in Latin America it was the prevalent oligarchic and aristocratic export-oriented system which entered into its terminal phase. It was this economic collapse which precipitated the political crisis of the old system and which eventually led to new national populist regimes and to an incipient and partially successful import-substituting industrialization process.

The process of incorporation of the middle classes was not the same all over Latin America. In Argentina, for instance, the middle classes were directly incorporated into the hegemony of the exporting bourgeoisie. In Brazil, by contrast, the newly emerging middle classes formed alliances with sectors of the bourgeoisie to set up a new kind of political leadership. In countries such as Chile and Peru, where domination was not purely oligarchic, the middle sectors found that their incorporation into the political system was more difficult and they had to resort to alliances with peasants and workers to breach the system. In some countries, such as Mexico, Venezuela and Bolivia, with large exploited peasantries, where an oligarchy of traditional hacienda owners clearly dominated, the middle classes were totally excluded and resorted to a mobilization of the peasants in order to break the oligarchic system by means of revolutionary movements.[2]

This stage of crisis and change in Latin America was accompanied by important cultural changes which brought into question the nineteenth-century positivist orientation towards Europe and the United States as the only possible sources of Latin America's civilization and its neglect of and contempt for Latin America's own racial characteristics. These cultural changes were characterized by the emergence of an anti-imperialist consciousness, by a new revaluation of *mestizaje*, by a new indigenista kind of consciousness critical of the discrimination against the Indian communities, and by a growing social consciousness in relation to the problems of the working class. In general most of these trends showed a renewed interest in Latin America's specific cultural identity and opposed the kinds of modernity offered by the North American or European models.

Anti-imperialism and the realist novel

In the first thirty years of the twentieth century the winds of change brought about by the explosion of the 'social question' and the emergence of the middle classes as political forces in the context of a crumbling oligarchic power were accompanied by two literary tendencies. On the one hand, in the decade of the 1920s there emerged in Brazil a movement of the literary avant-garde which, twenty or thirty years after the emergence of Hispanic American modernism, was also named modernism. This movement had basically aesthetic concerns and wanted to assimilate the novelties of the European literary avant-garde. The widely influential Mario de Andrade's *Macunaima* and Oswald de Andrade's novels (*Memorias sentimentales de Juan Miramar*, 1924) and revolutionary manifestos (*Manifesto Antropofágico*, 1928) are its best representatives. Unlike Hispanic American modernism, Brazilian modernism linked its will to modernity with the construction of a Brazilian national identity.[3]

On the other hand, there was also a consolidation of a realist tendency in the writing of novels which expressed in a literary form the turbulence of these times. This realism had several dimensions. There emerged novels of a rural and regional character, for instance *Zurzulita* (1920) by the Chilean Mariano Latorre and *Los gauchos judíos* (1910) by the Argentinean Alberto Gerchunoff, which showed the hard life of rural workers. Mariano Azuela's *Los de Abajo* (1916) not only portrayed the events of the Mexican revolution, but also showed the heroic virtues of the humble Mexican peasants. The best two expressions of this regional or rural type of novel praising the values of the countryside are undoubtedly the Argentinian Ricardo Güiraldes' *Don Segundo Sombra* (1926) and the Venezuelan Rómulo Gallegos' *Doña Bárbara* (1929). In both cases the authors sought national redemption on the basis of the spiritual renovation that was meant to come from the Argentinian pampa or the Venezuelan plains.

An interesting though limited variant is the naturalist realism of *La Vorágine* (1924) by the Colombian Eustasio Rivera, and *Cuentos de la Selva* (1918) and *Anaconda* (1921) by the Uruguayan Horacio Quiroga. They highlight the struggle of human beings against a hostile and savage nature, mostly represented by the tropical jungle. There is also the social realism of Baldomero Lillo (*Sub Terra*, 1904 and *Sub Sole*, 1907), who describes the sufferings of the Chilean coal miners, and the indigenista realism of the Bolivian Alcides Arguedas (*Raza de Bronce*, 1919) and the Ecuadorian Jorge Icaza (*Huasipungo*, 1934), who show the brutal treatment of the Indians in the haciendas. These novels of denunciation question the legitimacy of the Latin American power structures. In general, the various forms of realism were related to the difficult times of change in which the Latin American old order was beginning to be challenged, thus producing a crisis of identity. These novels do not offer clear-cut solutions to the problems of identity but hint at different possibilities stemming from the virtues of popular characters and geographical places.[4]

At the beginning of the century, in the context of North American expansionism, a series of intellectuals raised their voices against the United States and its hegemonic aspirations in relation to Latin America. Among others one can mention José Martí (Cuba), Rubén Darío (Nicaragua), José Vasconcelos (Mexico), Rufino Blanco Fombona (Venezuela), Manuel Ugarte (Argentina), Pedro Henríquez Ureña (Dominican Republic) and José Enrique Rodó (Uruguay). Martí, for instance, is critical of Sarmiento's famous opposition between civilization and barbarism and praises 'natural men' who have defeated the artificial men of letters in Latin America. As he puts it, 'the battle is not between civilization and barbarism, but between false erudition and nature.'[5] He warns against the 'excessive importation of alien ideas and formulae' and against 'iniquitous and impolitic contempt for the aboriginal race'.[6] Yet he is not radically against all foreign influences as long as they respect Latin America's being: 'let the world be grafted on to our republics, but the trunk must be of our republics.'[7]

In *El Modernismo y los Poetas Modernistas* (1912), Blanco Fombona, a sharp literary critic, castigated Latin American modernist writers and poets because they seemed to have no roots in Latin America and were bent on finding an intellectual home elsewhere. They were very keen on imitating the European literary fashions but unable to create a native Latin American art of their own:

> We have not been able to see, like and understand our nature and our societies. We have not even been able to descend to the bottom of our soul. We ignore our own self. We have often been monkeys, parrots. That is to say, *imitators, repeaters of Europe* . . . We are not creators. We possess a feminine spirit. We need impregnating to give birth. We are fertilized poets.[8]

Rodó, in his turn, achieved enormous influence with his book entitled *Ariel*, which was published in 1900. Rodó started a critique of what he called *'nordomanía'*, the Latin American inclination to copy foreign models, especially North American, and advocated a return to its own – superior – reality. He uses Shakespeare's counterpointing of Ariel to Caliban. Ariel is Latin America's own spirit: 'idealism and order in life, noble inspiration in thought, disinterestedness in morals, good taste in arts, heroism in action, delicacy in customs'.[9] Caliban, on the contrary, represents the spirit of North America, which is not refined or spiritual but pragmatic and shallow.[10] Thus Rodó celebrates the feelings and virtues of the Latin race by contrasting its greater cultural sensitivity and idealist sense of life with the materialism, utilitarianism and vulgarity of the United States.

Against the positivist idea that *mestizaje* brought degeneration to the race, Vasconcelos celebrated the values and newness of *mestizaje* and of the Latin race[11] and opposed them to the characteristics of the Anglo-Saxon race. The attitude towards the Indians is crucial. Whereas Anglo-Saxon colonizers 'committed the sin of destroying those races . . . we assimilated them, and this gives us new rights and hope of a mission without precedent in history.'[12] This mission is the formation of a new fifth 'integral race', 'cosmic race' or 'synthesis race', produced by the fusion of whites, blacks, Indians and Mongols. In this fifth race all the peoples of the world will eventually fuse, and the honour of accomplishing such an integrating mission belongs to the Latinos.[13] This idea of universality is also present in Henríquez Ureña, a collaborator of Vasconcelos, who argues that Latin America must approach 'the creation of the universal man, through whose lips the spirit may freely speak'.[14]

In general, Vasconcelos and the others mentioned above seem to define Latin American identities in terms of the greater culture and idealism and the universal mission belonging to the mestizo race in contrast to the imperialist and materialist 'other' which is the United States. As Henríquez Ureña puts it, 'Latin America must affirm its faith in its own destiny, in the future of civilization.' But if Latin America has a future it is not because of its potential material wealth, nor because of its industrialization: 'it is the spirit that has saved us . . . the spirit alone and not military force or economic power.'[15] The majority of these authors regard the Hispanic cultural legacy with sympathy as a fundamental and integral part of the Latin race. Thus they become precursors of a more systematic critical review of the liberal-positivist pole.

But it was not only anti-Americanism that was the leading motivation of many writers of the time. There was also a new concern with discovering and studying the social reality of Latin American nations from a more sympathetic point of view, instead of systematically ignoring it or condemning it as inherently deficient. João Cruz Costa[16] has studied the evolution of Brazilian intellectuals in the first years of the twentieth century and has shown how, starting from Euclides da Cunha and his book *Os Sertões* (1903), a new intellectual direction was given to Brazilian thought which was less oriented to the contemplation of things European and more open to seeing the social plight of its own poor people. This was a trend that da Cunha initiated with his sympathetic account of the Canudos revolt, and after the First World War it acquired more importance among Brazilian intellectuals. This trend affirms a sense of Brazil's own identity, the idea that it is necessary to start from Brazil's own way of being.

However, da Cunha basically belonged to the generation of late nineteenth-century Brazilian authors who, influenced by positivism, were still trapped in racist premises. His account of Canudos showed the beginnings of a change of epoch in its social progressiveness, but still could not rid itself of the idea of a white racial supremacy. In this sense a clearer change of direction can be noticed in Manuel Bonfim, who also published his *America Latina: Males de Origem* in 1903 and was also heavily influenced by positivism. Bonfim proposed a different explanation of Brazilian problems that was hinged on the idea that Portugal had lived parasitically off Brazilian labour. Contrary to Euclides da Cunha, Sílvio Romero and Nana Rodrigues, who saw many defects deriving from *mestizaje*, Bonfim 'considers the racial mixture as restorative, in the sense that it would tend to rebalance the negative elements inherited from the conquerors'.[17] The worst two elements of this negative inheritance from the Portuguese were conservatism and a lack of a spirit of observation. Thus there is in Bonfim an anti-imperialist attitude and a positive evaluation of *mestizaje* which entitles him to be considered together with Martí, Vasconcelos, Rodó, Ugarte and other authors of this new stage.

Indigenismo

During this stage there also emerged the works of the indigenista movement, a broad current of thought which encompassed politicians, novelists, anthropologists, painters and journalists, advocating a return to Indian values and customs in opposition to the European cultural heritage. They wanted to change the prevalent negative view of the Indians as backward and called for social reform to favour the impoverished Indian communities. This movement flourished in those countries like Peru and Mexico where the most important Indian civilizations had existed and where the biggest Indian communities survived. However, Indigenismo was far from being a uniform position.

Manuel Gonzalez Prada, one of the first indigenistas of Peru, argued that there was an alliance between the bourgeoisie and the landowners of Peru in order to exploit the Indian: 'if the gamonal from the mountains serves as political agent to the gentleman of Lima, the gentleman of Lima defends the gamonal from the mountains when he abuses the Indian in a barbaric way.'[18] The problem started with the Spanish who, according to González, decimated the Indians by allocating them out to work for conquistadors without payment in their mines or on their land (by means of the mita and the *repartimiento*). But the abuses, cruelty and exploitation continued after Peru got its independence. Just as during colonial times the viceroys condemned the abuses and tried to implement protective legislation, republican presidents in their discourses advocated the redemption of the oppressed Indians and issued orders which were never to be obeyed. Landowners, prefects, governors and priests, equally greedy, would continue to exploit the Indians, knowing that 'the lack of compliance will result in no harm to them.'[19]

Luis Eduardo Valcárcel, in his turn, took a more radical position by lamenting the profound ethnic division of Peru as the gravest problem of its social and political life, a problem tending to 'aggravate itself with the extension of the racial phenomenon: the *mestizaje*'.[20] The mixture of Spanish and Indian produces nothing good, 'but a new hybrid being: he does not inherit the ancestral virtues but the vices and impediments. The *mestizaje* produces nothing but deformities.'[21] Thus Valcárcel defended the purity of Indian blood and culture as the only reservoirs of the millenary virtues of the race. Against Vasconcelos, he appealed to the pure race as the only entity that could create culture, so that even mestizos must make themselves Indians to achieve anything, 'by purifying whatever we have of Indians', because otherwise 'we shall never create anything, as nothing has been created by hybridism so far. The cosmic race can only be born from Indian entrails.'[22]

Indigenismo, as Leopoldo Zea has maintained, did not originate in the Indian communities themselves, but was 'part of a program to incorporate the Indian' into the national life controlled by criollos and mestizos.[23] This is especially true of Mexico where the Instituto Nacional Indigenista was created and directed for many years by Gonzalo Aguirre Beltrán, having as its goal the full integration of the Indian into the Mexican nation.[24] Aguirre Beltrán argued that the term 'Indian' was more an expression of the social condition of those who had been vanquished and subjected to servitude than of an ethnic quality. Hence Indians had to be incorporated into national culture and treated as citizens with their full rights, but care had to be taken that they were not uprooted and that their own cultural expressions were incorporated into the national culture.[25] The only difficulty with this, as Zea points out, is that with the incorporation of the Indian into the national culture the original Indian culture disappears.[26] Yet for Aguirre Beltrán this is an objective and ineluctable historical process: even though part of the Indian culture is continually assimilated by national culture, in the end the integration of the Indians presupposes their disappearance.

In many authors Indigenismo tends to be rather naive and romantic in that they depicted the pre-Columbian Indian civilizations as idyllic and as possible models for the future. Degregori accuses Indigenismo of 'exoticism', a tendency to describe the Indian with exotic and stereotyped features, not as a concrete reality; 'pasadismo', a tendency to overrate the historical Indian and not rate the present one; 'paternalism', a tendency to have compassion for the Indian; and 'populism', a tendency to utilize the Indian in political movements.[27] However, other authors such as Mariátegui consider the Indian problem to be an economic problem based on the regime of land ownership and capable of being solved by socialism.[28] One can see then how Indigenismo oscillates between the absolute and essentialist affirmation of the Indian race (Valcárcel) and its dissolution into the national culture (Aguirre Beltrán), but on the whole, and with the exception of Mariátegui, it wanted to affirm identity against modernity. The influence of Indigenismo has survived until today, as can be seen in several articles celebrating the five hundredth anniversary of the discovery of America.[29]

The national populist stage

By 1930 new populist regimes emerged in Latin America which sought to widen the franchise and to incorporate the middle classes into government. Processes of import-substituting industrialization were initiated. The incorporation of the middle classes as a new force in the political system was linked to the necessity of complementing the export economy with the development of the internal market that could be satisfied by local industry. Industrialization began to be seen as the key to providing new sources of employment as the export industries declined. But political changes occurred prior to industrialization and this had important cultural and political consequences. As Mouzelis has argued, the end of the oligarchic regime occurred in a preindustrial context and therefore the new openness of the political system did not include the active participation of organized working classes, as in Europe, and tended to incorporate just the middle classes into the power structures.[30]

When the crisis of the exporting economy started, Latin America, unlike Europe, did not have a powerful bourgeoisie capable of defeating the landowners on its own in order to create a fully fledged capitalist system that represented its interest. In Latin America the bourgeoisie was incipient and weak and in order to attain power it had to enter into alliances with other groups and class fractions. Modernization and industrialization were thus attempted by a combination of the state and of various groups, mainly the emergent middle classes, some modernizing sectors of the old aristocracy, the incipient bourgeoisie and sectors of the working class. As a result, the bourgeoisie was only one group among others, none strong enough on its own to impose its interests on society. A fully fledged bourgeois revolution or industrial revolution was never possible, and the old regime was not entirely replaced by a new one.

This peculiarity helps explain the emergence of populist regimes and the survival of paternalist and clientelistic political forms. The oligarchic state was in crisis and yet the process of change and modernization was only possible through a very complex system of alliances between different classes and groups. This is why some authors refer to this period as the stage of 'compromise'. Whereas the European working classes were more autonomous and very well organized by the time democratizing political changes were occurring, the Latin American working classes were very dependent on middle-class leadership and on state-promoted and state-controlled forms of organization. They could be more easily manipulated and used by the middle classes. Yet in order for this strategy to be successful, they had to be offered some social gains, and this is what populism was all about.

National popular regimes achieved power in the 1930s in Brazil, Argentina and Chile. These regimes initiated what has been called import-substituting industrialization, the development of the internal market, or what the Economic Commission for Latin America has called 'inward-oriented development'. Since the export economy controlled by the landowners was in crisis and the numbers of those unemployed grew dramatically, a change in economic direction was necessary. Simultaneously, as political participation in the old oligarchic regime was very limited, populism was also about political change and incorporating the middle classes into the administration of the state. Widening the franchise and mobilizing the formerly excluded masses were also a means for the middle classes to secure the stability of the newly formed regimes. Both the middle classes and the working classes saw the state as a crucial level of society. Controlling the state was conceived as the only means by which they could redistribute economic and political power in their favour. In this context a state-led and state-promoted policy of industrialization was the key economic policy advocated.

The main tools used to promote import-substituting industrialization were high tariff protection for those manufactured goods being produced internally in order to make them competitive against the same goods produced abroad; and special incentives, cheap credit, tax exemptions and easy access to cheap foreign exchange in order to facilitate the importation of crucial raw materials and capital goods for manufacturing industries. In addition the state expanded public investment in infrastructure oriented towards complementing and supporting industrial production. The state also created institutions for the promotion of industry. A typical case was CORFO (Corporation for the Promotion of Production) in Chile, created during the presidency of Pedro Aguirre Cerda, head of the Popular Front, a populist coalition which was swept to power in 1938. CORFO was intended to assist and promote the industrialization process by investing in new technologies, providing credit and supporting ailing productive ventures. The state therefore took an increasingly significant role in the economic process, becoming an important productive agent and controlling most of the national investment process. It actively sought to compensate for the weaknesses of the incipient bourgeoisie, which did not have the strength, the capital or the will to carry out the industrialization process on its own.

Populism in Latin America was thus a specific kind of political phenomenon that cannot be confused with similar processes elsewhere. The Russian narodniks were considered populist in the sense of wanting a type of socialism based on the masses of the peasantry. The politics of Nyerere in Tanzania was also considered populist in the sense of avoiding the dangers of fully fledged industrialization, the preference for small enterprises (small is beautiful) and for agriculture as the basis of development. In the context of Latin America, populism emerged at a time of massive social and political dislocation and was connected to urban multiclass political alliances and political movements presided over by charismatic leaders and seeking to incorporate the middle classes into the political system by organizing the working classes as a support base. They also wanted to industrialize their countries in order to create jobs and achieve a kind of development which would be an alternative to the former oligarchic 'outward-oriented' type.

The populist agenda was really about anti-aristocratic and pro-bourgeois objectives; it was not about socialism, although the rhetoric about the promised changes was usually very radical and inflammatory. In reality, though, few populist movements were able to change the old landowning system and radically oust the aristocracy. Even more, according to Valenzuela and Cousiño, populism would have sought to reconstitute in the cities the kind of social bond that existed in the rural hacienda. The paternalist and personalist figure of the populist leader would have substituted for the paternalist and personalist figure of the hacendado. Both demanded the same personal loyalty and had a predisposition to spend in extravagant and profligate ways.[31] The only two countries where the emergence of the middle classes in alliance with revolutionary peasantry of Indian origin acquired revolutionary connotations were Mexico and Bolivia. In those two countries there were true revolutions which more radically expropriated and destroyed the oligarchy: Mexico in 1910, Bolivia as late as 1952.

In the rest of Latin America what the oligarchy lost was basically political power: they lost the control of the executive, which in most Latin American countries is a separate power from the parliament. However, as they were not expropriated, they kept their economic power almost intact and indeed their exporting capability became crucial to earn the hard currency necessary to sustain the process of import-substituting industrialization. Additionally, for a long time they managed to keep a very important presence in parliaments, from where they blocked all attempts at passing any legislation that might have affected their interests. So the political situation that followed the oligarchic crisis was eminently unstable and fluid. It was a compromise between several groups, but this did not mean that tensions and confrontations among them did not continue.

This situation gave the state, in addition to its economic role, a crucial importance: it was at the level of the state that the bargaining between the different groups took place and where the agreed policies were implemented favouring different groups. The state was perceived as a superior entity from which every participant group expected protection and the fulfilment of its own interests. This applied as much to the working classes, who wanted jobs, social legislation and welfare, as it did to the bourgeoisie, who wanted state-led policies of protection and the promotion of industrialization, as it did to the middle classes, who wanted secure state jobs and careers.

What the populist alliances and movements sought was to initiate a process of change which widened the franchise and democratized the political structures, which up to that moment had been entirely controlled by the oligarchy. These populist coalitions succeeded in controlling the state but were not powerful enough to challenge the economic power of the landowners. In order to get hold of political power they sought the support of popular pressure, which they directed against the old state and political structures. They achieved the support of the masses by offering them new jobs and forms of welfare state and social legislation, indeed by organizing them too. But the populist coalitions did not radically change the system: rather their leadership, which was entirely bourgeois and middle class, was incorporated into the system. The working classes, having until then hardly any organization and legal protection, were only a subordinate partner wishing to gain some autonomy, and were manipulated by the populist coalitions.

As a result of the populist policies of the 1930s, the internal market of many Latin American economies was increasingly consolidated. Governments in which the middle classes and the industrial and commercial bourgeoisie increasingly participated led the process of import-substituting industrialization. In some countries such as Argentina, where the export economy had remained under national control and where industrialization was already well on its way, the new policies were based on the expansion of private enterprise. However, in Brazil, where the entrepreneurial groups were not hegemonic, the state assumed a more important role in the creation and regulation of industries. In countries such as Chile and Mexico the state was used 'as an instrument in the formation of an industrial class, which eventually would share entrepreneurial functions with the state-owned enterprises'.[32]

Despite these different emphases, the private sector grew and the state played an important part in the creation of basic industries and infrastructure and in protecting the new industries behind tariff barriers. A new urban proletariat emerged, but so did a growing sector of 'marginalized' urban dwellers without employment, because the creation of new jobs by the industrialization process always lagged behind demographic pressures and internal migration from the countryside. The developmentalist policies of the state and the growing aspirations of the urban masses were expressed best in nationalist and populist ideologies which represented conflicting interests. The most typical cases were the ideologies fostered by Peron in Argentina and Vargas in Brazil.

Most political regimes and ideologies of this period insisted on the originality or difference represented by the Latin American situation. Thus, for instance, the Mexican revolution, Getulio Vargas's 'new state' in Brazil, Peronism in Argentina, and Haya de la Torre's APRA in Peru all asserted the peculiarity of their situation or appealed to some special national essence which would require steering a course in between socialism and capitalism. This is what Villegas has called 'political originalism'.[33] In general, most populist regimes of the time adopted a reformist position which, while developing a socialist, nationalistic and anti-imperialist rhetoric, in practice kept a capitalist system moderated by some forms of social legislation.

Culturally speaking, this is a complex period which in spite of the modernizing thrust of populist alliances saw the emergence of a series of traditional intellectuals who were critical of the direction national development was taking. Some concentrated on the problems of the Latin American character, others advocated a return to Hispanic values, while still others were nostalgic of the rural society that was disappearing and considered populism a kind of fascism.

The 1930s essayists and the Latin American character

Anti-imperialism and Indigenismo had been a way of affirming that Latin America was different. Another way of doing the same in the

1930s, in the context of the Great Depression, was a series of very pessimistic discourses propounded both by foreign visitors and Latin American writers, underlining the peculiar and negative features of the Latin American identity as against the European pattern. José Luis de Imaz[34] has synthesized the thought of visiting foreign writers like Ortega y Gasset, Keyserling and Waldo Frank, who more or less concurred in the view that the characteristics of the Latin American culture were: (1) prevalence of the emotional over the rational and the overrating of sentiments; (2) propensity to imitation coupled with a tendency to lie – this tendency being facilitated by the contradictions of the Latin personality; (3) a weak will as an aspect of the Latin personality, oscillating between monotony and violence, tenderness and rudeness, passivity and melancholy; it is divided between the desire for external modernity and a very poor internal life, which produces envy and moral relativism; (4) the overwhelming influence of natural forces leads the culture to favour determinism, fatalism and improvidence.

Count Keyserling, no doubt influenced by Buffon's theses, published in 1932 *Meditaciones Sudamericanas* in which he describes Latin America as a continent of exuberant vegetation, threatening reptiles and unlimited sexuality. Hence his idea that 'the South American is totally and absolutely a telluric man. He incarnates the opposite pole to the man conditioned and penetrated by the spirit.'[35] Ortega y Gasset, in his turn, leaves aside the 'telluric mysteries'[36] to speak of the youth and immaturity of Latin America. The Spanish conquerors arrived in an empty land: 'the Indians who populated it were few given the magnitude and the possibilities of the lands, and besides, so inferior in their culture to the colonizers that it was as if they did not exist or as if they were merely usable objects for them.'[37] It is this youth that allows passions to dominate without control. Whereas in Europe 'we have become used to not counting on our passions . . . in these young peoples, instead, all the passions operate with energy, without inhibition, without a brake . . .'[38]

Zea, closely following Gerbi, accuses Ortega y Gasset of believing that Latin America has no future and suffers from an 'incurable organic infantilism'.[39] I do not think that this is a fair interpretation of the thought of the Spanish philosopher. True, Ortega thinks that Latin America is just coming out of adolescence, with all its defects and immaturity, and it is clear that he believes that the future will not be easy; but he does not feel dismayed about the existence of a future. That is why he says to the Argentinians: 'now the history of America will commence in the strict sense of the word: that first youth, which is adolescence, is over, and the uphill road starts. Adam gets out of Paradise and begins his pilgrimage. Good luck Argentinians, in this history that is beginning for you.'[40]

The Latin American writers and essayists of the time also identified some cultural peculiarities. Martínez Estrada, for instance, focused on the idea of resentment as best expressing the Latin American ethos. Resentment would have first characterized the Spanish conquerors who could not find the mythical Indian city of gold. Resentment would have been the reaction of the Indian women raped by the Spaniards and of the male Indians exterminated or enslaved. The problem with Latin American culture is that it has repressed that feeling and constructed a false superstructure concealing that basic resentment.[41] In his monumental work *Radiografía de la Pampa*, one finds devastating descriptions of the different Argentinian strata and characters throughout history. No group escapes the ferocious and profoundly pessimistic critique of Martínez Estrada. Be they the gauchos, the Argentinian people, the sons of immigrants or the natives, all seem to want to conceal a truth that is profoundly resented:

> the psychology of the gaucho and the soul of the anarchical Argentinian multitudes will never be fully understood if one does not think of the psychology of the humiliated son, of what an inferiority complex irritated by ignorance could come to produce in an environment which is propitious to violence and arbitrariness.[42]

> The immigrant's son . . . is excessively patriotic; he dissimulates our defects, overlooks the bad . . . praises national institutions to a ridiculous point, thus affecting their prestige . . . and thus, against the native, who because of other defects works in the same task of misleading, by inherited subconscious pressure . . . destroys without willing it.[43]

In a much-altered 1937 re-edition of his *Pueblo Enfermo*, Alcides Arguedas accentuates his critique of mestizos and makes them responsible for the duplicity of the Bolivians. In every Bolivian he argues, there are two personalities, because a lie is institutionally established in the country, thanks to simulation. Hence the series of revolutions, betrayals, envy and political hatred which characterize the history of Bolivia.[44] Bolivia for Arguedas has a sick people in the sense that it pretends to be what is non-existent and is 'chronically unable to direct its activities for its own conservation'.[45] Fraud, hatred and envy are common among Bolivians, 'nothing produces enthusiasm or respect in them; perhaps they are more sensitive to a vilifying fear.'[46] It is interesting to note that these authors' pessimistic description of the Latin American character still has an echo in Octavio Paz's writings twenty years later. He too describes the double personality of the Mexicans, who show one face that conceals a deep emptiness and resentment. The well-known machismo of Latin Americans is seen as an attempt to deal with the problem of the raped Indian woman through an overrating of the paternal image. The Mexican negates his past and his hybridism: 'he turns himself into nobody's son' and because of this, 'each time he affirms a part of his person, he negates the other.'[47]

In general, in these Latin American authors, similar notions abound, such as resentment, resignation, passivity, inferiority feelings, self-deception, etc. Although these harsh self-criticisms did not seem to leave room for any pride in the Latin American identity, these writers still wanted to emphasize the peculiarities of the Latin American cultural identity as against the European pattern. The point was to explain why Latin America was different and why modernity could not succeed. And yet it is quite obvious that in spite of, or maybe because of, the crisis, many modern and progressive changes were successfully introduced in the region. But the supporters of identity against modernity did not properly recognize this.

From these accounts two fundamental things stand out. First, how incredibly pessimistic their assessment of the vices and limitations of the Latin American cultural identity could be. Second, there appears to be a surprising convergence of views between foreign and local authors, showing how some of the Latin American self-perceptions mirror prejudices and stereotypes conceived elsewhere. In strict logic one could envisage a mere coincidence of opinions. But our discussion in chapter 1 about the construction of identity by means of the internalization of significant others' expectations and attitudes allows the hypothesis of a closer connection: the assessment of others appears to have become, unconsciously, Latin America's own self-evaluation.[48]

The literary novel of the time contributed, although from a different angle, to enhancing this image of difference tinged with pessimistic or at least unusual features. Miguel Angel Asturias' famous novel *El Señor Presidente* (1936) symbolically established the prototype of the Latin American dictator. *Mamita Yunai* (1941) by Carlos Luis Fallas and *El papa verde* (1954) by Miguel Angel Asturias constructed the image of Central America (Guatemala, Honduras, El Salvador) as the land of 'banana republics'. In *El Mundo es ancho y ajeno* (1941) Ciro Alegría describes through the mythical town of Rumí how its isolation is the key to its survival and way of life. The moment modernity arrives and isolation is lost, happiness and the ancestral way of life are destroyed.[49] It is precisely as this period came to an end that Miguel Angel Asturias spoke of 'magic realism' and

Alejo Carpentier referred to 'the marvellous real' to express the idea that Latin America was unusual, unexpected, in short 'different', possessing a reality that cannot be understood by the European rationalistic worldview. These terms have been widely used to refer to Latin American identity as expressed in the literature.[50]

The Brazilian essayists of the 1930s still conceived of the national identity in terms of some essential features which constituted the national character. But in contrast to their Spanish-speaking colleagues, they were far more positive in their assessment of Brazilian identity. Two influential masterpieces were written at the time: *Casa Grande e Senzala* by Gilberto Freyre (1933) and *Raízes do Brasil* by Sérgio Buarque de Holanda (1936). But they differed in the way in which they approached the Brazilian character. While Buarque saw the roots of Brazilianhood in 'cordiality', Freyre went back to the racial mixes to define it. Buarque had a more progressive approach which saw the importance of the changes introduced by the *Estado Novo* (New State), whereas the more conservative attitude of Freyre insisted on the wisdom of the old traditions as against the dissolving effects of industrial technology and the dictatorial elements of the new populist government of Getulio Vargas.

In effect, Freyre conceived of Brazilian identity as based on the *mestizaje* of three races, Indian, black and white, but instead of deriving from it the catalogue of character problems such as indolence, moral inadequacy, improvidence and apathy which had been highlighted by nineteenth-century authors, he accentuated the positive side, the harmonious contribution of each group to a syncretic Brazilian identity. He celebrated the ethnic and regional plurality of Brazil as the basis of its unity. For Freyre national unity was built upon diversity. He did not see major conflicts or contradictions between the various component parts. Difference and complementarity were enough for a balanced and harmonious society. Yet to this harmonious and traditional Brazil he opposed the anti-democratic and fascist tendencies which he detected in the *Estado Novo* and the modern tendencies of the industrial order which began to be developed in Brazil in the decade of the 1930s. As Ortiz remarks, for Freyre the Brazilian modern state is thus foreign to Brazilian history.[51]

Hispanism

Another form of traditionalism emerged in the Spanish-speaking Latin America of the late 1940s. For many authors, the key to the

Latin American problem of identity was the conscious neglect of the Hispanic matrix. New theories emerged which tried to rescue the Hispanic features of the Latin American character, thus confirming the idea that Latin America was different from the rest of Europe and the United States.[52] In Pike's opinion it can be said that Hispanism, as a current of thought which values the distinctive character of the Hispanic lifestyle, traditions and culture, has existed in Latin America from the time of independence.[53] This may be true in a sense, but the initial strength of such a movement was small, especially while the independence wars and their consequences were relatively close.

A certain form of Hispanism acquired strength at the beginning of the twentieth century with the works of Rodó, Blanco Fombona, Vasconcelos, Henríquez Ureña and others who tried to oppose the Latin race to the Saxon race and struggled against North American imperialism. Vasconcelos, for instance, argued that 'we will not grow up for as long as the Spaniard of America does not feel as Spanish as the sons of Spain.'[54] But the Hispanism of these authors was quite moderated by a strong Americanist feeling and the valuing of *mestizaje*. In other cases, the attempt to fight against Indigenismo fed the Hispanist current and this assumed a more radical character. The most typical case is that of José de la Riva Agüero, Peruvian historian, who in 1905 affirmed as against the indigenista current of González Prada: 'for criollos of Spanish race [the pre-Columbian civilizations] are foreign and alien, and nothing links us to them; and foreign and alien are also mestizos and cultivated Indians, because the education they have received has totally Europeanized them.'[55]

By the end of the 1940s, a more elaborated and systematic Hispanist current appeared in Chile which tried to respond to the questions about identity raised by indigenistas and essayists of the early twentieth century. It adopted two basic forms, one historical and the other philosophical. Jaime Eyzaguirre and Osvaldo Lira were its most distinguished representatives. For Eyzaguirre, Iberoamérica (notice the intentional use of the word) would not have existed without the presence of Spain, and the first sense of the Iberoamerican identity had to be found in the Hispanic cultural root. The Spanish preserved all the values possessed by the native cultures, and, in their turn, contributed more culturally than they destroyed:

the Spanish is not one element more in the ethnic conglomerate. It is the decisive factor, the only one that was able to tie everyone together, that manage to harmonize the 300 different languages of Mexico . . . The Spanish cleared the hurdles of the difficulties that geographical distances, tribal particularisms and racial diversity imposed, in order to produce the miracle of the American cohesion. That is why to try to forget the Spanish name in these lands and to try to oppose to it a hyperbolic revaluation of the Indian will be directly to attack the vital nerve which unites our peoples.[56]

It is not surprising, therefore, that Eyzaguirre should see the struggle for independence as a process of the disintegration and uprooting of a unity formerly achieved, although it is explicable and also shows the idealism of the criollos. For Eyzaguirre it is even more disappointing that 'the dismembering of the body was followed by a rejection of the old collective soul and the laborious search for a life reason in exotic sources.'[57] Latin America turned its back on its true being and ran after other cultures, sometimes antagonistic to its own, to imitate alien political and social models which could not be successful in such a different context. Hence the failed attempts at copying North American federalism, French Jacobinism and British parliamentarism, instead of using as an example the old Castilian 'fueros'.

As Eyzaguirre sees it, the true Latin American historical tradition consists in being conscious of human dignity and of the moral law which rules international life, all this founded on a Christian conception that subjects the individual to the state in matters temporal, puts the state at the service of the human being and considers the latter as essentially ordered towards God. Whereas the sense of justice in other cultures is based on what is useful for each person, in the Hispanic culture it rests on the right to salvation which all human beings have, which makes them basically equal. From these general principles are derived more specifically the feeling of independence and freedom, respect for the law and openness to dialogue.[58]

These are the principles that Latin Americans have betrayed in a true act of apostasy, which as a consequence can only bring on them contempt and ridicule. Eyzaguirre could be as hard in his judgement of Latin America as the essayists of the 1930s or the European intellectuals of the nineteenth century. But his hardness is guided more by the rage and sadness provoked by the abandonment of the Hispanic culture than by racism. It is possible to explain in this way some of his expressions which otherwise would seem to evoke Hegel's racist stereotypes: 'In one hundred years of free life Iberoamérica has not said one word to the world that deserves to be remembered. Its vegetative and grovelling walk has only attracted universal contempt.'[59] Elsewhere he adds, 'How can one say something truthful, something original and authentic if one is disloyal to its own essences?'[60] Still, Eyzaguirre is not a pessimist and thinks that in the youngsters of his land 'an instinct to revalue the cultural patrimony'[61] is already appearing which will allow progress towards a true independence, which is the basis of any original cultural contribution. But in order for all this to happen, it will be necessary to abandon alien models: 'the day on which, by reconciling with the substance of our collective soul, we ask it and not alien souls the answer to our anguish . . . on that day we shall have conquered an authentic, and therefore respectable, site in the world of culture.'[62]

From a more philosophical and scholastic point of view, Osvaldo Lira tries to prove that 'Hispanic American nations constituted from the beginning and continue to constitute today a perfectly homogeneous whole of culture among themselves and with Spain.' For him, 'all and every one of the perfect elements which the Hispanic American culture contains derive exclusively, as from its intrinsic essential first principle, from Spanish culture.'[63] The starting point is to consider every nation as a substance with its own essence, with a soul that explains its unity and its maintenance over time. Such an essence does not come from a biological-ethnic purity, because there is no nation in the world which does not have a mixed population, but comes from a form of culture which is shown to be superior to others. Hispanic American nations are *mestizas*, but their cultural essence is provided by the Hispanic culture, which is clearly superior to the indigenous cultures in so far as the latter ignored 'the conjunction of eternal values of which, due to a natural condition, the human being is a necessary bearer'.[64] The immense superiority of Spanish culture led indigenous cultures to remain in a relatively passive situation

> very similar to that of marble in the face of the creative activity of the sculptor. In this case, the only thing marble can show itself able to do is reduced to not imposing goals on the chisel, but simply imposing some determined conditions of work; its influence will not be of the positive type, like that of an engine, but of the negative type, like passive resistance.[65]

Hence Lira considers the Indo-American cultures in existence at the time of conquest as pseudo-cultures, incapable of contributing any central value or orienting principle, in the face of which the Spanish culture never conceded a single principle of its own. The mistake of the indigenista is to fail to understand this, Lira argues, for it is not enough to have participated in the origins of the Hispanic American nations – an assessment must be made of its participatory strength. For Lira it is clear that 'indigenous values have been purely and simply a passive subject'[66] with very little to set against the Spanish language and the Catholic religion contributed by the Spanish. Following in the steps of Eyzaguirre, and indeed of all essentialism, Lira also laments the treason committed by the majority of the leading sectors in Hispanic America. In his view, these sectors, 'far from keeping themselves irreducible . . . to foreign influences, have allowed themselves to be seduced by them, forgetting and in many cases reneging on the very values which gave birth to their historical existence'.[67] This betrayal of the national soul has gone so far as to put Hispanic America at a dangerous crossroads, from which it must take the right turning at all cost. This task will be facilitated by the fact that many of the foreign values, especially those having to do with liberal democracy, are decadent and about to die. When this happens, 'that will be the moment when the indestructible truth of Spanish values will impose itself.'[68]

With Indigenismo and Hispanism were born, almost at the same time, the essentialist versions of the Latin American identity. The historical moment was particularly apt, for it was a time of confusion and uncertainty, a time of a new adaptation of Latin America to the international context, a time of enormous social problems. The old oligarchic structures of power were beginning to fall and the outward orientation of the regional economy was questioned. It was a period spattered with social and economic crises. It is at these times that essentialist answers are tempting: all the problems can be blamed on the supposed abandonment of the true national being and the alienated search for foreign models to bring solutions.

What is that true collective self that has been unrecognized and lost? For indigenistas it lies in the Indian traditions buried and oppressed by centuries of exploitation since the conquest. For Hispanists it lies in the Christian-Spanish values which have been forgotten since independence. Both propose to go back to the past to recover the cultural matrix, the lost essence (Indian or Spanish) of Latin American being. We shall see how other forms of essentialism arising in later crises, although abandoning the simplicity of the Indian or Spanish factors and highlighting the process of *mestizaje*, nevertheless maintain a similar vision, that the Latin American inner being has been betrayed by the uncritical following of foreign ideas.

The sometimes naive and anachronistic belief in the social economic virtues of the Indian pre-Columbian civilizations typical of the indigenista movement, and the pessimistic accounts of the double and resentful personality of Latin Americans typical of the essayists of the 1930s share equally with the Hispanist versions of the supremacy of Spanish values a total lack of trust in the Latin American ability truly to assimilate the rational European pattern of culture, and the conviction that such a model should have never been adopted. To put things in their proper context and proportion, though, it has to be clarified that these ideas never became dominant and widely accepted in Latin America, and that throughout the twentieth century the European cultural experience continued to be crucial for Latin American identity, as it had been for its independence.

In this way, a period of many crises and of important economic and political changes was accompanied by new forms of social consciousness and by a search for identity which tried a variety of avenues, but which, in any case, had abandoned the nineteenth century's certainties, and in some significant instances had attempted to affirm a Latin American identity against modernity. Nevertheless, the main thrust of modern industrialization and of the widened political participation and social rights which populism brought about continued to be the focus around which the great national debates revolved, thus influencing in practice the construction of cultural identity. Where the nineteenth-century positivists wanted modernity at any cost but remained trapped in some forms of the old identity they wanted to abandon, so the essayists and critics of modernity in the first half of the twentieth century wanted to recover an old identity, a sense of originality, and could not recognize the important new changes and modernization which were occurring in practice with the end of the oligarchic period.

5

Postwar Expansion
1950–1970

Economic development and modernization

With the end of the Second World War, a new period opened. Three main characteristics of the international context are worth mentioning. In the first place, this was a time of booming capitalism, actively led by the state. The war effort had necessitated a greatly increased role for the state in organizing the economy and mobilizing the population. This form of interventionism became widely accepted and was continued by the first postwar European governments in their support for a mixed economy. The application of Keynesian techniques, the introduction of welfare, the incorporation of the organized labour movement into the management of the economy, the expansion of education and the dissemination of the ideals of growth and equal opportunities for all constituted the main hegemonic planks of the new consensus constructed through the state. More direct management of the economy was also an attempt to manage the political class struggle. Securing popular consent through the interventionist state was more than ever the only basis of legitimacy.

During this stage the most dynamic sector of the world capitalist system was the production of modern consumer goods (cars, fridges, TV sets, etc.), which was increasingly controlled by big transnational corporations. The production of raw materials ceased to be something carried out almost exclusively in Third World countries and was shifted on a massive scale to the industrial centres.[1] International capital in the metropolitan centres mainly flowed to other metropolitan centres, but in so far as a proportion of it went to Latin America, it was no longer directed only at raw material production but, above all, at the production of modern consumption goods which could be sold internally at monopolistic prices or exported cheaply to the metropolis.

In Europe the state concessions on welfare and full employment secured a measure of the popular support required for the revival and expansion of capitalism. From this central ground the development of a popular consumers' capitalism was launched. The adoption of Keynesian instruments of economic regulation made possible the high-wage, mass-production, consumer-oriented economy of the 1950s and 1960s, successfully counteracting the capitalist tendency to uncontrolled boom and recession. This kind of capitalist development required a major refashioning of the capitalist state. It was through the state that the market could be coordinated, consumption could be regulated and the working class could be incorporated and contained. This is the phase of European modernity which Peter Wagner has called 'organized capitalism'.[2]

In the second place, an important process of decolonization started all over the world and new independent nations emerged everywhere. The new wave of nationalism in the Third World coupled with the expansion of socialism brought about by the Soviet war effort became a matter of great concern for the Western industrial societies. Issues of social progress and economic development which had been taken for granted during the previous eighty years were forced back on to the agenda. For the first time the poverty and economic difficulties of less developed countries came to the fore and were recognized as genuine problems by the developed world. This is connected with the third characteristic of this period, which is the construction of a bipolar world dominated by the United States and the Soviet Union, confronting each other in a cold war.

In this context, development could no longer be taken for granted, and a renewed academic interest in the study of the necessary conditions for, and obstacles to, development arose in the metropolitan centres. The direct investment by international companies accelerated some processes of industrialization in Latin America, but it nevertheless remained heavily dependent on the metropolitan centres, both technologically and financially. Due to the payment of royalties and interests, the repatriation of profits and payments for imported capital goods, the net flow of capital favoured the metropolitan centres. The Latin American nations suffered from chronic deficits in their balances of payment, inflationary processes and widespread unemployment. In these circumstances socialism appeared as an

appealing experience, an example the Latin American nations could
follow in order to develop their productive forces. The Cuban revolution became an influential example throughout Latin America. This
reinforced the belief in the West that the Soviet Union was out to take
advantage of Latin America's growing pains, thus giving a further
impulse to the Cold War.

In Latin America this was a period which consolidated democracies through wider participation and important processes of modernization of the social economic base. García Canclini has selected
five types of structural changes: (1) industrial and employment
growth coupled with more consistent economic development allowing an expansion of the consumption of durable commodities produced in Latin America; (2) expansion and consolidation of urban
growth; (3) a widening of the artistic and cultural goods market, due
especially to the expansion of education; (4) the introduction of
new communicational technologies such as television; (5) progress of
radical political movements seeking profound structural reforms.[3]
Most states developed interventionist and protectionist policies which
controlled most of economic life, but they also introduced some
aspects of a welfare state in health, social security and housing. In
spite of all this, the benefits of modernity continued to be highly concentrated and the masses of the people continued to be excluded.

The beginning of television in the 1950s and the wider consolidation of radio, which had started as a more restricted and non-
commercial medium in the 1920s, marked the starting point of the
increasing impact of the electronic media on Latin American culture.
This was the beginning of the consumer society and of an incipient
mass popular culture. This was intimately connected with the industrial and urban expansion of the time, but also with the new commercial opportunities. In Brazil, for instance, a new law in 1952
allowed publicity time on radio to reach 20 per cent of daily pro-
gramming, and this allowed radio to become the basis for the expansion of a mass popular culture. It was also at this time that North
American films became widely available for consumption, and the
market for magazines, newspapers and books grew considerably.[4]
The same happened all over Latin America. Television followed suit,
but a bit later. By the end of this period, in 1972, TV advertising
expenditure in Latin America was higher than printed and radio
advertising expenditure, in contrast to Europe and the United States
where printed advertising expenditure was still far ahead.[5]

So, alongside education and industrialization, the increasing impact
of electronic media and the expansion of print undoubtedly helped in
the transmission of modern values and the creation of an incipient
mass culture by means of the constitution of a massive cultural

market. It can be said that the process of the mediazation of culture described by Thompson,[6] whereby the media increasingly shape the way in which cultural forms are produced and transmitted, considerably expanded in Latin America during this time. As radio and television became the main sources of popular entertainment and culture, they also facilitated the construction of new forms of self-recognition and struggle for the masses, and this can be connected with the emergence of urban popular radical political movements.[7]

Even though this stage in Latin America coincided with the phase of organized capitalism in Europe and some common features can be found, there are also important differences. In the first place, the role of the state in the promotion of industrialization in Latin America was much more accentuated than that of private initiative. Second, the participation of foreign capital in the Latin American process of development became increasingly more important than that of national capital. Protectionism brought more benefits to international corporations than national ones. Third, the elements of the welfare state introduced by governments and the progress of industrialization did not cover or reach most of the population, by contrast with Europe, and a sizable number of excluded and marginalized poor people began to cluster around big cities.

The comparison with the Asiatic trajectory to modernity is interesting on this point. While in Asia, Japan and other countries built sophisticated and highly automated and flexible technologies, strongly supported by the state, with a view to exporting industrial products on the international market, in Latin America the process of industrialization contented itself with second-rate technologies, partly because its horizon was limited to the protected national market, and partly because the state failed to assume the role of promoting a national technological capacity. This is why the success of industrialization depended, to a great extent, on the size of the internal market. Thus, in the cases of Brazil and Mexico, the countries with the largest internal markets in Latin America, competition and economies of scale allowed international levels of competitiveness.[8] In the rest of Latin America industrial production had high costs and little demand.

The new theories of development and modernization

It is not surprising that all these processes of modernization and change should have been accompanied and promoted by modernizing ideas and theories coming from abroad. The emphasis on mod-

ernization was best expressed in development economics and structural-functional sociology. They propounded the dismantling of traditional agrarian cultural identities and their replacement by modern
values and institutions. Thus, after the Second World War some stages
can be distinguished where important European and North American intellectual traditions held sway. The adoption of these theories
in successive stages by the Latin American elites meant that the predominance of essay writing, which had prevailed up to the Second
World War, began to decline and was replaced by an eruption of the
social sciences. From then on most analyses of Latin American culture
were to acquire a sociological or anthropological expression and,
ceasing to be concrete and historical, were to be seduced by the
abstraction of models or paradigms. There was little interest in issues
of identity but much interest in the normative structure of Latin
American societies. The field of culture was reduced to the normative element of social and economic transformation: analyses of
culture which went beyond the abstract structures of society became
scarce and weak.

First it was the ideas of the North American sociology of development, usually called 'modernization theories',[9] which cropped up
in the late 1940s and beginnings of the 1950s. They put forward the
idea that Latin America was in transition from traditional society to
modern society and that the very advanced (North American or European) industrial societies were the ideal model which backward
countries would inevitably reach. The modernization process was
conceived as a historical necessity which, following a transitional
route, repeated the same stages previously passed through by
advanced societies. The obstacles presented to this transition by a traditional culture underpinned by an oligarchic system controlled by
the old landowning aristocracies would be inevitably overcome.

The best representative of this kind of analysis in Latin America
was, without any doubt, the Argentinian sociologist Gino Germani,
who published his widely known *Política y sociedad en una época de
transición* in 1965. In Germani's analysis, what remained to be dismantled in order to reach a truly modern democracy were the traditional cultural values of both the elites and the masses in Latin
America, presenting stiff resistance to modernity especially through
what he called traditional and ideological authoritarianism.[10]
Germani describes the two polar ideal types existing in Argentina and
Latin America in terms of some changes occurring in three main areas
of the social structure: the type of social action, the attitude towards
change and the degree of institutional specialization. These changes
entail that

I. The type of *social action* is modified. From a predominance of *prescriptive* actions to a (relative) emphasis on *elective* actions (mainly of a 'rational' type).
II. From the *institutionalization* of the *traditional* to the *institutionalization* of change.
III. From a *conjunction of relatively undifferentiated institutions* to their increasing *differentiation and specialization*.[11]

In proposing the dichotomy between prescriptive action and elective action, Germani replaces the Weberian distinction between traditional and rational action. Unlike Weber, the rationale of Germani's distinction is the normative framework: prescriptive action takes place within a very rigid normative framework which fixes the course of action, whereas elective action takes place within a normative framework which is less rigid and determines a choice instead of a preordained course.[12] Germani's thesis is that in preindustrial societies most actions are prescriptive, whereas in industrial societies there is a predominance of elective actions. As for the second dichotomy, Germani proposes that in traditional societies change tends to be a violation of traditional norms and therefore is abnormal and rare. In a modern society, on the contrary, change becomes a normal phenomenon which the normative framework promotes and regulates. Finally, traditional societies possess an undifferentiated structure, with a few institutions performing many functions. In industrial societies each function tends to be performed by a specialized institution, resulting in a differentiated structure.

All these changes occur asynchronically. Germani distinguishes several types of asynchrony: geographical, institutional, intergroup and motivational. Regions, institutions, social groups and values change at different speeds and therefore coexist with one another in traditional and modern forms. Two important phenomena accompany the process of asynchronic change: the demonstration effect and the fusion effect. The former refers to a situation where some people, once they know the level of consumption and standard of living of other people, develop similar aspirations. This affects the pattern of consumption and savings and may in itself constitute an incentive to change. The fusion effect, on the other hand, gives rise to an ideological traditionalism which consists in the fact that

> when ideologies and attitudes which are an expression of advanced development processes encounter areas and groups which are characterized by traditional features, they are not interpreted in terms of their original context, but may reinforce those very traditional features,

which now seem to acquire a new credibility, not in the name of the old structure, but as 'advanced products'.[13]

The demonstration and fusion effects are responsible for a variety of problems in Latin America. For instance, popular classes develop economic aspirations similar to those of the working classes of developed countries. Since the productive structure is underdeveloped, those aspirations cannot be satisfied. The middle classes, on the other hand, may develop consumption patterns typical of highly industrialized nations and hence those patterns and corresponding attitudes may be fused with the conspicuous consumption pattern of traditional elites. Germani's point is that in underdeveloped countries consumption attitudes typical of developed economies coexist with underdeveloped productive structures. Similarly, popular classes develop egalitarian political aspirations which in the developed world arose only after the economy had diversified and modernized. In general, Germani's idea is that due to asynchronic change and, particularly, the demonstration and fusion effects, contemporary developing countries suffer from many cleavages and problems which did not exist in countries which developed earlier. Still, he does not lose faith in the inevitability of the process of transition and argues that despite many problems it is taking place at a quicker pace than in the past.

For Germani, therefore, culture becomes the 'value system' of society and this structural-functional idea is applied to Latin America as an abstract scheme whereby the transition is supposed to mean the progressive abandonment of religious values and old rural traditions and their replacement by the values of reason, freedom, progress and tolerance. Modernization theories of Germani's type reintroduced a concern for the institutional framework and the social aspects conditioning the process of development in Latin America. However, they did this in an abstract and ahistorical manner. They defined in general and taxonomic terms a series of dichotomous variables which by aggregation and juxtaposition constituted abstract models of a developed society or underdeveloped society. There was hardly any theoretical analysis of the connection between these factors. There was no real analysis of society in terms of a complex set of social relations which determined a type of domination, a productive structure, a class system and a cultural domain, all in correspondence with one other.

The process of transition is assumed to happen through successive changes in a number of variables, and the more variables are affected the more rapid the process of modernization. When modernization theorists identify the entrepreneur as the motor force of change they do it rather arbitrarily, not as a result of an analysis of social relations and in the context of other groups and classes struggling in pursuit of other interests, but as an abstract definition, the embodiment of many variables. The entrepreneur is the agent of development because of being in theory innovative, achieving, deviant, universalist, hard-working, rational, willing to take risks, etc., not because entrepreneurs as a class and within certain conditions have historically succeeded in imposing their interests on society. Hence these analyses assume a prescriptive character and instead of studying historically the structural context and the development of the bourgeois class with its specific features, they only seek to establish whether the ideal model of an entrepreneur is present or absent in Latin America. Modernization theories reduce the study of sociohistorical processes to the construction of abstract models of universal applicability.

The thought of the Economic Commission for Latin America

At the beginning of the 1950s the Economic Commission for Latin America (ECLA), an international organization created by the United Nations, under the chairmanship of Raul Prebisch, an Argentinian economist, developed an original body of thought which challenged some of the assumptions of the theory of international trade.[14] ECLA wanted to promote the modernization and industrialization of Latin America, but saw certain problems stemming from international trade. According to its analysis the terms of trade were consistently deteriorating for raw material exporters because they sold their products at international prices which were below their real value, whereas industrially powerful countries sold their industrial products at prices above their real value. There was therefore unequal exchange between centre and periphery, a terminology they were the first to introduce.

The pioneering economic work of the Economic Commission for Latin America[15] then focused on the existence of a centre–periphery world system which favoured the central industrial countries. According to ECLA's analysis those countries specializing in the production of industrial goods grew faster than those specializing in the production of raw materials, and therefore the gap between the central and the peripheral economies was steadily growing. This is why it propounded the idea that the countries of Latin America had to modernize their societies by switching from an economy oriented to the export of raw materials to an economy led by industrial output, in order to lessen their dependency on the external demand for raw materials and substitute for it the expansion of internal demand.

This meant for ECLA a change from a model of development 'towards the outside' to a model of development 'towards the inside'. At the centre of the latter model is a process of industrial diversification which is considered to be crucial to any process of development. This process appears in the Latin American context as an 'import-substituting industrialization' because it replaces those imports which these nations cannot afford with the available hard currency. Although this process had already started in the 1930s, there was the danger, after the Second World War and in conditions of industrial expansion in the main developed centres, of a relapse into the old outward-oriented pattern. The political and economic initiative to bring about modernization and industrialization had to be mainly in the hands of the state. ECLA contended that given the many difficulties which a process of industrialization had to face it was crucial that the state took the initiative of organizing, promoting and supervising all the industrializing efforts in order to guarantee the continuity of the process.

Industrial development had to be carefully planned, both globally and by sectors, and the state had an important responsibility especially in the fields of energy, transport and some essential industries. In order to be able to achieve a higher rate of growth, ECLA also recommended the assistance of foreign capital. Additional resources were necessary because a process of industrialization increased the need to import equipment and technology from abroad, and the relatively deteriorating price of primary exports did not allow the developing countries to keep pace with the expansion of necessary imports. Finally, ECLA proposed regional integration as a long-term goal which would allow an expansion of national markets and would increase the opportunities for the import-substituting industrialization. The model of development 'towards the inside' would work better if the markets were extended and Latin American countries could specialize in certain areas, thus expanding regional trade and avoiding having to substitute for all imports separately.

ECLA's position was a mixture of modernization theory, a belief in capitalist development and foreign investment and a perception that, nevertheless, the capitalist world was divided into centre and periphery, that the latter had had a raw deal in the international markets and that many economic analyses about developing countries elaborated in the industrial centres were inadequate. ECLA shared with modernization theories both their optimism about the viability of development and their faith in the capitalist road to development. But, on the other hand, its views about the centre–periphery division of the world coincided with some of the tenets of the Marxist theory of imperialism concerning the opposition of interests between industrial and underdeveloped countries. This is why in many Western academic centres ECLA's views were regarded with suspicion. Nevertheless, they were also recognized as the first original contribution to the development debate coming from the periphery. Together with theories of dependency and the literary boom in the Latin American novel which I shall explore further below, the thought of ECLA is considered to be a major Latin American contribution.

Theories of dependency

By the end of the 1960s new theories arose in Latin America which were critical of both the theories of modernization and ECLA's policies. These were the theories of dependency. They partially drew on the classical theory of imperialism, but challenged some of its assumptions by focusing more specifically on the problems caused by the world capitalist system in the periphery. Both ECLA and Marxist orthodoxy since 1928 had supported the progressiveness of the national bourgeoisies and had considered industrialization as a process fundamentally antagonistic to and opposed by the imperialist centres. The new theories of dependence were sceptical about the liberating role of national bourgeoisies and suggested that the processes of industrialization in the Third World were the vehicle of imperialistic penetration and of a new kind of dependence on transnational companies.

There are various kinds of dependency theory. The best known is that of A. G. Frank, a North American of German origin who elaborated his theory while working in Chile.[16] It had a great intellectual impact partly because it was the first to appear but more fundamentally because it radically questions what had been until then a received truth of both Marxist and liberal theories, namely, that capitalism is essentially a mode of production able to promote development everywhere. Frank rejects this idea and maintains that capitalism is to blame for the continuous underdevelopment of Latin America since the sixteenth century. He conceives of capitalism as a world system within which the metropolitan centres manage to expropriate the economic surpluses from satellite countries through the mechanisms of the international market, thus producing simultaneously the development of the former and the underdevelopment of the latter. Latin American countries are underdeveloped because they are dependent within the world capitalist system. Hence development can only occur when a country breaks out of the system by means of a socialist revolution.

Despite its appeal and widespread impact, Frank's theory has been severely criticized. First, because it defines capitalism in terms of orientation to the market and not as a mode of production. Second, because it overemphasizes the exploitation of certain countries as a whole and pays less attention to the exploitation of their working classes. Third, because it confuses dependency with underdevelopment, whereas it can be shown that some countries such as Canada are dependent and developed. A more sophisticated theory of dependency is that of Cardoso and Faletto.[17] For them dependency must not be used as a blanket concept which can explain all the evils of underdevelopment everywhere. For a start they propose that even within Latin America the situation of dependency is not the same for every country and that although the conditions of the international market and the strategies of international capital may be common to them, they are negotiated in different ways by different countries depending on their internal class struggles. This means that there is a specific mode of articulation between internal class structures and the manner of incorporation into the world market. Thus in certain countries a path of dependent capitalist development is possible, whereas in others stagnation may result. The advantage of this approach is that it allows the study of concrete situations of dependency rather than uncovering a single universal mechanism of exploitation applicable to all peripheral countries.

The emergence of dependency theories coincided with a resurgence of Marxism and of hopes placed in socialism in the 1960s and early 1970s. The influence of the 1959 Cuban revolution was certainly instrumental in promoting these ideas. The disillusion with the results of import-substituting industrialization processes, the lack of dynamic economic growth and the increasing number of contradictions surfacing, mainly due to the widespread poverty and destitution of growing sectors of the population, gave rise to a powerful critique of the capitalist system as unable to deliver economic development in the conditions of the periphery. The failure of the capitalist modernization process was mainly blamed on imperialism. But the critique of capitalism and imperialism did not prevent the adoption of new foreign models prevalent in the socialist countries. The resurgence of Marxism and socialist projects was directly related to the need to struggle against dependency and bring about national development.

The idea of a national development was mainly explored from an economic point of view, except in Brazil, where the thinkers of the ISEB[18] set the idea of national development in opposition to an alienated culture. Outside Brazil, Sunkel was one of the few authors in Latin America at this time who also considered culture as an important dimension to be taken into account in any idea of a national development. For him transnational capitalism through the agency of transnational corporations causes a process of cultural and national disintegration in Latin America, a truly segmented social structure. But he does not develop the point much further, except to say that segmentation at the cultural and ideological level manifests itself 'by overwhelming and systematic publicity for the model of consumerist civilization'.[19]

Even with its deficiencies and problems, the postwar advance of modernity was notable and showed the continued cultural importance in Latin America of European and North American rationalistic and developmentalist ideas. In spite of the differences between these modernizing theories, their basic premise continued to be development and modernization as the only means to overcome poverty and/or dependency. Even socialism was considered more as a new road to development than as a means for the emancipation of the working class. Nevertheless, in all these positions, except perhaps in the thought of the ISEB in Brazil, the idea remained that modernity was something essentially European or North American, which Latin America ought to acquire by repeating their historical experiences. There was little consideration of local specificities and cultural differences, and therefore they tended to reduce all differences to uniformity. This is why institutions and values could be transferred from the European or North American reality to the Latin American reality without many problems. The Latin American acquires meaning only in so far as it becomes an instance of a universal process. The idea also remained that the traditional agrarian cultural pattern in Latin America had to be dismantled in order for modernization processes to succeed. This is why agrarian reforms were considered so crucial to the modernization process.

The problem of national culture and identity

Implicit in the various modernizing approaches there was, nevertheless, a project for a new identity, a kind of developmentalist identity whose goal was economic development of an industrial kind, with the state playing a central role and the value of equality having great importance. Political struggle in this period was about how to achieve development and welfare for all. It was crucial to raise the consciousness of the people, to abandon the profligacy of populism and to adopt a new work ethic. The economic system continued to be capitalist but the modernizers wanted to humanize it, and by following interventionist policies they wanted to protect the workers and redistribute national income in their favour. The new identity had therefore a developmentalist and egalitarian matrix which combined industrial development with state support and workers' rights.

Although ECLA was perhaps the most crucial institution for the reception, creation and elaboration of many of these ideas, the Latin American universities were also very important for the reception and dissemination of all these theories. In every period, the universities, through research but mainly through teaching, were decisive in the expansion of the new ideas about modernization, dependency and Marxism. This new role of the universities was supported by the introduction of social sciences such as sociology, economics, psychology and political science, which are now established as autonomous and professional degrees. At every stage the ideas of modernity were promoted as against identity. In spite of some isolated doubts, Latin America came back to believing in and applying the ideas and traditions of modernity that came from Europe and other intellectual centres of the world.

One of the few exceptions worth mentioning is the case of Brazil, where in addition to economic and sociological abstract analyses, some authors grouped around the ISEB developed a consistent line of cultural analysis which had a vast influence in many fields including anthropology, cinema, pedagogy, theatre, literature and music. Their basic project was both critical and forward looking in that they characterized Brazilian culture as alienated by mental colonialism, but wanted to establish the premises for the construction of an authentic national culture. Prestigious intellectuals such as Alvaro Vieira, Paulo Freire, Carlos Estevan Martins, Darcy Ribeiro and many others were influenced by these ideas. They all detected cultural alienation in their fields of work and linked the idea of alienation to a colonial situation in which an authentic culture could not be produced. For a culture to be authentic it has to be elaborated from a starting point in a country's own being and reality, whereas inauthenticity can be compared to a colonial situation in which culture reflects the metropolitan culture.

Following these ideas some authors identified an alienated Brazilian theatre, an alienated Brazilian cinema and alienated

Brazilian sociology, and they advocated a 'national theatre', a 'new cinema' and a 'national sociology' characterized by their authenticity. All this was connected with the idea of a true national development, which could overcome the situation of mental alienation characteristic of underdevelopment.[20] A notable expression of these trends was 'Cinema Novo' in which distinguished film directors like Glauber Rocha, Carlos Diegues and Leon Hirszman made important contributions. They not only started from the situation of underdevelopment with a view to questioning its reality of inequality and injustice, but also advocated a new and original aesthetic approach. Cinema Novo wanted to be socially and aesthetically subversive. One of the first films made with these new ideas was a collective work, *Cinco Vezes Favela*, produced in 1962 by the National Union of Students, which was inspired by life in Brazilian shanty towns.

In spite of the widespread prevalence of social analyses centred on the Latin American economy and social processes, it is also possible to find during this period a few works which more directly tackle the issue of culture and identity.[21] Yet it is not surprising to find that, as in the second half of the nineteenth century – another period in which modernity predominated over identity – Latin American identity is again defined in terms of an opposition to Europe, which represents, if not civilisation *per se*, at least a culture with a positive self-affirmation and self-confidence that Latin America lacks. The Venezuelan Ernesto Mayz Vallenilla, for instance, published *El problema de América* (1957),[22] in which he tries to define the essence of the Latin American, or, as he puts it, the originality of Latin America. He does not think that it can be found in the Indian traditions or in the special character of Latin American nature, but rather the novel element is to be found in the inhabitant of this world.[23]

The Latin American human being is permanently searching for the new and is dissatisfied with the present because it is not as new as they expected. By using Heideggerian terminology, Mayz Vallenilla tries to show that the most basic attitude of the Latin American human being is that of expecting to be, that of 'not-being-still'. This permanent dissatisfaction with the present and projection into the future is regarded as an essential feature of the Latin American's mode of being-in-the-world. As he puts it, 'the peculiar, original or novel of this *world* . . . is to be found in the disposition of radical expectation, which, as a fundamental ingredient of its ethos, distinguishes the Latin American man.'[24] Thus Mayz Vallenilla not only falls into a form of essentialism but also reduces Latin American identity to a psychological attitude or disposition. What is interesting from my point of view is the fact that this Latin American 'forever-not-being-still' looks defective by comparison with the implicitly satisfied European 'being-in-the-present'. A state of permanent dissatisfaction cannot be better than a state of satisfaction.

Even clearer is the comparison in the case of Alberto Caturelli's *América Bifronte* (1956), which has heavy Hegelian overtones.[25] Latin America appears in this work as a being still not fertilized by the Spirit, as opposed to Europe which is the kingdom of the Spirit. The Latin American, Caturelli argues, 'is the unrealized, the purely virtual, the imperfect, the immature, the essentially primitive'.[26] Latin America is seen as suffering from two alienations, retrospective alienation, a fixation with the European cultural tradition, and projective alienation, an excessive patriotism. The former is a kind of evasion, an unconfessed nostalgia for the absent European culture. The latter is a disproportionate elevation of the Latin American.[27] However, in order for Latin America to create a culture that has universal value, it has necessarily to integrate European culture with its own original primitivism. Even more, since European culture is excessively intellectualized, only Latin America can make that culture fructify.[28] So Caturelli, rather implausibly and contradictorily, goes from a pessimistic assessment of the Latin American original being to an exaltation of its special role in redeeming European culture.

In a similar way, H. A. Murena's *El pecado original de América* (1954)[29] describes Latin Americans as the pariahs of the world, as dispossessed 'because we left *everything* when we came from Europe or Asia, and we left *everything* because we left *history*'.[30] Once again by evoking Hegel, Murena argues that Latin America is a continent without history, without the Spirit. Latin Americans once inhabited Europe, the land of the Spirit, but they were expelled from it as from paradise and were thrown into another land, America. This expulsion was due to a second original sin which Latin Americans are not aware of: 'America is a punishment for a guilt we do not know . . . to be born or die in America means to be burdened by a second original sin.'[31] The curious thing is that for Murena, even if Latin America is the expelled European soul, redemption cannot come from a return home. Latin America must definitively break with Europe in order to acquire an autonomous life.

Octavio Paz's classic *The Labyrinth of Solitude* (1950) was another expression of these feelings of uprootedness and abandonment which appeared at this time. It describes the plight of Mexicans in ways which can be applied to the rest of Latin America. According to Paz, the Mexican is in search of his origins, is like an orphan who is conscious of having been uprooted and starts a passionate search.[32] But the Latin American identity is not just a search for roots; it is at the same time a rejection of the past, a condemnation of origins, a reneging on hybridity:

> The Mexican condemns all his tradition as a whole . . . The Mexican does not want to be Indian or Spanish. He does not want to descend from them either. He negates them. And he does not affirm himself as a mestizo, but as an abstraction: he is a man. He turns to be a son of nothingness. He begins in himself . . . The Mexican and Mexicanness are defined as rupture and negation. And at the same time as search, as a will to transcend this state of exile.[33]

In such a search, no particular historical form or tendency can fully express Mexicanness. We have been pro-French, Hispanists, indigenistas, liberals and Catholic, Paz argues, but none of these forms constitute the answer to the search. They only represent a permanent 'oscillation between various universal projects, successively transplanted or imposed and all useless today'.[34] Paz seems to despair that any answer will be able to be found, but gets some apparent comfort from the fact that the situation of the rest of the world is not entirely different: 'we live, as the rest of the planet, in a mortal and decisive conjuncture, orphans of the past and with a future to invent. Universal History is already a common task. And our labyrinth is that of all human beings.'[35]

There are of course many differences between these authors, but at a time of rapid modernization, dominant development theories and renewed prestige of European influences, they all express an interest in identity, which is by no means widespread in Latin America, and a conflictual view in which an admiration for European culture is mixed with a feeling that Latin America's identity cannot find its own course. Hence the ambivalence which in some cases leads to a proposal for total rupture (Murena), and in others to one for total fusion (Mayz, Caturelli, Paz).

The Latin American novel 'boom'

Corresponding to the Latin American postwar economic boom there emerged a notable literary boom which gave Latin America's literature a universal dimension. It was as if the modernizing dreams of going quickly through the same stages of development as the Europeans first achieved some credibility by the world recognition given to the Latin American novel. As Ainsa has remarked, in just seven years, from 1960 to 1967, major works of what was called the Latin

American literary boom were published: Augusto Roa Bastos's *Hijo de Hombre* (1960), Carlos Fuentes' *La muerte de Artemio Cruz* (1962), Ernesto Sábato's *Sobre héroes y tumbas* (1962), Mario Vargas Llosa's *La ciudad y los perros* (1963) and *La casa verde* (1966), Joao Guimaraes Rosa's *Gran Sertón: Veredas* (1963), José Lezama Lima's *Paradiso* (1966), Julio Cortázar's *Los Premios* (1960) and *Rayuela* (1963), Juan Carlos Onetti's *El Astillero* (1961) and *Juntacadáveres* (1964), Alejo Carpentier's *El siglo de las luces* (1963), and Gabriel García Márquez's *Cien años de soledad* (1967).[36]

Most of these works were innovative in that they did not respect the boundaries between traditional genres, thus combining myth with social criticism, narrative with essay writing, novel with poem. There was a new concern with the materiality of language which bridged novel and poem. The best two examples of this would be *Paradiso* by Lezama Lima and *El Gran Sertón: Veredas* by Guimaraes Rosa.[37] Experimenting with language was a hallmark of these works. Ainsa has spoken of a veritable 'linguistic insurrection' in which 'paradox, humour, ambiguity, language games, popular, literal, prosaic or poetic idioms question and criticize language at the very heart of the text, thus giving the novel an unexpected metalinguistic dimension and, above all, proclaiming what we call "the right to heterogeneous imagination."'[38] Martínez Blanco also detects innovations in the structure of the literary work. According to her the Latin American writer was influenced by a series of European and North American authors such as Joyce, Faulkner, James and Woolf whose revolutionary techniques they have incorporated. Hence the experimentation with new forms of expression which lack linearity in the narrative, which disregard chronology and conventional rules, which introduce internal monologues, etc.[39]

On the occasion of the emergence of this new literary wave the expressions 'magic realism' or Carpentier's 'real marvellous', which had been used to refer to Latin American literature in the 1940s, surfaced again. In the new novels fantastic and incredible things very frequently occur. Mythical cities like Comala, Macondo and Santa María appear, symbolizing Latin America's isolation disrupted by the external forces of modernity, or representing in a concentrated form relevant parts of its historical past. According to Martínez Blanco what is meant by magic realism is the idea that there is a typically Latin American worldview which 'consists in the counterposing of two planes: that of everyday, superficial reality and that of the other non-rational reality which encompasses the world of myths and beliefs – Indian or African – of dreams, of the supernatural, of the unusual or extraordinary'.[40] It can be said that Juan Rulfo's widely influential novel *Pedro Páramo* (1955) is, at an early point in this period, the first important work of the new Latin American novel. It concentrates all the elements that characterize the new approach: the appearance of a mythical town, Comala; a narrative structure which, according to Franco, is more poetic than logical; an unconventional arrangement of chapters; a permanent interplay between the real world and an illusory world of hopes and dreams; a lack of linear development, etc.[41]

Another interesting aspect of this new Latin American novel is that most of the authors know and influence each other, thus giving their novels a specific character or hallmark which is recognized all over the world. Fernández Retamar argues that the new Latin American novelists 'come from one another'. What Martí said of the modernists in 1893 can be said today of these novelists: 'It is like a family in America.'[42] The fact has also been mentioned that in one way or another most Latin American novelists have had a connection with journalism,[43] not just as a job which provided them with economic security at the beginning, but as a genre they go back to from time to time – as García Márquez and Vargas Llosa do – which goes to show the increasing importance of the mass media for the novel.

The commercial success of this literary movement was certainly connected with the new modern economic and commercial conditions emerging in Latin America, but was not a mere manifestation of such conditions. In fact, in its content the Latin American novel of this time did not necessarily reflect favourably on the processes of modernization underway, but rather critically questioned the injustices and problems suffered by Latin American peoples. Although the new novel broke with the realism and social denunciation typical of the first half of the twentieth century, it clearly had a political dimension. Carlos Fuentes has defined this dimension in terms of an interest in exploring 'the problem of power in the Hispanic world' using the resources literature possesses:

> I am not alien to this problem in *Terra Nostra*. Neither is Carpentier, or Roa Bastos, or Uslar Pietri, or García Márquez with his *Otoño del Patriarca*, and even at another level Vargas Llosa in *Conversación en la Catedral*, which is also a novel on the exercise of power, or in a different manner, José Donoso in *El obsceno Pájaro de la Noche*... There is always a background about the use of power in the Latin American novel...[44]

A different version is that of Mario Benedetti. He sees a relationship between the creative revolution in the narrative field and the Cuban revolution in the political field:

Narrators and poets, playwrights or essayists are the Latin American revolution's sons (putative or natural, prodigal or parricidal) . . . With the Cuban revolution a new experimental and imaginative manner of carrying out an anti-imperialist policy started. Curiously, Latin American literature . . . broke with the old patterns, with the old rhetoric, with the old routine and launched itself enthusiastically into experiment.[45]

In this sense the Latin American novel of the boom is a politically progressive kind of literature which in its own unsystematic but aesthetic fashion critically anticipated the end to this period of economic development and modernization, and the resurgence of some dark forces which were lurking from the past. Vargas Llosa has argued that this is precisely the reason why great novels emerged in Latin America at this time: great novelists often appear at moments which precede profound historical transformations, 'when the world they reflect finds itself in a state of decomposition, when its foundations are eroded and when that world will justly disappear'.[46] Be that as it may, the novel of this time was one of the crucial areas of culture which acted as a critical conscience, both espousing the situation of the downtrodden and casting some doubts on the possibilities of success of the modernizing logic of this period. But paradoxically, it itself became universally recognized thanks to the very modernizing boom of which it was so suspicious.

6

Dictatorships and the Lost Decade

1970–1990

The crisis of the 1970s and 1980s

By 1973 a new phase had set in which was characterized by a slowing down of economic growth and a falling rate of profit in industrial nations. Everywhere in the capitalist world profits fell, trade contracted and unemployment became very pronounced. This was compounded by the sharp rise in oil prices in October 1973. By 1974–5 a generalized recession was hitting the world capitalist system for the first time since the Second World War. What was new about this recession and the period that followed it was that the anti-depression policies followed by most governments produced inflation without adequately stimulating the economy, thus provoking high levels of unemployment. Throughout the developing world the recession had damaging effects: it aggravated the chronic deficits of its balance of payments by bringing down the prices of raw materials and raising the prices of oil and other essential imports, thus producing inflation, unemployment and stagnation.[1] This marked the beginning of the huge expansion of the Third World's international debt, which soon became an impossibly heavy burden for its very weak economies, with the result that several countries defaulted on their obligations.

Authors of what has been called the 'regulation school'[2] have argued that the deep economic crisis of the early 1970s was not just or simply a temporary phase of late capitalism, but a manifestation of the break-up of the old and rigid Fordist–Keynesian regime of accumulation and its replacement by a new, more flexible regime of accumulation which is usually called post-Fordist. They are talking of the emergence of an important new stage of capitalism. The Fordist–Keynesian regime of accumulation presided over the long postwar boom from 1945 to 1973, and was built on certain consumption habits involving mass-produced commodities, industrial modes of organization favouring huge and bureaucratic corporations, rigid labour control practices and mass-producing technologies. The new regime of accumulation was characterized by the emergence of entirely new sectors of production, new ways of providing financial services, new markets and, above all, greatly intensified rates of commercial, technological and organizational innovation. Flexible accumulation implied relatively high levels of 'structural' unemployment, the rapid destruction and reconstruction of skills, and the rollback of trade union power – one of the political pillars of the Fordist regime.

At this time in Latin America the processes of industrialization and development entirely lost their dynamism, economic growth came to a standstill and even became negative during the 1980s, and as a consequence social unrest and labour agitation became widespread. The international recession resulted in unemployment, inflation and increased political instability everywhere. While in Europe right-wing governments were elected which sought to limit trade union power and state expenditure, in Latin America the challenge of the Chilean socialist experiment and the exhaustion of other political experiments of the left precipitated a wave of military dictatorships which proceeded in a more drastic and authoritarian way. It started with the 1964 military coup in Brazil and was followed by coups in Argentina, Peru, Bolivia, Chile and Uruguay. This showed the precariousness of Latin American modern political institutions as compared with the European ones. They were incapable of channelling and absorbing the political turmoil within a framework of stability.

In the late 1970s and 1980s the neoliberal and conservative theories of the free market started to gain ascendancy and the socialist dreams collapsed. The military dictatorships swiftly changed the direction of economic policies by opening up their countries to foreign investment and foreign goods. The main ideas were now to export, to abolish tariffs, to abandon an inefficient industry and to let market forces produce development by means of a more rational allocation of resources. Dependency was no longer blamed for lack of development, but rather excessive state intervention in the economy became the new culprit that had smothered growth. Capitalism was still dynamic if it was allowed to work according to market forces. What had failed in the past was not capitalism but socialism.

From 1981 international interest rates began to rise dramatically due to Reagan's economic policies of expansion, especially in military expenditure. The rise of interest rates was a disaster for Third World countries, heavily in debt. Service charges on the debts became an impossible burden. Between 1978 and 1984, Latin America's total interest payments increased by 360 per cent. By 1984 every 1 per cent rise in interest rates added $700 million to the annual servicing of the Brazilian debt. It is no wonder that in August 1982 Mexico declared that it could no longer keep up its interest payments. In early 1984 Argentina declared a six-month moratorium on interest repayments. In July 1985 President Alan García of Peru announced his unilateral decision to limit debt repayments to 10 per cent of the value of Peru's exports. In February 1987 the Brazilian government suspended any further interest payments on its debt, which had reached the figure of $110 billion. Thus the debt crisis started.

It is true that in many cases, and most definitely in Chile, dictatorships opened the way to a new globalized stage of development and economic modernization in Latin America, changing the direction of economic policies by opening up their countries to foreign investment and foreign goods, and putting into practice the first neoliberal ideas. But it took many years before the new stage of expansion began to yield some economic fruits.[3] It has to be remembered that during the 1980s, the so-called 'lost decade', Latin America suffered negative growth. Besides, from the point of view of political and social modernity, dictatorships meant a major regression in so far as they abolished democratic institutions, systematically violated human rights, dismantled forms of social participation and consistently sought to destroy social organizations representing the poorest sectors of society. The exclusion of wide social sectors was increased as unemployment levels soared and salaries plummeted.

If in the 1950s Latin America had witnessed the beginning of a mass popular culture helped by the introduction of television and the wide accessibility of radio, it was in the 1970s that a true market-oriented consumer society of material and symbolic goods was consolidated. The novelty of the situation was that a massive expansion of the media, including television and records, and of advertising coincided in Latin America with a time of dictatorship and repression. As Ortiz has argued for the case of Brazil, 'the cultural movement post-1964 is characterized by two sources which are not exclusive of each other: on the one side it is defined by political and ideological repression; on the other, it is a moment in Brazilian history when more cultural goods are produced and diffused.'[4] This was also true of other Latin American countries such as Argentina and Chile, but it was in Brazil that the preoccupation of the authoritarian state with the field of culture was most notable, especially through the creation of new cultural institutions: Conselho Federal de Cultura, Instituto Nacional do Cinema, EMBRAFILME, FUNARTE, Pró-Memória, etc.[5] The main idea of the military government was that communications and the media in general were crucial for national integration.

Everywhere in Latin America the production, distribution and consumption of a 'mediazed' mass culture underwent an enormous expansion. A rough indication of this can be given by the growth in the number of TV sets in Latin America from 31.2 million in 1980 to 64.8 million in 1990. In Brazil the leap was from 15 million to 30.8 million in the same period. Television became an increasingly important means of cultural consumption in Latin America.[6] At this time there was a consolidation of the leading local and international conglomerates controlling the media and the popular mass culture of the continent. It became possible to talk of a true cultural industry in Latin America, producing cultural goods for the mass market. Perhaps its best expression is the *telenovela*, a genre which Chile, Mexico, Brazil, Argentina, Venezuela and Colombia perfected and exported. Unlike the North American soap opera, in Latin America the *telenovela* is not just for the afternoons and addressed mainly to a female public, but is a massive 'prime-time' product.[7]

The ambivalence of Latin American modernity

The exhaustion of the modernizing, state-led, heavily protectionist and developmentalist pattern of industrialization in the 1970s, and the succession of military coups which occurred as a consequence, started a process of reappraisal among intellectuals which was reinforced by a sense of continuous failure. The deep crisis explained in part, and went hand in hand with, a profound identity crisis, which was marked by pessimism and renewed doubts as to whether the road to modernity that had been followed could be wrong. The rise and fall of so many intellectual fashions and the persistence of enormous economic problems and widespread poverty, not to speak of the brutal activities of military dictatorships, could not but raise doubts as to whether the relentless pursuit of Western modernization ideas could bring about any real solution. The exhaustion of the dreams of rapid industrialization and Westernization in the 1950s and 1960s, the collapse of the hopes of economic independence and socialism, drowned in a sea of blood in the military coups in Brazil in 1964,

Chile in 1973, Argentina in 1966 and 1976, and Uruguay in 1973, and the years under terrible right-wing dictatorships were bound to raise again the questions about the nature of Latin American modernity and about the nature of the theories that had underpinned the modernizing aspirations.

Three main types of critique emerged which emphasized, first, the opposition of modernity to Latin American identity, second, the lack of authenticity of Latin American modernity, and third, its unexpected results due to telluric factors.[8] In practice these three critiques tended to overlap. Part of the third was what Brunner has aptly called 'Macondismo',[9] which grants a special explanatory power to Latin American literature.[10] The idea is that in its narratives a reality profoundly influenced by telluric factors of a portentous and enigmatic character is expressed. Macondo is a metaphor for the magic and marvellous character of Latin America, full of mysteries, challenging a purely rational understanding of it. As Brunner puts it, Macondo means that 'they (foreigners) will not be able easily to understand us' (the Latin Americans), which also entails that 'they will not be able to impose upon us a pattern of modernization which does not fit into our mystery.'[11] Macondism is therefore more defensive than conservative. It does not deny the possibility of modernization, but suggests caution, because Latin America is supposed to be the world of the unexpected and of uncontrollable telluric forces.

In a way, it can be suggested that this was the implicit position of the authors belonging to the so-called literary boom of the 1960s who continued to publish their novels during the 1970s and 1980s. I have already suggested in the last chapter that the novels of the 1960s were deeply suspicious of modernizing processes. In this respect there was little difference between them and the novels of this later period, apart from the fact that the new novels, or sometimes shorter stories, were able to focus on the reality of dictatorships with more emphasis than before. Works like *El cumpleaños de Juan Angel* (1971) by Mario Benedetti, *La Casa de los Espíritus* (1982) by Isabel Allende, *El jardín de al lado* (1981) by José Donoso, and *No habrá más penas ni olvidos* (1978) by Eduardo Soriano are deeply marked by the tragic events, human rights violations and exile brought about by military dictatorships. Yet the reality of these terrible events continued to be treated within the framework and with the peculiarities of the new novel, except that there was no longer the same interest in experimentation as in the 1960s. Ainsa has called these works the 'narrative of internal resistance'.[12]

Seymour Menton has argued that at this time, and more particularly since 1979, a new kind of novel made its appearance in Latin America, which he calls 'the new historical novel', and which was characterized by a story located in the past, a distant past that the author had not directly experienced, usually with a historical figure as the protagonist. The authors were sometimes the same ones who had belonged to the 1960s literary boom, but now, at a time of dictatorships and hopelessness, they seemed to look back into the past to try to find a ray of hope. Within this trend Menton places Alejo Carpentier's *El arpa y la sombra* (1979), Antonio Benítez Rojo's *El mar de las lentejas* (1979), Mario Vargas Llosa's *La guerra del fin del mundo* (1981), Germán Espinoza's *La tejedora de coronas* (1989), Abel Posse's *Los perros del paraíso* (1983) and several others. This type of novel did not seek fully to reproduce a past historical time, but to use the past and the fictionalizing of historical figures to present certain philosophical ideas.[13]

Octavio Paz, Carlos Fuentes (literary men who also write social essays) and Richard Morse, in their turn, highlight problems of authenticity. They maintain in various ways that Latin America has had fundamental difficulties in modernizing in accordance with the European model; its modernizing processes have not been entirely genuine and authentic. For Paz the main cause of this is that Spain and Latin America did not have an eighteenth century, that is to say, an Enlightenment, and therefore they could not carry out in depth the Weberian process of rationalization. Thus Paz holds that

> at the moment that Europe opens up to the political, scientific and philosophical critique that heralds the modern world, Spain closes itself in and encloses its best minds in the conceptual cages of neo-scholasticism. We, Hispanic peoples, have not succeeded in being really modern because, unlike the rest of the Western peoples, we did not have a critical age.[14]

For Paz there is a great difference between North America and South America. North America speaks English and is the daughter of the tradition that founded the modern world, especially its three fundamental processes: the Reformation, democracy and capitalism. South America speaks Spanish or Portuguese and is the daughter of the Catholic monarchy and the Counter-Reformation.

In a similar way Carlos Fuentes affirms that Latin Americans are children of the Spanish Counter-Reformation, a veritable barrier to modernity, and that they often prefer 'preserving the weight of anachronistic societies'. Thus he asks himself: 'how could we be modern then?' However, he also suggests that Latin Americans have often reacted violently against tradition by adopting the latest version of Western modernity in an uncritical fashion: 'we are a continent in desperate search of its modernity.'[15] For Fuentes there exists a strong contrast between the 'progressive impatience', which leads to the frequent Latin American political and economic ruptures, and the 'cultural patience', which maintains a line of continuity with the past.[16]

The ambivalence of Latin American modernity is also Richard Morse's argument: the Weberian process of disenchantment of the world could never be completely internalized in Latin America, not even by its most modern sectors. Once more, the cause is sought in the Spanish rejection of the scientific and religious revolutions, which impedes a lasting implant of European individualism and utilitarianism.[17] The diagnoses of these three authors are quite similar, but their conclusions differ. Morse is somehow the most optimistic; he believes that as a result of the lack of complete assimilation of what he calls 'the great Western design',[18] Latin Americans develop a rationality of 'compromise';[19] and that, on the other hand, the structure of their character is better suited to 'preserve humanity' within industrial society.[20] Fuentes suggests that Latin America's cultural continuity will provide the only solution for the future, but he still has some doubts and wonders whether 'we could transpose the strength of cultural life into political life and between them both create development models more akin to our experience, to our being.'[21] Paz is more pessimistic and concludes that Latin America has reached only a pseudo-modernity:

> the liberal revolution, initiated with independence, did not result in the implant of a true democracy or the birth of a national capitalism, but in a military dictatorship and in an economic regime characterized by the latifundia and the concessions to foreign consortia and enterprises, especially North American. Liberalism was sterile and produced nothing comparable to the pre-Columbian creations or those of New Spain: neither pyramids nor convents, neither cosmogonic myths nor poems of Sor Juana Inés de la Cruz . . . The old values crumbled not the old realities. Soon they were covered by the new liberal and progressive values. Masked realities: the beginning of inauthenticity and of lies, endemic evils of Latin American countries. At the beginning of the twentieth century we were already installed in full pseudo-modernity: railways and latifundia, democratic constitution and a caudillo in the best Hispanic-Arab tradition, positivist philosophers and pre-Columbian caciques, symbolic poetry and illiteracy.[22]

Finally, modernity has also been attacked for supposedly negating Latin American identity. Methol Ferré and Morandé criticize the modernizing efforts in Latin America for they would negate its true religious identity. Modernization, as it has occurred in Latin America, would be antithetical to its most profound being in so far as it has sought its ultimate foundation in the European enlightened rational model.[23] According to Morandé, Latin America's leading intellectual elite was unable to recognize its deepest cultural roots, and because of that led their countries into modernizing experiments which, by ignoring Latin America's true identity, could only fail. I shall show further below that for Morandé and Methol Ferré the identity denied by an atheistic modernity has a privileged reservoir in popular religiosity.

These critical theories emphasize the cultural differences with Europe to the point that any possible common basis is lost. Enlightened modernity would be an eminently European phenomenon which can only be understood from the European experience and self-consciousness. Which means that it is supposed to be totally alien to Latin America and can only exist in the region as a mask, as pseudo-modernity, in conflict with its true identity. As Touraine puts it, the bottom line is a spurious option between modernity and identity:

> To pretend that a nation or a social category has to choose between a universalist, destructive modernity and the conservation of an absolute cultural difference is too gross a lie not to conceal interests and domination strategies. All of us are embarked on modernity . . .[24]

Even if one does not agree with Touraine that there are power interests behind such theories, they are certainly crude and improbable. For these critics of modernity Latin America's own being would not be made of calculus and money, but religion, fiesta and ritual waste. As Brunner puts it, these positions are infiltrated with a subtle sense of superiority, analogous to that which the aristocrat holds *vis-à-vis* the merchant. This is why he maintains that these theories constitute 'the last aristocratic gesture of a semi-developed continent' which is finally faced with the need to recognize itself in modernity.'[25]

It may well be that Latin American modernity is not the same as the European one, but neither is it totally disconnected from it. Latin American modernity is a hybrid that is neither purely endogenous nor totally imposed from without. García Canclini has expressed this reality by saying, 'we do not arrive at *one* modernity, but at several unequal and combined processes of modernization.'[26] Cristián Parker has compiled a useful synthesis which shows the double face of modernizing processes.[27] Statistics are clear: life expectancy at birth, per capita consumption and the net rate of completion of primary education substantially progressed between 1965 and 1985; child mortality dramatically dropped from 12.51 per cent in 1950–5 to 5.51

per cent in 1985–90; the illiteracy rate came down from 44.9 per cent in 1945 to 17.2 per cent in 1990; industrialization and urbanization processes accelerated.

On the other side, however, industrial growth did not increase industrial employment and the tertiary sector of the economy became predominant, especially with the growth of the so-called informal sector. Latin American economies continued to be unable to absorb the growth of the economically active population, and, consequently, poverty continued to be a very serious problem. Estimates by the UN Development Programme for the end of the decade of the 1980s tell of 270 million poor people in Latin America, more than 60 per cent of the population. This shows the heterogeneous and specific character of modernization in Latin America. The problems pointed to by Paz, Fuentes, Morse and Morandé are not necessarily an expression of the failure of modernity in Latin America, but an expression of Latin America's specific manner of being in modernity. And yet, all the same, they do express a sense of unresolved crisis which is quite objective.

Identity crisis

The doubts about modernity, exacerbated by economic problems, were also lived as an identity crisis. Many authors underline either the incomplete nature or the abandonment of Latin American identity. The former reject the idea of an already constituted identity and emphasize its precarious and problematic nature; Latin America is still searching for a cultural unity which has so far eluded it. The main idea of this current is the belief that there is a Latin American identity that could be constructed. The latter, on the contrary, believe in a different, supposedly original kind of cultural identity, of which Latin Americans are not always fully conscious. The idea of originality is usually, but not always, accompanied by a forceful and bitter critique of Western instrumental rationality. Whereas this approach believes that there is a Latin American essence which can be recovered, the former seems to have nostalgia for a true and adequate identity. To this extent both seem to take a position which I have defined as essentialist in chapter 1.

It is not surprising, therefore, that these currents of thought should be clearly influenced by the debates that occurred between the two world wars in which Indigenismo was set against Hispanism. Nevertheless, latter-day thinking is not exactly the same. Whereas the original Indigenismo had a strong anthropological influence and Hispanism a strong historical slant, the more recent essentialism has a sociological character. Maybe because of this it has a preference for the construction of models. In this way it has arrived at the idea that there is an opposition between two different cultural patterns: the European rational enlightened and the Latin American symbolic dramatic.[28] The former strongly believes in instrumental reason, that is to say, in reason as a means to master nature and bring about progress. The latter is suspicious of instrumental reason and has a religious-aesthetic approach to reality.

The rational enlightened pattern emphasizes abstract and conceptual discourse and appeals to reason; the symbolic dramatic pattern emphasizes images, dramatic representations and rites, and appeals to sensations. Parker thinks that the nucleus of this model is popular religion, which is characterized by its vitalism in the face of the intellectualism of the enlightened pattern, by its expressionism in the face of the ruling cultures' formalism and by its sense of the transcendental in the face of Cartesian-positivist scientism.[29] In this way these positions emphasize the difference and specificity of the Latin American cultural experience and stress what separates that experience from other cultural models, especially the enlightened one.

Among the theories that conceive of an original identity – one that has been abandoned and has to be recovered – three kinds stand out. The first is neo-Indigenismo, the thought of some left-wing intellectuals who, in the middle of the theoretical turmoil resulting from the crisis of Marxism, resort to a revaluation of Indian traditions as a new source of critical thought and a reservoir of cultural identity. Then there is the rekindling of the idea of cultural *mestizaje* as a source of originality which has not always been fully recognized by the Latin Americans. Finally, there is the religious thought of more traditional intellectuals who highlight the decisive Catholic influence over the mestizo culture formed during the colonial period and its supposed long-lasting effects thereafter. Hence, the identity crisis is expressed by the emergence of four different approaches: the search for a true identity, neo-Indigenismo, cultural *mestizaje* and Catholic fundamentalism.

The search for a 'true' identity

This approach denies the existence of an already constituted identity and describes the Latin American situation as a permanent search for an identity that cannot easily be found. This position can be traced back to Octavio Paz's classic *The Labyrinth of Solitude*, where, as we saw in the preceding chapter, the Mexicans and also by extension all Latin Americans are in a passionate search of their origins.[30] During this period of crisis, other authors like Bifani, Langon and Gissi can be mentioned as trying to elaborate a similar line of thought, although their language is more sociological and formal.

For Bifani the problem is that the colonization of America destroyed the Indian social systems and created a new hybrid structure which is not well integrated. The Latin American identity has to be reconstituted by recuperating the lost cultural integration. This could be achieved by 'a symbiotic organization of what is one's own and what is someone else's in the context of a self-focused and self-determined social system'.[31] Langon, in his turn, argues that the very question about identity presupposes a destructuration, an inability of Latin Americans to define themselves: 'we are not Indians, nor Spanish, nor anything. We are in dissolution, bordering on extinction, without a place for a project of our own.'[32] Latin America was destructured by colonial powers in order to be integrated in a subordinate position into a global structure of domination. However, there is a Latin American 'deep identity' which could be recuperated and manifests itself in many forms of survival and resistance. But such identity does not refer to a fixed, essential content; it has to be conceived rather as a process. What has to be found is more a mode of identification, which shows the presence of an energetic centre of one's own.[33]

Jorge Gissi, in his turn, starts from the idea that Latin America does not even have a true name since all its names are colonial or neocolonial. In effect, the word 'Indian' given to the new world's inhabitants already entailed a mistake: Columbus believed that he had arrived in India. The very word 'discovery' is equivocal because its inhabitants had discovered America many centuries before the arrival of Columbus. Even today, the word America is used to name the United States. The term 'Latin' is also of neocolonial origin: the first author to refer to South America as Latin America was French, and then it was adopted in the United States. From this Gissi derives that Latin America has no identity, or rather that it has a precarious identity. This is both the consequence and the main cause of Latin America's past and present economic and cultural domination. From all this Gissi concludes that Latin America has to construct its identity.

Gissi argues that the Spanish identity and culture impose themselves over the autochthonous ones by destructuring them and causing a pyschosocial disarticulation among the Indians that still persists. The Indian self-image and self-esteem deteriorated as a consequence of the process of deculturation. The predominant Indian reaction was apathy or resignation once defensive aggressiveness became unviable. But even so they created a culture of resistance and distrust. As a consequence of all this, Latin America has not seen itself with its own eyes, it has not been able to assume itself. Latin America for Gissi has been a people almost without historical memory. Latin America does not want to see itself as it is: as a mestizo and mulatto continent. It is ashamed of being so. Its ruling classes, in order to raise their self-image, internalize in a non-critical way European and North American fashions and live alienated, negating what they are.

Despite all this, Latin America gained consciousness of itself in the second half of the twentieth century. The best in cultural creation, Gissi avers, has been the Indian, black or mulatto music, painting and poetry. Latin America has gained a place in the world in so far as it has presented itself as Latin America. Gissi argues that paradoxically the fundamental cultural alternative for Latin America entails an opening up to its true culture and a questioning of the anti-democratic hegemonic international culture which is reproduced in the countries of the area. To construct its identity is thus to come back to what is its own, to what Latin America always was, but did not want to recognize.[34]

The tradition that encompasses all these authors is quite different from the other three essentialist approaches that I shall explore, in that identity seems to be conceived as a project to be constructed, as a task which will define the Latin American future. Still, the language used continues to betray a certain form of essentialism or perhaps a longing for the true 'deep' integrated identity that has to be recognized. True, identity is no longer conceived as an essence waiting to be discovered, since it has to be constructed; but these authors have faith that this task can be accomplished or must be accomplished if Latin America is to survive. They start from the fact that Latin American identity is precarious, destructured, decentred, not well integrated, and that all this is the result of colonization and cultural transplants and foreign impositions. But there is no acceptance of these realities. There is a longing for integration, for a fully structured identity. One can doubt whether this nostalgia for the 'true' identity will ever give way to the satisfaction of having found it.

Neo-Indigenismo

The emergence of neo-Indigenismo in the 1980s was related to the economic and political crises of the time, but different versions of it were developed depending on whether anthropological, ecological, anti-liberal or anti-mestizo visions were privileged. In some cases it was also related to the cultural problems of so many intellectuals who were in great disarray after the crisis of socialism and Marxism and desperately looked for new and fresher arguments to oppose to the successful wave of neoliberal ideas which swept Latin American countries. Not feeling able to use the traditional Marxist arguments, some authors resorted to exploring Latin American origins and the forgotten cultural patterns present in the Indian communities as a new possible basis for a critique of neoliberalism, sometimes with an ecological dimension.

The influence of Indigenismo seems in this way to have acquired a new lease of life. Thus, for instance, Galeano, a most percep-tive Uruguayan author, writes that America must discover itself by redeeming its most ancient traditions: 'It is out of hope, not nostal-gia that we must recover a community-based mode of production and way of life, founded not on greed, but on solidarity, age-old freedoms and identity between human beings and nature.'[35] Galeano argues that many traditions which enhance freedom and respect the ecology can be found in the Indian communities and that to that extent America can find its energies to construct the future in its most ancient sources:

A system lethal to the world and its inhabitants, that putrefies the water, annihilates the land and poisons the air and the soil, is in violent contradiction with cultures that hold the earth to be sacred because we, its children, are sacred. Those cultures, scorned and denied, treat the earth as their mother and not as a raw material and source of income. Against the capitalist law of profit, they propose the life of sharing, reciprocity, mutual aid, that earlier inspired Thomas More's Utopia and today helps us discover the American face of socialism, whose deepest roots lie in the tradition of community.[36]

The view of Luis Guillermo Lumbreras is that 'the victorious Spaniards introduced an alien technology' which belonged to and had been successful in a different (European) ecosystem and that 'much of our continent's economic weakness and dependency can be traced to that fateful decision'.[37] The point is that Latin America's 'tropical and mountainous lands were not necessarily suited for the procedures of the prairies and cold forests'. So the whole process of development in Latin America has been misdirected from the beginning and the only solution is to recover 'the knowledge of our ancestors' and 'to make use of that knowledge'.[38]

Quijano, in his turn, finds in Latin America a historical reason which differs from European instrumental reason: it is a reason which focuses on 'ends rather than means and on liberation rather than on power'.[39] In the earlier history of Latin America there existed a different concept of the private and the public. Indian communities represented 'a unique environment, one characterized by reciprocity, solidarity, democracy and their corresponding freedoms', and they are private. Although Quijano explicitly says that he is not advocating a return to 'an agrarian communal life', he still maintains that 'the socially oriented private sector and its non-state public sphere' as found in the early Andean communities could serve as a basis for a non-instrumental reason and 'show us the way out of the blind alley into which the ideologues of capital and power have led us'.[40]

Quijano dreams of a utopia constructed on the basis of an alternative reason. This reason comes from the past and was cultivated by the Indian communities, but it has its reality in the present: 'among us, the past is or can be an experience of the present, not its nostalgia. It is not a lost innocence but . . . what the past defends in ourselves, against instrumental rationalism, as the basis for an alternative proposal of rationality.'[41] This different rationality, based on solidarity, collective effort and reciprocity, remains alive in the mass of the urban poor, in their popular kitchens, in their cooperatives and in their forms of organization for survival.

A somewhat aggressive form of neo-Indigenismo can be found in the work of Helio Gallardo, who castigates 'ladinos'[42] for their treatment of Indians. For this author the very notion of 'ladino' entails an attitude rather than anything substantial, and this attitude is one of contempt for, and rejection of Indian values. The 'ladino' attitude is the attitude of the dominator, destroyer or victimizer before his or her victim. Gallardo argues that 'the ladino attitude appears to be sustained by a false spirituality, a spirituality of death. The ladino is therefore an actor of destruction and death. Ultimately, of self-destruction.'[43] No one can behave like a ladino or become a ladino without accepting an identity which cannot be outside the system of domination. Because the ladino is an attitude, it is not confined to the rich or the poor, to adults or children; anyone could have it. For the ladino the Indian is a non-person. The ladino searches for his or her own identity by breaking with and rejecting his or her own social roots.

Gallardo finds the 'ladino attitude' not only in authors such as Sarmiento, who quite openly propounded racist ideas and wanted to improve the Latin race by means of white European immigration, but also in authors such as Vasconcelos, Rodó and Paz whose 'racism' is far more difficult to detect, if at all possible. Vasconcelos, as we saw, put forward the idea of a new integral race in which all the world races would fuse. Yet Gallardo believes that this new Latin race was conceived by Vasconcelos as a variety of the white race which is different from the Anglo-Saxon race, but that it does not really acknowledge the Indian and black cultures of its past. So Vasconcelos' discourse would have come under the 'ladino attitude'.[44]

Equally in the case of Rodó, who criticized the tendency to imitate North America as a case of 'nordomanía', Gallardo argues that this opposition was still between two white races and two white cultures, the Latin and the North American, but that the very existence of blacks and Indians was ignored by *Ariel*.[45] According to Gallardo, Octavio Paz too falls under the heading of the 'ladino attitude' with the abstract humanism of his *Labyrinth of Solitude*, 'a classic of "ladino" psychology'.[46] He sees Paz as fusing the problems of Mexican identity with the problems of universal 'man' and the latter with Western civilization. Thus Paz's is a uniform world which merges diversity and eliminates social roots, a world in which the specificity of Indians, noble Europeans, black old people and ladinos is lost.

A different variant with an anthropological slant seeks to show the enormous capacity for survival of Indian cultures in spite of colonization and other Western influences. Thus, for instance, Daniel Eduardo Matul wants to demonstrate that the Mayan ethnic identity remains unscathed after five hundred years of historical process and that there is no syncretism or significant incorporation of Western cultural elements.[47] Bonfil Batalla, in his turn, argues that the basic form of cultural identity in Mexico is an ethnic identity in the specific sense of Meso-American identity. Although he denies that the Meso-American identity is an 'Indian identity', he maintains that in the pre-Columbian period a basic identity of all Meso-American cultures was constituted. Once constituted, this identity remained unaffected by acculturation, by the influence of other cultures and, in general, by historical changes.

Bonfil Batalla recognizes the diversity of the original cultures that correspond to the various Meso-American ethnic groups and is aware of the fact that colonizers consciously sought to fragment the various original ethnic groups through a process of regionalization and division into small villages and localities. Nevertheless, in spite of this process of fragmentation, regionalization and localization, in spite of the Spanish effort to diffuse their own culture among the indigenous peoples, in spite of the efforts of the Western sectors to 'civilize' the Mexicans during the two centuries of republican history, the Meso-American civilization has succeeded in preserving its essential component parts. This is not only the common basis of the various ethnic cultures with a peasant character, but further, it comprises the majority of the present Mexican population. This civilization includes a conjunction of religious beliefs, cultural values and practical bodies of knowledge, especially traditional agricultural techniques adapted to the Mexican environment.[48]

In a similar way, Emilio Mosonyi tries to recover the Indian values and put them at the centre of the Venezuelan cultural identity. Although in some essays Mosonyi recognizes historical cultural changes and the fact that the Venezuelan identity is in the process of being formed, ultimately his thesis is that the Venezuelan identity exists in an irreversible and evident manner, despite a strong tendency to voluntarily forget it, repress it or inhibit it: the proto-identity of the Venezuelan – like that of almost all the peoples of the continent – is contributed by the American Indian. The Indian constitutes for Mosonyi the oldest, most constant and most specific human factor of Latin American history. The historical basis and the fundamental point of reference for the identity of the Latin American peoples is the Indian population, because it is older, has had an uninterrupted presence and because it has served as a receiving matrix for all the other populations as they arrived. This does not detract from the merits and contributions of subsequent epochs, nor does it mean that the present Indians are the same as those found by Columbus. What Mosonyi asserts is that despite the fact that the Indians have suffered profound transformations, there has not been a total loss of continuity and they continue to constitute the principal basis of identity.[49]

In all these contemporary Latin American writers one still finds the idea that Latin America's future depends on its being true to some age-old Indian traditions or principles which were forgotten or ignored by instrumental reason, alienated enlightened elites and neoliberal modernizing attempts. These traditions constitute a truly distinctive type of rationality, which still finds some expression in the Latin American people and which ought to be the basis for the construction of the future. The basis of Latin American identity is therefore already constructed and it has been there, in the Indian communities, from pre-Columbian times. But it is not recognized by modernizing elites in Latin America and is waiting to be recovered.

Cultural *mestizaje*

Just as the crisis of the 1920s gave rise to *mestizaje* theories which competed with Indigenismo, so the crisis of the 1970s rekindled the idea of *mestizaje* and new theories came to the fore, which opposed both Indigenismo and Hispanism. Two fundamental tendencies can be placed within it: one which emphasizes cultural *mestizaje* in general, and another one which underlines the religious factors of mestizo culture and which, because of this, I shall treat as a separate current.

The most distinguished representative of the cultural *mestizaje* thesis as a source of Latin American identity in the 1970s and 1980s is Arturo Uslar Pietri (Venezuela). In a 1974 essay on 'El mestizaje creador'[50] he distinguishes between a *mestizaje* in the biological sense of a mix of blood, and a cultural *mestizaje*. The former was discredited in Latin America due to European racism. The latter has given *mestizaje* a more positive slant in the twentieth century and a creative capacity. For Uslar Pietri 'the mestizo, the impure, the capacity to absorb and encompass the contraries, [is] one of the characteristics which mark the Hispano-American the most.'[51] From the time of the conquest a process of *mestizaje*, not only biological but also cultural, spontaneously occurred which expressed itself in the transformation suffered by the conquerors and colonizers who became 'Indianos'. Because the American environment was so different from the European one and had very specific characteristics, all cultural European features could not but transform themselves. But the Indian world vision suffered similar transformations.

With respect to Latin American mestizo identity Uslar Pietri highlights three aspects. First, the idea that Latin American identity is mestizo even if the Latin Americans are not aware of it and even if they believe in a different kind of identity. Latin Americans have not so far become aware of their own rich cultural reality and therefore the first fundamental task they have to accomplish is 'to recognize and assume our past in its totality, without exclusions, in order to be able to be reconciled with ourselves and assume the plenitude of our multiple inheritances'.[52] Uslar Pietri provides an example of an important literary contribution of *mestizaje* which is nevertheless not recognized by the author:

> The case of Rubén Darío, like that of all great figures of the so-called literary modernism that he headed, constitutes one of the best examples of cultural *mestizaje* and of the fate of the New World. He could deceive himself and believe that he was a loyal follower of the French poetry of the Parnassians and Symbolists. But he was not. He was a marvellous creator of poetry, with the elements of cultural *mestizaje*, of which he was the product and expression.[53]

Uslar Pietri tries to show that Latin American art is indebted to *mestizaje* in other ways. On the one hand, he argues that the Baroque, as an expression of Latin American art which favours intricate ornamentalism and a convoluted style, is a mixture of European Baroque and some specific features of Latin American reality and sensitivity. It is not just an expression of Latin American art but a most adequate form to express the process of cultural *mestizaje*. On the other hand, Latin American literature shows the coexistence of heterogeneous tendencies from different periods; it is a kind of 'alluvial' literature in which elements from an infinite variety of origins are integrated in a mix in continuous flow, within which nothing ends and nothing is separated.

Second, Uslar Pietri proposes the idea that such mestizo Latin American identity exists because it is the result of a historical evolution. For him, Latin America has the important task of 'assimilating the past and accepting its identity in order to know who we are and make good who we are'.[54] We are who we are because the historical process has made us thus. In this sense the Latin American cultural identity is a destiny which must be radically assumed, independently of our preferences and projects. Third, Uslar Pietri maintains that the mestizo cultural identity has a conflictive or dramatic character. By means of an analysis of the life and work of a famous mestizo, the Inca Garcilaso de la Vega, he tries to show how difficult it is to live the experience of cultural *mestizaje*, because its component parts are not only different, but also contradictory.

Otto Morales (Colombia) and Gustavo Vega (Ecuador) put forward similar ideas in favour of a mestizo identity. The former argues that the European cultural elements were spontaneously transformed in Latin America, sometimes because they could not be reproduced as in Europe, for instance the house-building techniques, other times because the natives gave them their own character, as happened with native artists and baroque forms.[55] The latter underlines the mestizo character of the popular culture's numerous expressions, especially in Ecuador, and proposes to stimulate the development of a 'mestizo utopia'. Vega analyses mestizo expressions in medicine, art and daily life and shows that the Latin American *mestizaje* is more varied than is usually supposed; and not only because of the important European migration to Latin American countries on the Atlantic coast during the twentieth century, but also because of the presence of migrants from other countries.[56]

Identity and popular religiosity

A new Catholic sociological discourse emerged and thrived during the 1970s and 1980s, precisely at the moment when church attendance was rapidly declining, Pentecostal churches were experiencing a major expansion and the traditional role of the Catholic Church was being questioned by liberation theology. This discourse sought to demonstrate that Latin American cultural identity had an inherently Catholic substratum, so that the need to renovate a declining religious identity was replaced by the certainty that the very essence of Latin Americanness was Catholic. The official documents of the Latin American Catholic Church of the time show the impact of this kind of discourse. Thus, for instance, the Puebla document stated:

> In the first stage, from the sixteenth century to the eighteenth century, the basis of Latin American culture and of its real Catholic substratum is constructed. Its evangelization was profound enough for the faith to become constitutive of its being and of its identity, thus providing a spiritual unity which subsists despite the later division into diverse nations . . . with all its deficiencies and in spite of ever-present sin, the faith of the Church has put a seal on the soul of Latin America, thus marking its essential historical identity and constituting itself as the continent's cultural matrix . . .[57]

Unlike Indigenismo and neo-Indigenismo this tendency focuses on the process of cultural *mestizaje*, but finds in the adoption of the Catholic religion its most important characteristic. It appeared with special force in Uruguay, Argentina and Chile at a time when these countries were under military rule. Its three most eminent representatives are the Uruguayan Alberto Methol Ferré, the Argentinian Juan Carlos Scannone and the Chilean Pedro Morandé. Scannone is a Jesuit priest; Morandé and Methol Ferré are, to use a Gramscian expression, organic intellectuals of the Catholic Church, and the official Church at that. Maybe for this reason they tend to be ignored in Anglo-Saxon accounts of Latin American culture. But they represent a movement which was, and still is, fairly influential in many countries whose peoples are still deeply Catholic in spite of the progress of secularization.[58] Part of the original appeal of this trend for many young people – not necessarily always practising Catholics – was due to the fact that it was able to channel a critique against the free-market and modernizing policies of the military rulers at a time when other forms of political critique were not tolerated.

For Methol Ferré the Catholic cultural substratum is expressed in the Baroque, the 'last great Catholic wave in Europe', which is linked to the Council of Trent and which constitutes the 'total seal' of Latin America. However, after independence and with the arrival of the Enlightenment, he sees a division as having been created between the baroque people and the enlightened elites. Since Vatican Council II, however, it has become clearer that modernity was not confined to the Enlightenment: this was only a variant, and the other variant was the Baroque, which today expresses itself in popular religiosity.[59] This marks the birth of the post-Council Catholic renewal of the 1970s and 1980s.

Scannone, in his turn, does not use the image of the Catholic substratum, but puts forward the idea that in Latin American culture there exists a special kind of rationality, different from modern instrumental rationality; he calls it 'sapiential' rationality and it coincides with evangelical teachings. This rationality is not anti-modern:

> but, because it is more radically and originally human, because it is the rationality most akin to the lifeworld, because it is essentially respectful both of differences and of the plural unity, it can take on the challenge of modernity, thus sapientially relocating the other forms of rationality without compromising their autonomy, their critical character and their differentiation, which are inherent parts of the modern inheritance.[60]

This sapiential rationality is characterized by a logic of gratuity and donation, by its promotion of a community that is more human and gives more respect to plurality and alterity. In the face of modern advances, but especially of certain alienating features of Latin America's modernizing processes, the people will tend to resort to their own sapiential culture. This culture reveals itself in impulses towards a basic communal solidarity at the economic level (cooperatives, popular kitchens, labour exchange associations) as much as towards multisector movements of civil society in defence of human rights, green spaces, justice, etc.[61] It is here that Scannone sees a coincidence between the Latin American cultural inheritance and evangelical teachings. In contrast to Methol Ferré and Morandé, Scannone emphasizes the fact that sapiential rationality is neither an exclusive feature of Latin America nor antagonistic to the autonomy of reason. Yet in presenting it as Latin America's own logic, a logic that differs from that of enlightened rationality, Scannone runs the risk of essentializing their difference.

In its boldest theoretical formulation – that of Pedro Morandé – this approach propounds the idea that what is typical of Latin American cultural identity was formed from the meeting of Indian cultural values and the Catholic religion brought by the Spanish. This meeting of cultures occurred orally because the Indians did not have writing and therefore the emerging cultural pattern was not a form of written culture but rather an ethos, a founding experience of togetherness, a shared understanding, a common feeling born from encounters among human beings. What crystallizes out of a cultural coming together which is spoken not written is not a form of coherent argument or ideology but a shared experience which lives off its constant memory.[62] The true subject of this encounter is the mestizo, a mixture of Spanish and Indian.

Contrary to many authors who emphasize the relationships of difference and opposition between Indians and Spaniards and who depict the latter as dominating and subordinating the former, Morandé argues that in order to understand the new cultural synthesis one has to highlight the relationships of participation and belongingness rather than those of domination.[63] According to him, Hegel's dialectic of master and slave is inadequate when applied to Spaniards and Indians. Not that Morandé denies the existence of domination, but he affirms that such domination is not crucial to Latin American identity. Other common experiences were much more important than the fact of domination. In fact, the confrontation was not between the Spanish on one side and the Indians on the other. As we have already seen, the Indians were very diverse culturally and many of them, oppressed by the ruling Indian people, entered into a series of alliances with, and fought alongside, the Spaniards. This is the reason why, for instance, it was the Indian chiefs themselves who offered the Spanish their daughters in order to establish alliances.[64] Hence, rather than construing the *mestizo* as a result of the forceful violation of Indian women by the Spanish, as Octavio Paz has suggested, the mestizo must be understood as the result of alliances cemented by intermarriage as practised by all primitive societies based on kinship.

Several other continuities, coincidences and common experiences were to be found between the two cultures.[65] Thus, for instance, the Catholic emphasis on rites and liturgy was matched by the Indian cultures having a cultic and ritual conception of life. Both the Catholic and the Indian cultic practices were based on ritual sacrifice carried out or represented in temples. The interest in dance, liturgy, theatre and rituals, the essential accompaniments of fiestas and religious festivities around which the year is organized, is also a characteristic in common. In both Spain and the Indian empires, work was organized by the liturgical calendar in accordance with the seasons. Time was given a religious organization through the liturgical calendar, and the agricultural cycle was in tune with the religious cycle.

Both cultures emphasized the tributary character of work. Just as the Indian empires were organized on the basis of tribute exaction from the dominated Indian nations, the Spanish crown wanted only gold and tributes from America. The encomienda was the servile system of labour through which the Spanish crown could secure the collection of tributes. The encomendero acted as a tribute collector for the crown and extracted tribute in advance from the Indians in order to send part of it to the king. This is the reason why, Morandé argues, a concept of work was developed in Latin America whereby payment of the tribute is more important than personal profit or personal duty.

In sum, Morandé argues that representation, liturgy and theatre best expressed the encounter between the Indian oral cultures and the Spanish written culture. This means that the place of the encounter, the cradle of Latin American culture, is sacred. Hence his conclusion that 'Latin American culture has a real Catholic substratum. This substratum is constituted between the sixteenth and the eighteenth centuries.'[66] The Latin American cultural ethos has, therefore, four important features:

1   It was formed before the Enlightenment and therefore instrumental rationality does not form a part of it.
2   It has a necessarily Catholic underlying structure.
3   It privileges the heart (sentiments) and its intuition, thus preferring sapiential to scientific knowledge.
4   It is best expressed in popular religiosity.[67]

One of the intriguing and interesting aspects of Morandé's approach, which is along the same lines as Indigenismo and Hispanism, is that, after patiently tracking down and putting together the main elements of the Latin American cultural synthesis, he comes to the conclusion that such a synthesis 'was not valued by the process of formation of the national states as its own patrimony'.[68] The elite which conducted the Latin American process of independence from Spain, very much influenced by a culture based on the written text brought from Europe, tended to liken the oral tradition, in which the new cultural synthesis was produced, to barbarism and Spanish domination. In this way the ruling Latin American classes never assumed their true identity and rejected their mestizo origins. They found refuge in the European rational enlightened pattern, well represented in the university system. But in doing so they became alienated from their own roots and launched their countries on modernizing programmes which could not succeed.

The idea that the betrayal by the Latin American elites of their true identity was the main cause of the failure of many economic and social projects in Latin America is not confined to this position and is shared by many Hispanist, indigenista and anti-North American authors.[69] This idea even influences authors whose vision of identity is far from being essentialist or religious, for example Leopoldo Zea: 'the origin of our ills is in the fact of wanting to ignore our circumstances, our American being. We have endeavoured, mistakenly, to become Europeans one hundred per cent. Our failure has made us feel inferior, neglecting what is ours, for we consider it the cause of our failure.'[70] To a great extent, though, the religious version tends to be more radical because it identifies European modernity with secularization and contempt for religion. Zea carefully maintains that we should not go to the other extreme, so 'that we feel alien to the European culture, wanting to erase all relationship with it. Whether we want it or not, we are children of that culture; this is something we cannot deny or avoid.'[71]

For the religious version, on the contrary, the attempts to repeat Weber's rationalization process were bound to fail, whether they took the form of modernization, the form of bureaucratic socialism or the form of the self-regulating market. Contrary to the Protestant ethic and the need to save and invest as a proof of salvation, the symbolic dramatic pattern put an emphasis on work as sacrifice and on religious festivities as ritual squandering. Basically, Latin Americans are not supposed to be motivated by technical progress, and the subordination of their ethos to instrumental rationality was a form of alienation, a mistake punished by chronic failure.

The thesis is, then, that since its independence Latin America has suffered from a cultural break: its true cultural identity has not been recognized by its own elites, and the rational enlightened cultural pattern adopted by the Latin American elites has not only been entirely different from but also inherently opposed to the true identity. If the adopted cultural pattern is alienation, where then can the true cultural synthesis be found? Morandé believes the answer lies in popular religiosity. While enlightened European reason praises the modernizing and rationalistic efforts of the elites and decries the backward religious beliefs of the alienated masses, Morandé praises the authenticity of the popular religious traditions and decries the failed modernizing attempts of a culturally alienated elite. According to Morandé, popular religiosity

> is one of the few expressions – although not the only one – of the Latin American cultural synthesis which stretches across all its epochs and covers simultaneously all its dimensions: work and production, human settlements and lifestyles, language and artistic expression, political organization, everyday life. And precisely in its role as the reservoir of

cultural identity it has had to undergo, perhaps more than any other institution, the attempts by modernity to subordinate particular cultures to the dictates of instrumental reason.[72]

According to Morandé this does not necessarily mean that the Latin American cultural identity is fundamentally anti-modern. What he argues is that it was constituted before enlightened modernity arrived, or rather that the Latin American cultural identity belongs to a different kind of modernity, baroque modernity. So what threatens this identity is not modernity itself but the modernity that entails a process of secularization, the modernity stemming from the Enlightenment. It follows that, given the Catholic substratum of this identity, secularization is not just a threat to the Church but, more fundamentally, a threat to Latin American culture itself. This irreligious threat succeeded in converting the Latin American elites, the criollos, to instrumental reason, but it did not succeed against the popular religiosity of the mestizos, which has resisted all attacks to remain to this day the most spontaneous and genuine expression of the cultural ethos.

In bringing his book to a close, Morandé argues that 'cultural syntheses cannot be chosen at will. If they are real, they impose themselves over the conjunction of individuals without asking if they are pleased. They may certainly be changed, but they cannot be denied. And if one wishes to change them, one has to start by recognizing their existence . . .'[73] This is perhaps the only place where Morandé recognizes, at least in principle, that the original synthesis can be changed. But the whole of the book's analysis denies that it has changed and confirms its continuous presence throughout history.

A variant of this conception can be found in Cristián Parker, for whom popular religion is the nucleus of the cultural *pathos* of the Latin American people and constitutes an alternative logic to the Western rationalist canon.[74] Parker finds in Latin America a popular culture with religious content, which constitutes a veritable counterculture to modernity. This counterculture is hemidern (semi-modern) because it has an ambivalent attitude with respect to modernity: it is anti-modern 'in all the alienating and dehumanized aspects of modernity and its instrumental rationality', but it is pro-modern 'inasmuch as it accepts all that modernity has brought about as an effective step forward in the conditions of life and in the satisfaction of man's authentic needs'.[75]

This ambivalent attitude with respect to modernity, however, does not prevent Parker from understanding this counterculture as 'another way of feeling, thinking and acting which is alternative to enlightened rationality', as 'a new emergent paradigm' 'which is at the other extreme from the paradigms of Western philosophy and science', as 'another logic'.[76] The structure of thought behind this new paradigm is not modern but neither is it mythical-traditional; it is, in Parker's opinion, 'syncretic'. Syncretic thought has for Parker a special meaning which goes beyond the traditional conception of religious syncretism. It is a symbolic process of the *bricolage* kind which constructs and reconstructs collective representations 'by using remains, rubbish and new contributions, apparently disparate, in such a way that from the composition of old and new works a new synthesis is produced'.[77] This type of thought has a neuro-physiological base in the brain's right hemisphere and in this way can be distinguished from the analytical and rationalist thought anchored in the left hemisphere.[78]

With these concepts, Parker wants to rethink Latin American identity, taking Christianity as a point of departure. Although he accuses Morandé of essentialism, that is to say, of postulating that the basis of Latin American culture is constituted by a 'Catholic substratum', he maintains that 'in the significant nucleus of Latin American popular culture . . . the dynamism of the Christian faith can be discerned, not in an exclusive, but in a decisive way.'[79] And it is this nucleus that he wants to project into the future. Instrumental rationality is seen as suffering from 'definitive fatigue' and 'the universe of values and categories which sustained an epoch of Promethean dreams' has crumbled, to give way to popular Christianity, to an alternative vitalist anthropology whose project is the 'integral man' based on a praxis of 'love-solidarity'. Christianity thus becomes the basis for the construction of the new Latin American civilization of the twenty-first century.[80]

Towards a critique of essentialism

Of the four essentialist currents I have explored, that of the neo-indigenistas, left-wing intellectuals in search of new weapons with which to attack the neoliberal version of contemporary capitalism in the periphery, is the least systematic.[81] The main criticism to be addressed to them is of their naiveté and anachronism, perhaps their temporary confusion in the middle of a crisis, which in some ways was also shared by the old indigenista movement. It is not that I deny that some specific cultural features of Latin American Indian communities could be of great interest, and perhaps also an example. Nor am I unaware of the cruel discrimination suffered by Indian communities right up to the present. But it seems rather difficult to believe that it might be possible to resurrect some form of socialism or a new pattern of development by looking back to the old ways. This is a mirage produced by desperation. The myth of the golden age is often resorted to in times of crisis, when the way ahead is not clear. However, I do not believe that these authors, if pushed, perhaps with the exception of Gallardo, would go down the same path as Morandé, by trying to identify an essential and originating cultural pattern whose observance would be the only way to guarantee a non-alienated and successful process of modernization.

Those who are in search of a true identity at least have a more dynamic conception of identity and do not consider it already established in a remote past. Still, their nostalgia for a 'true' identity betrays a certain essentialism in that they seem to believe that one day a true identity will be constructed or found. The implication is that once it is constructed or found, it will remain the same, given its 'true' character. But, of course, this is the typical mirage of all essentialism. There is no reason why any cultural identity should be fixed forever. The theories of cultural *mestizaje* in a way point to something obvious, that Latin American nations are mestizo peoples and that therefore it stands to reason that the Latin American cultural identity must be also a mixture of all ethnic component parts. Yet most of the time these authors emphasize the idea that in order to accept this cultural *mestizaje* one has to look into the past, as if this mestizo identity was constituted in the past once and for all. There is little sense of openness to the future, of the fact that identities, even mestizo ones, historically change. This is why they keep saying that we must 'accept' our mestizo identity by looking at the past, as if it were an already decided fate. Hence they fall into essentialism too.

Morandé's religious edifice is certainly impressive, passionately constructed with great conviction and persuasiveness. However, I believe its real contribution is limited to the analysis and description of the original Indo-Iberian synthesis. The great problem with his more general approach is that it reduces the problem of Latin American cultural identity to that originating moment. In effect, it is difficult to accept that Latin American cultural identity was fixed once and for all in the sixteenth century, in a symbolic-dramatic matrix standing fundamentally in opposition to the Enlightenment. As if cultural identity were an unchangeable essence with a birth certificate. It is also difficult to accept that academics and intellectuals in Latin America have always been profoundly alienated from their roots just because they were educated in the values of reason which the first Indo-Iberian cultural synthesis did not privilege.

It is true that Morandé's and Methol Ferré's criticisms can be applied to that generation of intellectuals such as Sarmiento, Alberdi, Prado, Ingenieros, and so on, who not only totally rejected the first Indo-Iberian cultural synthesis, but also blamed the Latin American's racial components for backwardness. But not all intellectuals went so far in their desire to adopt European rationality. It is true that differences must not be denied, nor must Latin America be reduced to an echo of the Old World, as Hegel propounded. But this is not a valid reason to think that our poverty and underdevelopment, our cultural specificity and failed dreams, are sufficient justifications to consider instrumental reason as alien to our cultural identity.

In the theories of Morandé and Methol Ferré there is hardly a balanced approach to enlightened modernity. It is not that modernity should be naively praised and exempted from shortcomings, but Morandé and Methol Ferré consider only its negative sides and have nothing positive to say about it. At the very least it is necessary to rescue its development of the scientific spirit, its defence of freedom and tolerance, its idea of democracy. It may be true that these values are not exclusive to modernity and that they have not always been practised within modernity as fully as they should have been. But modernity gave them particular relevance and pride of place. Even if enlightened modernity was altered and recontextualized in its reception in Latin America, it still had some positive elements to its credit, not least the attempt to construct new democratic republics able to overcome three centuries of authoritarianism and religious intolerance.

García de la Huerta has made an interesting analysis of Morandé's opposition between orality and writing. As we saw, writing, or the text, is associated with the modern, with ideology, in fact with what is inauthentic, whereas orality is associated with goodness and innocence, with the authenticity of the social bond in a relationship whose members are present. Textual or written culture is therefore linked to rationalist elites and their inability to recognize their true identity. By following Derrida, García de la Huerta shows how this opposition is a myth, and, paradoxically, 'a myth coined by the Enlightenment, in particular by Rousseau'.[82] It is a transposition of the 'noble savage' myth, later taken up again by Lévi-Strauss in his *Structural Anthropology*, in which the natural/original is associated with the authentic/true, while writing is related to inauthenticity.

Morandé and Methol Ferré introduce a totally unjustified cleavage into Latin America's history. Up to the moment of independence there is the process of the constitution of the Latin American identity, which is finally consolidated and fixed once and for all; from then onwards history stops, or rather becomes a travesty of what history should have been: it becomes the history of a major alienation, the history of the total failure of and betrayal by elites, intellectuals and rulers. If everything is not lost it is only because the torch of the true identity has been safeguarded in the realms of popular religiosity. Here it has resisted extinction and waits to be rescued by Catholic intellectuals who might one day convince the rest of society, and especially the elites, that their true heritage and identity has an ineluctable Catholic substratum which is different from instrumental reason.

Nothing of what the elites have done since independence, nothing of their intellectual production and ideological projects can affect or change the Latin American identity; all the complex history of development since 1810 does not really count for Latin American culture, or, if it does, it is only as alienation. Which means that not just the influence of the Enlightenment but also the formation of national states and the 180 years of their independent history are marginal to Latin American identity. This is not plausible. What is behind this conception is a form of essentialism supported by a narrow conception of cultural identity. According to this conception there is a Latin American essence, a shared experience of unity which solidifies before independence, a true self that provides an underlying continuity and stability to historical processes. This Latin American essence cannot disappear or be altered; it may be temporarily forgotten, but it can always be rediscovered and excavated from its privileged source, popular religiosity.

True, there is in Morandé's approach a critique of the abstract models of modernization theories and the intention to replace them by a conception that values the historicity of Latin American culture. But Morandé seems to limit historicity to the originating moment, to the past, at most to the first two centuries of colonial rule, and does not pay any attention to the contribution of the nineteenth and twentieth centuries. It seems as though the historicity of culture is reduced to the continuous manifestation of the same essence throughout history. In this respect Morandé's theory unwittingly replicates the very same problem the old modernization theories suffered from. They understood societies 'in transition' as deviations from the modern ideal type which they were bound to arrive at one day. The only difference would be that for Morandé those deviations are understood in relation to the model defined by the original synthesis. In this sense Morandé's critique of abstract model making does not prevent him from proposing a new model or paradigm against which all historical events are to be measured.

It is my contention that only the structural-historical conception of cultural identity[83] allows us to arrive at an understanding of the complexity of Latin American identity which does not exclude the best part of the last two centuries of Latin America's history and does not conceal the cultural diversity of the continent. No doubt, the first cultural synthesis produced out of the original encounter between Indians and Spanish is crucially important, but it did not totally eliminate cultural differences between various ethnic groups, nor has it remained the same; it has undergone transformations, not least the impact of enlightened thought since the time of independence. These new contributions and the various forms of cultural diversity which have helped shape what Latin America is today are not forms of alienation or betrayal of its 'true self'. They are simply important new inputs and transformations, or remaining divisions that have to be taken into account if we want to understand anything about the Latin American present complex cultural identity.

It may well be true that Latin America's first cultural synthesis had an important Catholic and religious input. But it is equally true that later on that cultural feature may well have lost importance in relation to others. This is not a problem of alienation, it is a problem of change, and it is the result of the Latin American identity being continuously and discursively constructed and reconstructed. Morandé's thesis is that secularization in Latin America succeeded among criollos but not among mestizos, who continue to be profoundly religious. Now, there is no doubt that strong elements of popular religiosity still exist in Latin America, but they no longer represent, by and of themselves, the nucleus of Latin American identity. They no longer have the centrality they had in colonial times. Secularization and modernization processes have also affected the popular religiosity of mestizos. There has also been a significant spread of Pentecostalism among the popular masses throughout Latin America.

It is in this new context that one has to examine the thesis of the 'Catholic substratum'. No doubt such a substratum or something of this kind existed in colonial times. But it has not remained untouched. Catholicism has ceased to be the central element of Latin American identity; it continues to be an important element among others, but it is no longer the decisive one. This is important in an increasingly plural and culturally diverse continent in which many ethnic groups, religions and different ways of life coexist. No particularity can pretend to represent the identity of the whole. The equation of Catholicism with identity is dangerous in any plural context because it seems to exclude from the properly Latin American everything which is not Catholic. By declaring the failure of modernity, one suspects that Morandé and Methol Ferré are trying to make up for the progressive displacement of Catholicism as the central element of Latin American identity and trying to justify a necessary return to a situation of Christendom as supposedly preordained in the Latin American culture itself.

Parker's variant is an interesting and well-researched work which must be appreciated as a rich source for any analysis or study of popular religion in Latin America. Nevertheless, from the point of view of an analysis of cultural identity it has serious shortcomings. Parker tries desperately to break with Morandé's essentialism, but he does not fully achieve it. Furthermore, his solution still finds the dynamism of the Christian faith in the central nucleus of Latin American popular culture, which makes him fall into a series of inconsistencies and contradictions.

In effect, on the one hand, Parker explicitly and quite rightly denies that culture can have an essence or spirit and, therefore, he does not accept that religion can be 'at the basis' of the constitution of culture; but, on the other hand, he affirms that 'Christianity is the nucleus of the popular cultural *pathos*' and that religion is the 'determinant factor in the formation of cultural patterns'.[84] On the one side, Parker rightly argues that culture is historical, 'the social product of historical collectives', but on the other, he speaks of an 'inheritance' or 'legacy' which we must seek in the past 'in order to detect those inspiring sources which may allow the reconstruction of an identity of one's own'.[85] So while Parker attacks with good arguments the geological metaphor of the 'Catholic substratum', he nevertheless accepts that 'to rethink the cultural identity of our continent starting from Christianity is not superfluous but necessary.'[86] Thus one can appreciate that in spite of his protest against it, an essentialist language infiltrates Parker's position.

True, Parker proposes that Christianity is only one of the factors in popular culture, not the only one. But at the same time he insists that such a factor is located in the 'nucleus' of that culture and that it manifests itself there 'in a decisive form'. He further identifies Christianity as a root of cultural identity. He might counterargue that to rethink the Latin American identity starting from Christianity is not necessarily a form of essentialism, since it is possible to consider any factor that forms a part of a complex cultural whole, not as an already constituted foundational essence, but as a nucleus to be developed, as a project for the future. This is the way in which Parker, in the last chapter of his book, invites us to construct such a Christian project of the integral man, of solidarity and love. I accept that in principle there is nothing wrong with wanting a society of love and solidarity. The problem arises when the reason why one wants to develop such a project goes beyond its intrinsic goodness and desirability and is, rather, ontologically rooted in a special mode of being, feeling and thinking which is supposed to be the property of a people, and one that others would not possess.

The whole of Parker's analysis tries to show the existence of a special mode of being, feeling and thinking, of which religion forms an essential part, and which is the opposite of Cartesian rationalism and the enlightened pattern. He goes to the extreme of proposing that at the basis of the religious mentality of the Latin American people a distinct anthropology throbs, which he calls 'vitalist', and which can be claimed to be 'an alternative to the Promethean anthropology of Western modernity'.[87] Could any stronger essentialism be conceived than to maintain that there exists a special anthropology which throbs at the deepest end of a mode of being and thinking? Were this to be true, the differences between Latin Americans and the rest would not only be of a historical, cultural and social-economic character, but would be determined by deeper roots affecting the very definition of the human being. The starting point, the basic conception of the human being, would be subject to variations which would go so far as to have a neuro-physiological basis. Latin American people would have a special syncretic mode of thinking rooted in the brain's right hemisphere, so different from the rational mode of thinking rooted in the brain's left hemisphere. The European would not be the same as the Latin American. In the former, a Promethean, Pantocratic dualist, a patriarchal anthropology would throb; in the latter, a vitalist, maternal, ecological and holistic anthropology would throb. One wonders whether Parker is aware that down this road of radical distinctions it is possible to fall into the justification of all kinds of racism and discrimination.

Essentialism neatly appears every time that one understands one's own culture as patrimony, inheritance or inherent legacy from a mode of being which is anthropologically defined. To this one can add the reference to the absolute and alien 'other': instrumental reason, logocentric discourse, Cartesian rationalism, Western modernity or any other way of calling it. It all unfolds as if instrumental rationality was totally alien to the Latin American popular mode of feeling and ethos; as if religious vitalism was totally alien to the European ethos. In sum, it is the idea that there is 'another logic'. To speak of another logic cannot but essentialize differences. The same danger surrounds Scannone's thesis of a Latin American sapiential rationality. But at least in Scannone's approach the 'sapiential rationality' is not considered to be the exclusive property of Latin Americans. It is true that here and there Parker struggles against the essentialism that invades him and tries to moderate his view, for instance by arguing that the Latin American mode of feeling is not anti-modern or anti-logical. But this does not prevent it from being absolutely different. That is why he speaks of 'another logic', of a 'new paradigm', of the 'alternative to instrumental reason': all are invitations to make fundamentalist distinctions.

Also paradoxical is the use which Parker makes of Lévi-Srauss's thought to support his idea of syncretic thought as the source of 'another logic'. According to Parker, Lévi-Strauss has shown that science and magic are not opposed, but coexist without contradiction.[88] Yet Lévi-Strauss's point is not so much that science and magic are not opposed, but rather that science and myth use the same logic. For Parker syncretic thought is neither mythical nor rational and consists in a kind of *bricolage*. The curious thing is that Lévi-Strauss maintains that symbolic production of the *bricolage* type is precisely the way in which myth is constructed. Yet, unlike Parker, Lévi-Strauss does not consider this mythical mode as 'far away from rational, formal, planned and systematic production',[89] or as totally different from science's way of working. On the contrary, he highlights their similarities: both science and myth catalogue, classify and search for an 'order' in the materials they examine.[90] Lévi-Strauss's point is precisely the contrary to the point Parker wants to emphasize: myth and science do not operate with a different logic; they use the same logic, applied to different realities and objects. In Lévi-Strauss's words, the difference lies 'not in the quality of the intellectual process, but in the nature of the things to which it is applied'.[91]

It is difficult to find in Parker's book a balanced evaluation of instrumental reason. The fact of Latin American modernization is recognized, but ultimately what comes first for Parker is the 'fact' that instrumental reason is in crisis and suffering from a 'definitive fatigue'. The values of modernity are asserted to be crumbling. The curious thing is that, despite all this, Parker maintains that the new logic constitutes only 'an underground and subaltern paradigm, which develops in the interstices of the underdeveloped modernity'.[92] This clearly indicates that Parker recognizes that the supposedly belittled enlightened logic is still dominant. One wonders how it is possible that a logic supposedly in crisis, fatigued, moribund and so alien to the Latin American people's inner being, could still have such a capacity for domination and such modernizing energy as it seems to have in contemporary Latin America. In Parker's picture this logic would be a mere artifice, without deep roots, without history and without any important role in the construction of the Latin American cultural identity.

Parker does not fall into Morandé's temptation of interpreting the pursuit of scientific reason as an alienation of Latin American elites. But his own explanation tends to reify two ways of feeling, two paradigms, two kinds of logic, as if they were separate and incommensurable worlds: the world of the people and the world of the enlightened intellectual community. I do not wish to minimize class differences, especially as they mark differential access to economic and cultural property. But not even Marx, who assigned great importance to class struggle, understood ruling and dominated classes as possessing totally different and separate cultures or a different 'logic'. An important lesson that can still be learned from his theory is that one must not confuse the contradictory character of the modernization process (treatment of subjects as objects, commodification of life and culture) with its content (production of machinery, consumption objects, art, techniques, natural sciences, etc.). In not considering this distinction, the radical critique equally with the naive apology in relation to modernization processes share a narrow point of view: apologists wish to perpetuate the contradiction on account of its results; critics are prepared to sacrifice such results in order to get rid of the contradiction.[93]

7

The Neoliberal Stage
1990 onwards

General mechanisms and tendencies
of late modernity

I would like to start this chapter by highlighting some characteristic mechanisms and tendencies of modernity, which have become more accentuated in late modernity, thus affecting the processes of identity formation in Latin America and the whole world. Many of these features appeared and matured in Europe earlier than in other places. In the case of Latin America they were consolidated only in the 1990s.

First, it is necessary to mention the increasing separation of time and space[1] in the sense that spatial distantiation no longer requires temporal distantiation. With the advent of modernity, time lost its spatial content and space became independent of particular places or regions. Time and space were constituted as empty and standardized dimensions that allowed the emergence of social relations with absent others, spatially distant from face-to-face interaction. Modernity increasingly disconnects space from place, from the local, by putting faraway places in contact through the expansion of the media and the means of transport. The increasing velocity of communications and means of transport alters our sense of distance and leads to what Harvey has called 'time-space compression'.[2]

Second, it is necessary to mention the 'mediazation of modern culture': 'the general process by which the transmission of symbolic forms becomes increasingly mediated by the technical and institutional apparatuses of the media industries'.[3] By this process, the media are increasingly shaping the way in which cultural forms are produced, transmitted and received in modern societies and the modes in which people experience events and actions which occur in spatially and temporally remote contexts. Mass media and transmission networks rapidly proliferate and reach an increasing number of individuals and in this way symbolic forms are both conditioned and transmitted by them. The technical means of transmission are not neutral in respect of the content, and the control of the content, of what is transmitted. They fix meanings and reproduce them widely, thus facilitating new forms of symbolic power.

Third, there is the reconstitution of the public sphere. A public sphere of debate and discussion emerged with modernity which was concerned with public affairs and important issues of civil society. This sphere, where public opinion was formed, was neither state nor privately controlled; it was a public area located in a space between the state and civil society where individuals could discuss the political affairs of the nation. Its public character was conferred by the privileged role that the media – being accessible to the public in general – played in its constitution. Habermas has explored this public sphere, which he sees as particularly connected with the emergence of the written press, and has regarded it as of great importance because through it the state and politics can be criticized and kept under surveillance by the public use of reason.[4] As Thompson has argued, with the consolidation of television the conditions under which public debate takes place have been radically altered. A new kind of public domain has emerged which, unlike the old cafés where people might discuss the newspapers, has no spatial boundaries (no shared locale) and no dialogical possibilities (no face-to-face interaction), reaching individuals in the privacy of their own homes.[5]

A fourth process typical of modernity is the creation of new social relations.[6] During most of the history of humankind, forms of human interaction occurred face-to-face, happening within the confines of a place physically shared by the participants. With the development of new means of communication, modernity fosters social relations with absent others, located in places far away from the local contexts of interaction. In this way, people can now interact without sharing the same space or time. Whereas face-to-face forms of interaction have a dialogical character in that they assume a flow of information in both directions, modern mediated interactions (especially those mediated by press, radio and television) have a monological character because the flow of information goes from the producer to the receiver, who cannot directly reply.[7] And yet they are still forms of interaction. Thompson has shown that individuals may even establish intense relationships of intimacy with television personalities, singers and idols, whom they have never met personally, by following their lives in minute detail and by adopting their tastes, gestures and clothes. These forms of 'non-reciprocated intimacy'[8] between the fan and the star clearly entail a form of interaction and have, undoubtedly, an impact on the construction of identities.

Fifth, one has to mention the phenomenon of globalization. Modernity is 'inherently globalizing' in that worldwide social relations which link distant localities have intensified 'in such a way that local happenings are shaped by events occurring miles away and vice versa'.[9] The social processes of modernity operate 'on a global scale . . . cut across national boundaries, integrating and connecting communities and organizations in new space-time combinations, making the world in reality and in experience more interconnected'.[10] All over the world, what happens in one corner affects the situation in another faraway corner in practically no time. Globalization entails not only an expanding multiplicity of relationships between places but also an increasing density in the levels of interconnectedness.[11]

Globalization has existed for a long time but in recent times it has intensified and the pace of change in various dimensions associated with it has accelerated. Giddens has analysed the existence of four dimensions that push globalization forward.[12] The first and most crucial one is the world capitalist system, which manifests itself in a growing trend towards the internationalization of the economy. Both the financial and productive spheres are increasingly controlled by multinational companies and are globally oriented and internationally articulated. Important developments particularly noticeable in this area are the extraordinary growth in international trade coupled with a spectacular growth of an increasingly globalized capital market and the deregulation of many national capital markets. There has also been a marked growth in the role of multinational companies and an acceleration in the process of technological change.

The second dimension is the system of nation-states which quickly extended itself throughout the world and which transformed the nation-state into the dominant agent of the global political order. The appearance of a complex system of international relations between the nation-states is clearly a factor advancing globalization. Third is what Giddens calls the 'world military order'. Modernity has brought about the industrialization of war and the same techniques of war have spread throughout the world.[13] Fourth to be noted is industrialization and the increasing international division of labour, creating a productive interdependence that is progressively extended. But together with this dimension, the emergence of global ecological interdependence is more and more evident. The radioactive rain caused by Chernobyl did not affect only the Soviet Union. The over-exploitation of the tropical rainforest in the Amazon will not affect only Brazil.

Nevertheless, there is another dimension of the process, the globalization of culture, which plays a central role even for the other dimensions, inasmuch as symbolic relations can more easily be abstracted from space. From this it is possible to derive the observation that the more that political and economic exchanges are realized by symbolic means, the better their chances for globalization.[14] It is not therefore surprising that economic globalization is more advanced in the financial markets, where the means of exchange is money. It cannot be surprising either that cultural globalization, mediated by electronic media, is even more advanced than political and economic globalization.

The expansion of the media has been crucial for this dimension of globalization. A new universal mass culture arises which affects even the most remote regions of the world. The new form of global mass culture is sustained by technological developments in the developed world, especially the United States, and manifests itself predominantly in television and film. Entertainment and leisure are now dominated worldwide by electronic images which easily cross linguistic and cultural barriers and which are absorbed more quickly than other cultural forms.[15] Modern culture is increasingly mediated by electronics. Cable and satellite TV are the spearhead of this dimension of globalization, and signal the fact that electronic media are rapidly replacing written and oral media. Visual and graphic arts, especially through computers, TV sets and electronic games, reconstitute popular life and its entertainments everywhere.

The universal language of this new global mass culture is English. But English does not totally displace other languages; it only has hegemony over them. This form of global culture has an ability to recognize and absorb cultural differences. It exercises hegemony over other cultures without dissolving them; it operates through them. It does not destroy local cultures; it uses them as a means.[16] This is why it is important to understand that the dialectic between the global and the local continues to exist. There is a tendency to homogenization, but also a fascination with what is different. The global does not replace the local, but the local operates within the logic of the global. Globalization does not mean the end of cultural and ethnic differences, but their increased recognition and conscious utilization or rejection.

The sixth process typical of modernity is a consequence of the phenomenon of globalization: the deterritorialization of modern culture. With globalization the link between culture and territory has been gradually breaking up and a new electronic cultural space has been created which has no precise geographical location.[17] The media increasingly mediate the transmission of modern culture, thus replacing the local and personal forms of communication and introducing a break between the producers and the receivers of symbolic forms.[18] The emergence of international communications conglomerates monopolizing the production of news, television series and films is a relevant aspect of this break. Culture is increasingly breaking with national and time-space boundaries and is becoming internationalized. However, this does not mean the end of territorial culture. In Latin America it is clear that the emergence of a deterritorialized culture, especially through television, has gone hand in hand with an expansion of the consumption of locally produced culture. In other words, access to global culture is always achieved through local culture.[19]

Further still, in seventh place, there is the commodification of modern culture. Culture is increasingly being conducted by the logic of profit and competition for consumers. This is the logic of the transnational networks and megacorporations that increasingly control the world market of communications. As Adorno and Horkheimer anticipated, culture has become yet another industry dependent on its market in an implacable competition to get consumers.[20] Thus it is possible to speak of a commodification of symbolic forms which are exchanged, sold and acquired in highly competitive markets. Art and cultural forms are standardized and commodified as a consequence of the emergence of the leisure and entertainment industries.

Cultural industries transform individuals into consumers. Cultural products are gathered from all over the world and transformed into commodities for consumption in the big metropolises.[21] It is possible to speak of a consumer culture in which the exchange of cultural commodities is determined not only by their capacity to satisfy certain specific basic needs but also by their ability to provide a sense of belonging or identity. Consumption as a means of identification allows people to be seen wearing certain labels, or being with certain people, or being in certain places that identify a certain group, which itself is sometimes a creation of the media. Going to a concert or an exhibition can satisfy aesthetic needs, but it can also satisfy the need to be in the company of a certain group with which one identifies. Equally, buying certain brands of jeans or cars does more than allow one to be clothed or mobile: it provides status and a sense of being someone belonging to an identifiable group.

Eighth, there is the revaluation of local and regional cultures. In the face of globalization and of the deterritorialization of culture it is possible to detect reactions (sometimes of a fundamentalist character) and forms of resistance arising everywhere. As McGrew has rightly argued, globalization is not a teleological phenomenon that might inexorably lead towards a universal culturally integrated human community. It is rather a contingent and dialectical process which engenders contradictory dynamics as it goes. It simultaneously universalizes some aspects of modern life and fosters profound differences; it introduces similar practices and institutions everywhere, while reinterpreting and articulating them in relation to local practices. On the one side it creates international associations and groups, but on the other fragments already existing communities; it favours centralization and the concentration of power, but also generates decentralizing tendencies; it brings about hybridity of ideas, values and bodies of knowledge, but also creates prejudices and stereotypes that divide.[22]

Finally, in the ninth place is what Thompson has aptly called the 're-mooring of tradition', which has to do with the fact that in modern society tradition has not been destroyed, as many theoreticians of modernity thought, but has been transformed because of the impact of the media. True, in modernity there is a gradual decline in the traditional grounding of action, but tradition retains its significance as a means of making sense of the world. Traditions do not disappear but become delocalized ('they lose their moorings in the shared locales of day-to-day life'), depersonalized ('detached from the individuals with whom one interacts in day-to-day life') and deritualized ('less dependent on ritualized re-enactment').[23]

Modernization, identity and neoliberalism in the 1990s

During the 1970s and 1980s the antagonism between supporters and detractors of modernity in Latin America reached its peak. Yet both sides seemed to share the idea that modernity was something external, which either had to be prevented from expanding in order to preserve identity or had to be brought about at all cost in order to change the old identity. By the end of the 1980s and in spite of the strength of attacks against modernity, which we saw in the last chapter, the project of rapidly advancing to modernity, even at the cost of identity, was becoming dominant in Latin America, supported by the increasingly overwhelming success of neoliberalism. The wave of military dictatorships was receding and democracy was making progress all over Latin America, but the neoliberal changes in the direction of economic policies, which had been swiftly introduced by dictatorships, remained firmly in place.

A new world order is still in the making and hence it is not easy to define its main characteristics. But in general one can say that some tendencies can be noted. In politics, there is the end of the Cold War and of the bipolar world, a reaffirmation of democratic principles throughout the world, the fall of various kinds of dictatorship and a renewed emphasis on human rights. In economics, one can point to the predominance of neoliberal policies in most parts of the world, a generalized attack on the welfare state in most countries, the abandonment of Keynesian policies, a reduction in the number of state-owned enterprises, and the triumph of a free-market export-led kind of development; and along with this, relatively high levels of unemployment, the rapid destruction and reconstruction of skills, few gains in the real wage, and a roll-back of trade union power. In international relations one sees a tendency to form large trading areas like the European common market and a new lease of life for international organizations which acquire a greater power to intervene in the life of countries, given the wider support they enjoy.

In Latin America, the stage that opens up after the end of dictatorships continues with, and accelerates, economic and political modernization under the influence of an already consolidated neoliberal ideology. Once more the concerns about identity recede as neoliberal optimism gets the upper hand everywhere. But this time, the modernizing wave is under a different banner from the postwar effort. Instead of protection for industry, economies open to the world market are advocated. Instead of an interventionist state, the tendency is to reaffirm reduced-size states with lower expenditure and greater control of macroeconomic variables to fight inflation. Instead of the welfare state, the privatization of health, education and social security is proposed. The main ideas are now to export, to abolish tariffs, to abandon an industry if it is inefficient and to let market forces produce development by means of a more rational allocation of resources. Lack of development is no longer blamed on dependency but rather on excessive state intervention in the economy, smothering growth. Capitalism is still dynamic if it is allowed to work according to the market forces. What has failed in the past is not capitalism but socialism.

The economic policies implemented by capitalist countries after the Second World War were very much influenced by Keynes in economics and social democratic ideas in politics. Two major objectives of these policies were the maintenance of full employment and the construction of a welfare state able to deliver social benefits such as education, health and unemployment benefits to everybody. Both goals demanded an important degree of state intervention to regulate the economy and high taxation to finance the increased public expenditure needed by such measures. Neoliberalism puts in question these goals and the level of state expenditure they require. It is argued that state intervention hinders private initiative and is normally inefficient. Full employment was maintained at the cost of low productivity and made industry uncompetitive. Too many regulations protected workers from dismissal and secured minimum wages, but the result was overstaffing, lack of productivity and general uncompetitiveness abroad. Such policies make export markets more difficult to penetrate and lead to deficits in the balance of payments.

In Latin America the neoliberal diagnostic was that the excessive size of the state and its mistaken interventionist policies had resulted in a very low rate of economic growth. The import-substituting industrialization promoted by ECLA and practised by almost all states in the region had led to a total distortion in the allocation of productive resources. Because of the high tariffs it was very attractive for internal resources to go into industry since profits would be high without the need to compete. But, at the same time, the high protection and the lack of competition fostered the inefficient production of goods at high prices and very poor quality for a very reduced internal market. Inflation was the result of high levels of state expenditure and reckless printing of money in a vain attempt to improve the situation of various underprivileged groups.

In line with this assessment, neoliberal policies in Latin America sought to curb excessive state expenditure, high tariffs and subsidies. They also devolved as many services as possible to the private sector and maintained the exchange rate at a level which would promote exports. In addition, they sought to reintroduce market relations into the sphere of labour. That is to say, salaries and wages were to be fixed by the law of supply and demand, not by government regulation. Firms acquired the right to get rid of excess labour in order to cut costs. They were also allowed to eliminate the trade unions' restrictive practices so as to manage a more flexible labour force which would adapt quickly to the demands of production and the market. So neoliberal policies curbed the excessive negotiating power of the unions in order to allow free market forces to rule over labour processes. Part of this strategy was a cutback in social security, not just because it was too expensive but also because it created a mentality of dependency on the state and discouraged people from seeking productive employment.

The free market and open economy policies produced in the first instance a significant diminution of industrial production and industrial employment. Some countries such as Mexico and Brazil managed, after a while, to expand their industrial exports, thus compensating for the flood of imports from foreign manufacturers. The rest, by contrast, followed a more radical laissez-faire model which did diversify the exports of primary products, but made more permanent the low level of industrial production and employment. In this the Latin American trajectory to modernity (with the exception of Mexico and Brazil) has been very different from the Asiatic one, where the state assumed a very important role in the acquisition and adaptation of leading technologies and in the promotion of industrial exports. In spite of this relative deindustrialization, the expansion of other activities and exports in Latin America has brought about a high rate of economic growth. However, growth coexists with an increased concentration of wealth in a few hands and the existence of extreme poverty in large sectors of the population.[24]

The new atmosphere of freedom and democracy in Latin America from the 1990s has made it imperative to begin to modernize and democratize the state. If one compares the newly elected regimes with former dictatorships, this process has made some progress and this continues. But many problems still remain, whether because many changes have been rather cosmetic, or because in some cases, as in Chile, the former dictatorship left a constitution and laws full of undemocratic elements which can hardly be changed. Rebuilding and democratizing the political structures which collapsed in the 1970s is one of the remaining tasks of the Latin American trajectory to modernity in the new century. But it is not an easy task, for it is far from being a priority for the dominant neoliberal worldview. This has a theoretical foundation in the inner structure of neoliberal thought.

Ruling classes in Latin America are frequently criticized for being truly liberal only in the economic sense, and illiberal, intolerant, authoritarian and traditionalist where politics, values and morality are concerned. Equally Thatcherism in Britain was accused of fusing neoliberalism with neoconservative ideas and in this way the advocated freedom of the market was not matched by an interest in political liberties. What these criticisms overlook is that neoliberalism in itself, at least in Hayek's version of it, prevalent in Latin America, inherently entails this duality of conservatism in cultural and political matters and liberalism in economic matters. It is not therefore that Mrs Thatcher in Britain and Pinochet in Chile were only half liberals: they were fully and consistently neoliberals.

Hayek made it quite clear that his brand of neoliberalism possesses three main characteristics. First, it has an evolutionist interpretation of culture and is inherently respectful of and compatible with tradition and religion. Second, it has a full understanding of the limits of reason, and consequently distrusts all attempts purposefully to construct a social order. It accepts the existence of a spontaneous order which is superior and more complex than anything human beings can intentionally create. Third, it does not confuse liberalism with democracy. The opposite of liberalism is totalitarianism. The opposite of democracy is authoritarianism. Hence it is possible to have totalitarian democratic governments and authoritarian liberal governments.[25] The latter are preferable to the former. Thus Hayek opposes the old kind of continental liberalism which is guilty of rationalism, constructivism and democratism. This last feature is interesting because according to Hayek democratism demands absolute power for the majority, thus transforming itself into a kind of anti-liberalism.

It is this opposition between democracy and liberalism which is at the heart of neoliberalism and which has allowed the ideological justification of dictatorships. How is it that this kind of thought could become so widespread in Latin America? Well, one can hypothesize that this is the result of a mixture, consolidated during three centuries of colonial domination, between Catholic religious traditionalism and political authoritarianism. The traditional Catholic hierarchy still exercises an enormous influence over political processes in Latin America, and with the exception of some worthy cases,[26] they have tended to back authoritarian regimes.

In spite of the democratizing influences of Enlightenment thought, which certainly achieved some partial moderation of authoritarianism from independence onwards, its cultural force has not easily been extinguished in Latin American social-political life.[27] Weber's classical thesis linked Calvinism and Protestant puritanism with the rationalistic spirit of capitalism. It may well be that, on the contrary, traditional Catholicism has a greater affinity with the Hayekian kind of neoliberalism. A certain kind of Catholicism, which is still quite prevalent in Latin America, is well known for its adherence to tradition and strict morality. It has also had historical problems with democracy and has a preference for very hierarchical and undemocratic structures.[28] This may help to explain the greater facility with which an overwhelmingly Catholic Latin America has adopted a more radical brand of neoliberalism, whereas in Protestant countries a stronger link survives between modernity, democracy and rational constructivism.

The identity of Archilochus' hedgehog

It is not surprising that it should be at this time that some authors openly propound the idea that Latin America must abandon its old identity in order to be able fully to enter modernity. It is just another instance of the old Latin American idea of modernity against identity which started in the nineteenth century and recurred between 1950 and 1970. Claudio Véliz is its best representative. He maintains that the main problem encountered by modernization in Latin America is the cultural resistance which the Latin American identity itself has set up against it. Véliz agrees with Morandé that the Latin American identity is baroque, but he sees it as an obstacle to development.

By resorting to a classical proverb from the Greek poet Archilochus, 'the fox knows many things, but the hedgehog knows one big thing',[29] which was used metaphorically by Isaiah Berlin to differentiate between writers who relate everything to a central vision and thinkers who deal with many diverse and non-related things, Véliz proposes the idea that this metaphor can also be applied to nations and societies. Latin America would be the world of the hedgehog, whereas the English-speaking civilization would be the world of the fox.[30] What characterizes the hedgehog is its resistance to change, the emphasis on order and unity, centralism, symmetry, organicity, tradition and the Baroque. What characterizes the fox is mobility, change, decentralization, asymmetry, diversity, the inorganic and the gothic. For the hedgehog there is one eternal and fixed truth; for the fox there are many changing truths. Hedgehogs and foxes, therefore, 'represent essential, definitive constituents of the dominant cultural traditions of the New World'.[31]

According to Véliz, all aspects of the conquest and colonization of Latin America by the Spanish and Portuguese carry the hallmark of the hedgehog: the construction of a centralized system of political control, commercial monopoly, the imposition of the Spanish language and Catholic religion. The unity of purpose had to be manifested in everything: only one God, one monarch, one economy, and one ancestry. Everything that was 'diversity, heterogeneity, adulteration, and discontinuity in any form were considered to be inimical to the flawless unity demanded for this elevated purpose'.[32] Spain played a central role in the Counter-Reformation and the Tridentine reno-vation of the Catholic Church.[33] The creation of the Jesuit Order, the definitive ascendancy of Thomism as the 'perennial philosophy' of the Church, the organization and leadership of the Council of Trent, the introduction of the Inquisition, baroque art and the rejection of the Lutheran idea of salvation by faith alone are all aspects in which the protagonism of the Spanish was crucial.

The Baroque contributed with a renaissance of art and images to the centralist and combative religious spirit of the Counter-Reformation, penetrating the whole social and political life of Spain and its colonies. The Baroque, Véliz argues, 'is a metaphor for Spain and her Indies at their triumphant best. It is a reminder of imperial greatness, an obstacle to dissolution, a technique for the preservation of unity, an alibi for the central control of diversity, a justification for the pursuit of glory.'[34] The Baroque, Véliz concludes, is the mode of the hedgehog, whereas the gothic is the mode of the fox. The gothic mode accepts diversity, change, the unexpected, the exotic. The baroque mode has aversion to change, to the new and foreign, and therefore takes refuge in the symmetric, in the durable, in the unitary, in intolerance of the different, in the centrally controlled. These are, therefore, the essential characteristics that define Latin American identity and one must not be deceived by the apparent volatility and irrationality of changes that occur there:

> in spite its reputation for frequent and violent political upheaval, the principal feature of modern Latin America is its overwhelming stabil-ity. There exists in the region a resilient traditional structure of insti-tutions, hierarchical arrangements, and attitudes that qualifies every aspect of behaviour and that has survived centuries of colonial gov-ernment, movements for independence, foreign wars and invasions, domestic revolutions, and a confusingly large number of lesser palace revolts.[35]

To this identity is opposed the mode of the gothic fox, typical of Britain and the United States, that is to say, an identity which thrives on uncertainty, risk, change and diversity; a mode of being that accepts disorder and improvisation, which rejects regularities and all attempts at centralist control; a conception that values and encour-ages individuality, personal initiative and self-sufficiency and distrusts bureaucracies, regulations and authorities. Whereas the baroque hedgehog has an urban character, the gothic fox loves the rural and nature. The former possesses rigid legal codes; the latter favours the 'common law' which is incessantly modified. What determines and expresses these totally different modes of being are those originating

moments which are located in the Catholic Counter-Reformation and
the industrial revolution. As Véliz puts it, 'nothing in the Spanish cultural tradition can compare with the prowess of the Catholic Reformation, and nothing that the English people have done can compare
with their Industrial Revolution.'[36] Whereas the Spanish peak
moment delivers the defence of the faith and closes itself to the exte-
rior, the English peak moment delivers a variety of industrial, cultural
and consumption artefacts which it wishes to export abroad and
which are avidly and universally accepted by other peoples.

Up to this point of the analysis one could think, with some reason,
that Véliz is contributing a new essentialist theory which opposes two
conceptions of life that are extremely durable and persistent.
However, he is to be distinguished from the religious essentialism we
have seen on two fundamental points. First, while religious essentialism blames Latin America's economic failure on the uncritical
adoption of European and North American rationalist cultural patterns, Véliz blames the Latin American identity itself and views the
English–North American identity with undisguised sympathy.
Second, while religious essentialism seeks in Latin America's own
identity, hidden and betrayed by the elites, the basis for a true and
durable social-economic recovery, Véliz observes how the very identity of the baroque hedgehog finally enters into a crisis as a consequence of the incursion of the cultural artefacts of the gothic fox. In
this way the solution to the problem of development seems to be in
the adoption of an alien identity.

Contrary to Morandé, Cousiño and Burns, Claudio Véliz argues
that the main problem the process of modernization has suffered from
in Latin America is the cultural resistance to it from Latin America's
own identity. All the intellectual efforts, the hundreds of thousands
of dollars spent in research, the hundreds of books and reports
written to find out the causes of, and to propose solutions to, Latin
America's economic problems have not only been unable to produce
any reasonable results, but they themselves have constituted a reflection, 'a distant echo of the legalism and bureaucratic prolixity of
Counter-Reformation casuistry'.[37] In spite of all these academic and
intellectual efforts, the economic health of Latin America has not
improved until very recently.

This is why intellectual tendencies have emerged which blamed foreigners or developed countries (theories of dependency), or a deficient
structure (structuralism), or incorrect economic policies (socialism),
instead of looking into Latin America's own cultural legacy, inherited
from Spanish Baroque. According to Véliz, development is not a
universal formula which any society or people can follow and adopt

at any time, under any set of circumstances. Latin America's failure is not due to dependency, deficient structures or socialist economic policies, but rather it is due to its own cultural identity, to its aversion to risk and change, to its distrust of the new, to its preference for stability and central control, to its respect for status and old loyalties:

> everything that sustained the imperial enterprise and the crowning achievement of the Counter-Reformation, every conceivable feature that favoured their eventual outcome, every personal trait and every social circumstance, every prejudice and every social virtue that nurtured the style of life that flourished in that sheltered world, was inimical to the establishment and growth of a modern economy.[38]

Latin Americans have lived imprisoned in their magnificent past, in their sensibleness and prudence, in their distrust of innovations, in their respect for status, in their immovable loyalties. All this indicates the stubborn presence of a mode of thinking and acting, of a cultural identity which was forged in the baroque Counter-Reformation. Nevertheless, after many centuries of resistance to change, the magnificent baroque dome has begun finally to deteriorate and crumble under the impact of thousands of banal cultural artefacts coming from the Anglo-Saxon world. The old Latin American identity finally gives way before the dynamic drive of Anglo-Saxon culture:

> the lofty dome of the Spanish cultural revolution has in the end proved defenceless against blue jeans, computer graphics, jogging shoes and electric toasters. It is now crumbling, not because it has been tested by rival doctrines or pulled asunder and brought down by ideological deviations but because it has been overwhelmed by the tidal heaving and pulling of an immense multitude of inexpensive, pedestrian, readily accessible, and unpretentious products of industrial capitalism.[39]

The fact that Véliz sees the beginning of the end of the baroque hedgehog's identity prevents anyone from accusing him of fully fledged essentialism. Stubborn and persistent for many centuries, finally this baroque cultural pattern has begun to break apart. No essentialist theory could accept the end of a collective identity. Véliz seems to see the end of the baroque cultural identity with ill-disguised satisfaction, because it will be replaced by the more versatile and pragmatic identity of the gothic fox. He does not wish to reconstruct the moribund identity: on the contrary, he maintains that 'the task at hand, therefore, is not to discover ways of restoring a crumbling dome to its former glory but to clear the rubble as expeditiously as possible.'[40] Ultimately, his point is that it is necessary to recognize the superiority of the gothic fox and to adopt its identity, to recognize in the culture expressed by the English industrial revolution the true essence of the modernity which Latin America must acquire.

The satisfaction with the crumbling of the baroque identity does conceal a certain essentialist vision of Anglo-Saxon modernity. The desirable cultural essence for Latin America would not come from the stable realm of the Baroque or from endogenous processes but would be the fruit of the infinite diversity and flexibility of the world capitalist market developed by the English world. It would not be a religious or autochthonous essence but an Anglo-Saxon essence. The very title of Véliz's book indicates either a programme of action or the verification of an ongoing process: the point is either to advocate entrance or to argue that Latin America is entering into *The New World of the Gothic Fox*. Véliz's position, with its unconcealed admiration for the English–North American cultural legacy, reminds us of the old positivist and liberal theories of the end of the nineteenth century, which in the works of Sarmiento, Alberdi and others appealed to the Latin Americans to get rid of their Indo-Iberian legacy in order to become the 'North Americans of the south'. In a similar way Claudio Véliz advocates in the 1990s an Anglo-Saxon kind of modernity. Which shows that in his view the process of modernization in Latin America is externally led and antagonistic to Latin America's own original cultural identity.[41]

Although Véliz's theory is pessimistic in relation to Latin America's own baroque identity, it has an optimistic side to it, which is the fact that it will be, or is being, overcome. This duality draws this theory near to some of the old theories of modernization in the 1950s and 1960s which detected a transition from traditional society to modern society. Many among them praised international trade for the beneficial impact it would have on the development of poor nations, especially through the so-called 'demonstration effect', whereby the conspicuous consumption in the West would become an object of desire in the developing world.[42] One wonders whether Véliz's theory, admittedly dressed up in a much better literary form and with the benefit of a more subtle historical analysis, has said something substantially different. I guess not.

Such a theory oversimplifies the problem and reduces the mechanism of change to the impact of foreign consumption goods, that is to say, to factors of a banal material kind. At least 'diffusionist' or 'acculturation' theories of modernization also considered the impact of Western values, technologies, forms of organization, skills and bodies of knowledge. Véliz is keen to dismiss all of these as having nothing to do with real change in Latin America: material artefacts alone are the main agents. But he also neglects all internal factors. Surely, the interplay of internal classes, political parties and interests in Latin America must have some impact on change as well?

Véliz's belief in the power of consumption goods is also missing the critical edge it might have had within modernization theory. At least in Gino Germani's analysis, side by side with the 'demonstration effect', there was the 'fusion effect' whereby modern values could be reinterpreted in new contexts in the developing countries in a way that could reinforce traditional structures.[43] One of Germani's examples was precisely that of conspicuous consumption, which in a highly developed context could be indispensable for boosting production, but which in an underdeveloped context could be an obstacle to the savings and investment necessary for enhancing production. Véliz, somewhat naively, grants too much power to consumption desires. This is the reason why he thinks that what has finally defeated the old Latin American identity, which resisted change for so many centuries, are jeans, sneakers, computers and toasters. But this is an illusion. The craving for refined Anglo-Saxon consumption products has existed in Latin America since at least the beginning of the nineteenth century, if not before, and this did not necessarily mean the industrialization or development of Latin America's economy.

The ambiguities of postmodernism

In the 1990s and even a bit before, a new current of thought developed in Europe began increasingly to be received in Latin American intellectual circles: postmodernism. But as is usually the case with cultural imports in Latin America, postmodernism was also recontextualized and re-elaborated according to the particular circumstances of the neoliberal stage. Because of its close connections with the issues of modernity and identity, postmodernism has become increasingly important in debates and discussions in the region. If one explores only the main tenets of European postmodernism, then one gets the impression that the content of this current of thought would be certain to support identity against modernity, and that this, at a neoliberal stage of dynamic development, would be a kind of anachronism.

In effect, the opposition of a Latin American cultural model to the enlightened European cultural model, so common in the 1970s and 1980s at times of crisis, seems to fit perfectly with the postmodernist critique of the absolute character of Western reason. Postmodernism questions the idea of objective truth and distrusts

totalizing theories or metanarratives which propose universal emancipation. The attack against the Enlightenment and modernity as
totalitarian processes would certainly ring true with those in Latin
America who during the 'lost decade' looked for the causes of the
region's failures in its indefatigable search for a modernity based on
instrumental reason and foreign models, thus betraying their own
identity. The uncritical acceptance and pursuit of the rationalist
enlightened cultural pattern would be accepted as at the root of Latin
America's problems.

The postmodernist discourse is thus very attractive for essentialist
conceptions of cultural identity in Latin America which reject enlightened modernity because it would be antagonistic or, at least, alien to
the Latin American self. The description of the Latin American
culture in terms of a different logic that is opposed to the Enlightenment fits all the requirements of Lyotard's language games: each has
its own rules and its own truth which is incommensurable with that
of other discourses. A powerful anti-modern alliance seems thus to
be struck between European postmodernism and Latin American
essentialism. Underlying this alliance there is also the typically postmodernist overintegrated conception of culture: each culture (language game) as pure, absolutely different, incommensurable. This can
be applied to the Latin American symbolic dramatic cultural pattern
vis-à-vis European Cartesian rationalism. They are supposed to be
totally pre-formed and mutually excluding patterns.

Postmodernism's distrust of totalizing discourses is also accompanied by tolerance for a plurality of discourses, and the belief that the
others have the right to speak for themselves in their own voice or
dialect. Basically this would follow from the new postmodernist
respect for cultural, ethnic, geographical, class, sexual and gender
differences. Postmodernism could be invoked to support Latin
America's right to speak for itself, to support the Latin American
discourse in its quest not to be reduced to European models and to
affirm its unique character and its own specificity. Additionally, the
distrust of instrumental reason and the revaluation of the aesthetic
experience might also be relied on to uphold the idea that Latin
America's identity can be defined in terms of a baroque culture which
privileges sapiential knowledge, rituals and drama.

The irony cannot but be noticed that the attempts at self-
affirmation by the Latin American other – for decades ignored by
Europe and the developed world – should appear now to be defended
by a European theory. The question arises, however, as to whether
postmodernist discourse truly defends Latin American specificity and
difference or whether a more careful and penetrating critical review

of its premises might show that all is not so clear-cut as it seems. Nelly Richard has developed a critical argument which precisely seeks to question the supposed openness of postmodernism to the case of Latin America. According to her, postmodernism appears to give Latin America a privileged position in so far as the heterogeneity and fragmentation typical of the postmodern era has been one of Latin America's long-standing characteristics. Besides, cultural peripheries like Latin America would benefit from a new centrality, as postmodernism would proclaim the end of Eurocentrism. However, Richard thinks that we 'need to *doubt* this new centrality of the margins':[44]

> just as it appears that for once the Latin American periphery might have achieved the distinction of being postmodernist *avant la lettre*, no sooner does it attain a synchronicity of forms with the international cultural discourses, than that very same postmodernism abolishes any privilege which such a position might offer. Postmodernism dismantles the distinction between centre and periphery, and in so doing nullifies its significance.

> Postmodernism defends itself against the destabilizing threat of the 'other' by integrating it back into a framework which absorbs all differences and contradictions.[45]

The critique seems to be that what postmodernism concedes with one hand, it takes away with the other, for it tends to abolish the traditional dichotomies with which modernity used to work and which gave specificity to the Latin American situation: the original and the copy, centre and periphery, colonial power and colony. My impression is that this is not a very fair critique and that it is based on a confusion of levels. Richard maintains that postmodernism tries to convince us about the obsolescence of oppositions such as centre–periphery, but when she tries to prove it the texts she cites do not refer to the elimination of such distinctions but only suggest a different assessment of their significance. Thus, for instance, one of the texts quoted as proof says: 'Why should it be true that what comes first is more valuable than what comes after, that the original is worth more than the imitation, that what is central is more important than the peripheral?'[46] This seems to be, precisely, a call for a revaluation of the copy, of the colony and the periphery, not an argument against these distinctions! The quote appears to come from Schwarz, and in effect, if one continues to read Schwarz's text, at least in its English version, one can see that he agrees with Foucault and Derrida and thinks that the revaluation of the copy 'could increase the self-esteem and alleviate the anxiety of the underdeveloped world which sees itself as tributary to central countries'.[47]

Hence, it is difficult to argue that postmodernism eliminates the traditional dichotomies; what it does is to evaluate them in a different way, one which is more advantageous for Latin America. To maintain that postmodernism defends itself from the 'other' by integrating it in a frame which absorbs the differences and contradictions is not an adequate interpretation. If anything, that was the technique of modernity and its totalizing theories. Postmodernism is always in favour of exaggerating differences, not of absorbing them. But my point is not to assert the total innocence of postmodernism. I agree that postmodernism tries to defend itself from the other, but not in the way Richard thinks; it uses a more subtle device which consists in exaggerating differences to the point that nothing is left in common and the essence of what is supposed to be 'Latin American' can no longer touch that other essence of what is supposed to be 'European'. The defence is by exclusion, not by integration.

Be that as it may, there is yet another problem with the idea of a perfect fit between European postmodernist tenets and Latin American anti-modern thought, and this problem has to do with the specific way in which Latin American authors have reinterpreted those tenets. It is, of course, well known that intellectual imports everywhere, but perhaps particularly in Latin America, are adapted and contextualized to specific realities and needs. In this case, though, such elaborations and modifications are enormously facilitated by the very nature of the postmodernist approach: its relativism, its distrust of absolutes, its aversion to rigorous logic, its rejection of metanarratives, its doubts about claims to absolute truth. All of this lends itself very well to the task of reinventing, adapting, changing, reinterpreting and contextualizing meanings.

It is not therefore very surprising that in the Latin American context, the fixing of the content of postmodernism should be a very difficult task indeed. Nelly Richard, a very good critical representative of this current of thought, has no problems in recognizing that 'some postmodernist texts activate (new) energies of resistance and critical opposition, while others deactivate them. Postmodernism lends itself to a multiplicity of significations.'[48] Latin American postmodernism is not part of a Postmodernist International and is certainly not reducible to European postmodernism. As she puts it, 'postmodernism signifies for us, instead, a *horizon of problems* in relation to which we can discuss local significations that are (unevenly) affected by the political, social, and cultural mutations of the contemporary world.'[49] She even celebrates the evasive and polymorphous character of postmodernism as a way of escaping ideological purism and all attempts at controlling discursiveness.[50]

This flexible and open attitude allows us to understand why postmodernism for most Latin American authors sympathetic to it is not necessarily connected with the end of modernity. On the contrary, for many of these authors postmodernism seems to be a particular way or modality assumed by modernity in the Latin American periphery. Brunner, for instance, argues that there was in Latin America, even before the arrival of postmodernism, a cultural heterogeneity which could be conceived as a kind of 'regional postmodernism *avant la lettre* that, nevertheless, is fully constitutive of our modernity'.[51] In other words, he is suggesting that postmodernism is the specific form modernity takes in Latin America. Brunner detects a connection between specific postmodern features and the dynamism brought by Latin America's new openness to the international market: 'the motor of modernity, the international market, provokes and then reinforces an incessant movement of heterogenization of culture, employing, stimulating, and reproducing a plurality of *logics* that act simultaneously, becoming interwoven.'[52]

Norbert Lechner, in his turn, maintains that one of the positive contributions that the postmodern turn makes to democracy in Latin America is the loss of the fear of heterogeneity, and a renewed trust in pluralism.[53] The postmodernist praise of heterogeneity does not entail 'a rejection of all ideas of collectivity' but only an attack on 'the false homogenization imposed by formal rationality'. Which leads him to the same conclusion that Brunner drew: 'postmodernism does not oppose the project of modernity as such but rather a specific modality of it'; which in politics means 'the managerial-technocratic style of doing politics'.[54] Lechner argues that modernity should not be confused with modernization and that postmodernism only involves disenchantment with the latter, not with the former. In a similar manner, Jesús Martín Barbero treats the postmodern phenomenon as the way in which Latin American modernity, 'loaded' with premodern features, becomes a collective experience. This is why he maintains that postmodernity in Latin America, 'instead of coming to replace, comes to rearrange the relationships between modernity and traditions'.[55]

Hence for many Latin American authors broadly but critically sympathetic to postmodernism there is no opposition between modernity and postmodernism, but on the contrary they even find in Latin America postmodern features *avant la lettre*[56] and tend to relate the new dynamism and openness of Latin America's modernization processes to these postmodern features. If one adds to these interpretations postmodernism's own evasiveness and polymorphism, it becomes easier to understand the fact highlighted by Hopenhayn that while many postmodernists in Latin America are not neoliberals and are interested in introducing cultural dimensions into the problematic of development, reorienting planning, reappraising democracy and tolerance, focusing upon new social movements, etc., many others have used the tenets of postmodernism to underpin neoliberal positions.[57] Hopenhayn describes very well how postmodernism has been used in Latin America to produce what he calls 'a strategic package of euphemisms' which covers up the real intentions, which are neoliberal. A discursive astuteness in postmodern neoliberalism is recognized whereby it talks about diversity when it means the market, it talks about desire when it means the maximization of profits, it refers to play to dress up conflict, and talks about personal creativity when it means private appropriation.[58]

Hence, all these authors not only do not see any opposition between modernity and postmodernist tenets, but also see postmodernism as positively collaborating with economic modernization by renovating cultural values; in some cases even celebrating neoliberal modernization. This is how the connection between postmodernism and the new neoliberal stage in Latin America can be understood. Whereas in Europe postmodernism may represent an option for identity against modernity, in Latin America postmodernism, barring some exceptions, supports modernization against identity. This is why during this neoliberal stage the problem of identity tends to recede and the theories that predominate praise the triumph of modernity over identity. Both Véliz's gothic fox and postmodernist talk of dynamic heterogeneity seem to fit into this picture very well.

To these authors one can also add those like Carlos Pérez who – this time following more closely the European postmodernist scepticism *vis-à-vis* integrated identities – declares that Latin America is the cultural history of a non-identity.[59] Strongly arguing against Latin American essentialism of the *mestizaje* kind, Pérez argues that there is no such thing as a fundamental identity with a mestizo character in Latin America because Latin America belongs to a tradition and possesses bodies of knowledge for which it is not the legitimate addressee: they are European bodies of knowledge. Thus Europe is Latin America's other, but an other of which Latin Americans inevitably form a part. So in the end the Latin American is 'a kind of European who is not the owner of his identity', 'he is nothing more than the recognition, under European form, of his non-European being.' This is why Latin America, considered in relation to its own culture, 'is the history of this non-identity, of this inappropriate identity'.[60]

Hernán Vidal has accused Pérez's thought of characterizing the Latin American as an ontological monstrosity. As he puts it, 'the negation of historical identity denounces the Latin American as a monstrous being that, in its creative capacity, only has the option of an infinite "game" of the "modification" and "distortion" of the originals.'[61] There is some truth in this critique because, after all, such lack of originality can be wider than we realize and may even affect the centre itself. The ideas of purity, authenticity and originality are dangerous when applied to national or regional identities in order to deny mixes, hybridity, and borrowings. Which nation or region, these days, can argue that it has an absolutely pure, authentic and original culture? Paradoxically, Pérez himself ends up recognizing this when he says that 'the shine of copies can be more spectacular than the old opacity of their models . . . the original, these days, does not exist anywhere, or, what is the same, it does not interest anyone.'[62] On the other hand, there is little doubt that this denial of an historical identity, even if it is not directly and necessarily connected with a desire for modernity and/or neoliberal development, at least, by default, leaves the field open to them.

Postmodernist positions are steeped in relativism and therefore seem never totally to discard positions which are at the opposite end to their own, being prepared to consider their efficacy in particular contexts and localities. This is why it is so difficult to pin postmodernists down to firm and clear-cut propositions. To some of them, like Richard, this is an advantage. I can see the advantages of this slippery nature for their own strategies of defence. But there are also overwhelming disadvantages in academic terms: what can be said of a mode of thought which can activate and deactivate resistance, which can be neoliberal and its opposite, which is opposed to modernity but then not in Latin America, which celebrates otherness, but dissolves its identity? The least one can say is that it is a confused and confusing mode of thought which nevertheless responds to real changes in the world and can still have some critical insights which help to rethink modernity. Ultimately, though, in Latin America postmodernism has frequently aligned itself with neoliberal modernization against identity.

Nevertheless, as in other times of accelerating development and economic expansion, a new kind of identity seems to be implicitly advocated and discursively constructed by the neoliberal project. Only that this time it is very different from the developmentalist identity that responded to the populist matrix in the 1950s and 1960s. Now a new kind of discourse on identity is being constructed which advances the idea of 'winner nations' whose main agent is the figure of the successful and innovating entrepreneur, and which offers wide-spread (credit card) consumption as the linchpin which could deliver the masses. The former values of equality, state-sponsored welfare, fairness and general austerity propounded by most developmentalist ideologies are now replaced by individual success, conspicuous con-sumption and privatized welfare. The point now is no longer justice, full employment or industrial development, but rather to become winner nations, comparable with the Asian tigers, ready to conquer the markets of the world.

The power of media and new trends in literature

The economic processes mentioned above occur now in a new politi-cal context which, after years of dictatorship and appalling abuses of power, revalues formal democracy, participation and respect for human rights. The role of television and other media in this respect cannot be overestimated. I have already shown that in the 1970s and 1980s a true mass culture emerged in which the consumer market for symbolic goods was consolidated everywhere. This new reality was instrumental in the return to democracy even though military cen-sorship and control strove to avoid it. There is evidence that in both Brazil and Chile, for instance, television served as a great articulating means for the construction of a hegemonic (in the Gramscian sense) democratic mass view which eventually forced the military out of office. TV Globo in Brazil, having been basically pro-military, even-tually sided with the idea of direct elections and from April 1984 vig-orously reported the pro-democracy rallies and supported the civilian candidate Tancredo Neves, who was eventually elected.

In Chile in 1987, Channel 13 managed to report the Pope's visit to the country in a manner which opened up a daily discussion which included members from the democratic opposition to the military rulers. Even more decisively, in the campaign for the 1988 plebiscite, which General Pinochet eventually lost, television played a major role by scheduling fifteen minutes of political propaganda for the demo-cratic opposition and another fifteen minutes for the military government every day. Even though the government forced the sched-uling of the programme very late at night in order to reduce the audi-ence, it achieved an enormous success in ratings and became crucial for the opposition's victory. Thus a mass communication medium such as television became instrumental in the construction of a hege-monic democratic worldview.[63]

The 1990s in Latin America continued to witness an enormous expansion of television and other communications technologies such as cable and satellite TV, video-cassette recorders, etc. An interesting aspect of the Latin American consumption of television in the 1990s is the fact that locally produced programmes outperformed US-produced programmes in the ratings. In Brazil seven of the top ten programmes in terms of home ratings in the first four months of 1997 were nationally made, and among them the highest two belonged to *telenovelas*.[64] In Chile, in 1998, more than 60 per cent of the 50,000 hours of transmitted programmes were nationally made. If prime time is taken into consideration (a time when more than 70 per cent of television sets are turned on), then during certain months of the same year 81 per cent of programmes were nationally made.[65] In Mexico, Argentina and Colombia something similar occurs. Television has also become the leading source of information about the news for Latin Americans. A survey carried out between 1994 and 1996 in nineteen Latin American countries showed that 87 per cent of the people obtained news from television, 65 per cent from newspapers and 41 per cent from radio.[66] As Marín has argued, the consolidation of television in Latin America 'has radically altered the conditions under which public debate takes place . . . the development of television has created a new kind of "publicness", more open and accessible.'[67]

In literature new trends are apparent. Of course the old guard who became famous in the 1960s continues to produce novels that sell very well all over the world, but in the 1990s it was possible to detect the emergence of younger authors writing novels and stories with a different perspective. They are authors who have been much more exposed to the impact of neoliberalism, globalization, the market economy, increasing mediazation of culture, depoliticization and modernization. They were born in the late 1950s or early 1960s, so they did not experience the turbulence and ideological hopes of the 1960s, nor could they do much when the era of dictatorships started. Politics is not one of their main concerns. They were shaped by the newly emergent individualism. All this is reflected in their outlook towards life and in the kind of literature they write. They no longer want to continue with the tradition of magical realism, nor are they concerned with nature, the rural society, left-wing politics or Latin American identity.

It is put like this by Fuguet and Gómez, the editors of a new compilation of stories and members of this generation: 'the great theme of Latin American identity (who are we?) seemed to give way to the theme of personal identity (who am I?). The stories of *McOndo* are centred on private and individual realities. We suppose that this is one of the legacies of the world privatizing fever'.[68] It is interesting to note that Fuguet started his literary career as an editor of a supplement of *El Mercurio*, the most important and most right-wing newspaper in Chile. The writers of *McOndo* are certainly not the top writers of the day and their literary quality may be questioned, but they show a new trend: they are all very conscious that they no longer live in a rural society and want to avoid 'reductionist essentialisms' and 'political correctness'.[69] They accept that they live in a world of McDonalds, malls and computers, that present-day culture is a mass hybrid culture controlled by the media. And they consider all of that as Latin American as the supposedly more genuine Indian, left-wing, folkloric or rural traditions. They write about modern life in the cities, about middle or upper classes.

This is a feature which is also shared by the more established novelists of this period: Fontaine and Contreras. The protagonists in their novels and stories come from the upper classes, like for instance the neoliberal economist in Arturo Fontaine's *Oir su voz*, or the retired doctor and womanizer who lives in a fashionable area in Gonzalo Contreras' *El Nadador*. Equally the Argentinian Juan Forn's novel *Frivolidad* features the editors of a Buenos Aires magazine who have holidays in the fashionable Punta del Este and have complicated personal lives. Fontaine has been mentioned as a good example of the new Latin American novel by Carlos Fuentes, yet he is politically more to the right than the old guard, perhaps with the exception of Vargas Llosa, and feels equally comfortable writing about Hayek's neoliberal revolution as writing fiction.[70] It can be said, therefore, that the fiction written by these authors, as much for its private topics and depoliticization as for its new kind of upper-class protagonists, is helping to shape the new forms of identity which are emerging out of the neoliberal period.

8
Key Elements of Latin American Modernity and Identity

The combined construction of modernity and identity in Latin America, which I have explored historically in six stages, has produced certain specific features and characteristics that can be presented more systematically. These cultural features should not be essentialized; they are the result of history and they can change, be modified or even disappear altogether. But they still have an important presence today and are the results of a specific historical evolution. I have selected those characteristics which seem to me most relevant and which mark a contrast with other trajectories to modernity. I make no claim that they are exhaustive.

Clientelism, traditionalism and weak civil society

The first feature I would like to refer to is clientelism or cultural and political personalism. As I mentioned earlier (pp. 100–4), this feature arose from very precise historical circumstances but its effects have remained up to the present. I differ in this view from Manuel Barrera, who has argued that with the kind of state that has emerged out of years of authoritarianism and neoliberalism in Chile, clientelism has disappeared.[1] I think his arguments only point to a probable diminution of clientelism, but by no means its disappearance. Recruitment of civil servants, university lecturers and mass media journalists continues to be done through clientelistic or personalist networks of friends and supporters. The processes of public competition for a job are absent, scarcely developed or work in a purely nominal fashion when procedures are 'fixed' to favour a preselected individual. Clientelistic recruitment flourishes in Latin America and shows the absence of normal channels of social mobility as much as it does the narrowness and sought-after nature of posts in political and cultural environments.

Education, acquired skills and personal achievements are not enough to secure access to certain political or cultural jobs. Well-placed 'contacts', 'godfathers' or 'friends' are required to facilitate entry. Because the system depends on the patronage of certain individuals who exercise institutional power, it secures the personal loyalty of the recruited and favours institutional immobility. Thus veritable institutional fiefdoms are created which, because of their discriminatory character, are almost impenetrable for those who do not belong to the group that controls them. By paraphrasing Habermas in a slightly different sense, one could speak of a true refeudalization of cultural and state institutions.[2]

A second feature could be called ideological traditionalism. In putting forward his theory of transition to modernity, Gino Germani, as we have already seen, spoke in the 1960s of the 'fusion effect' by means of which modern values could be reinterpreted in contexts different from developed societies, with the result that traditional structures were reinforced.[3] A particular form of this fusion effect was ideological traditionalism, when leading groups accepted and promoted changes necessary for development in the economic sphere, but rejected changes required for such a process in other spheres.[4]

In late modernity a similar phenomenon takes place in that certain leading groups advocate total freedom in the economic sphere but appeal to traditional moral values in other respects. Thus they emphasize an almost religious respect for authority and order, the traditional family and the national heritage, or they express doubts about democracy and oppose, for instance, divorce laws or the decriminalization of women's adultery. A good example of this is the position in Chile, where until 1995 adultery was a crime for which women alone could be punished, and where to this very day a divorce law has not been passed due to Catholic and conservative opposition. Renato Cristi has argued convincingly that conservative thought in Chile never opposed liberalism as such but rather 'the democratic element which took over its reservoir of ideas from the nineteenth century onwards'.[5] These fusions are not exclusive to the developing world. The emergence of a New Right in the United States and the United Kingdom has been also characterized by the way in which it has combined traditional conservative attitudes about authority, Victorian values, internal order and external security with a new emphasis on free markets.[6]

However, traditionalism in Latin America has stronger institutional bases than in Europe or the United States. One of them is the extraordinary power and influence of the more traditional Catholic Church over political and legislative matters. This can be explained by the privileged role which the Catholic Church has played since colonial times in the maintenance of social and political order. As I will show on pages 195–6, the church and religious mechanisms played a central role in the exercise of authority and the political control of people.

A significant phenomenon, which differentiates Latin American modernity from others, is the lack of autonomy and development of civil society. In Latin America civil society (the private sphere of individuals, classes and organizations regulated by civil law) is weak, insufficiently developed and very dependent on the dictates of the state and politics. This is one of the consequences of the absence of strong and autonomous bourgeois classes developing the economy and culture of society independently from politics and any state support. Brunner argues, with justification, that in contrast to the modernity of central countries, Latin American modernity suffers from a 'voracity of politics which swallows everything and behind which everyone seeks protection or justification: entrepreneurs, intellectuals, universities, trade unions, social organizations, clerics, the armed forces'.[7]

For instance, it is significant that some universities, institutes and even the media may lose a good number, or the best, of their members each time that there is a change of government and when recruitment of civil servants takes place in order to replace those who are leaving. At the same time, it is not unusual to see the functionaries of the outgoing government using their power to make advance plans for posts in particular universities or institutes, which in this way are further 'colonized' by certain political tendencies or power groups which only recruit members or supporters of their own sector. Neither is it rare to find that a good number of research and consultancy institutions depend almost exclusively on services rendered under contract to various state organizations. Many cultural centres are directly created by local governments and managed by the political majority controlling them. Hence politics exercises a disproportionate influence on civil society and cultural institutions. The lack of an autonomous civil society has been especially noted in the case of Chile by Jocelyn-Holt, who has argued that it was prevented from flourishing by the traditional social order in the nineteenth century and by the overwhelming presence of the state in the twentieth century.[8]

Politics, democracy and human rights

It is also necessary to refer to the fragility of political institutions in Latin American countries. Since their independence Latin America has appeared in the eyes of the world as a continent of revolutions and caudillos, military coups and conspiracies, where the institutional order is permanently under threat.[9] The wave of military dictatorships which began in the 1960s and persisted through the 1970s and part of the 1980s did not even spare countries like Chile which had a reputation for institutional stability. True, Latin America is now going through a period of return to democracy, but the symptoms of institutional weakness remain quite evident throughout Latin America, especially in Argentina, Venezuela, Colombia, Peru and almost all Central America.

A relatively recent feature of Latin American modernity, especially the Chilean one, is the relative depoliticization of society. Military dictatorships sought to depoliticize society by eliminating elections, abolishing political parties and closing down parliaments. Their policies of exclusion and violations of human rights, however, brought in the long term the opposite result: society became more intensely politicized against military governments. This led to a search for crucial agreements and coalitions which would allow a return to democracy. One of the conditions for this search for democratic consensus was to make the economic sphere autonomous in order to protect it from the ups and downs of everyday political discussion. In future the economic system was to be self-regulating in tune with the laws of the market, and a consensual economic policy acting on macroeconomic variables was to be introduced.

As Cousiño and Valenzuela have put it, 'once the economic system is made autonomous, politics loses the capacity to keep watch on and intervene in the economy and, therefore, abandons its claim to place itself in the perspective of totality.'[10] The consequence of this is that politics itself is converted into another functional self-centred system which turns away from intervening in the basic course of the economy. Hence something that had been an immense arena of disagreement and political disputation gets left out of discussion. It can be concluded from this that Latin America's democratization, mediated by the autonomy of the economy, has resulted in a considerable and significant depoliticization of society. For instance, the military dictatorship in Chile started the process of reorganizing the economy, but this could be consolidated only with the redemocratization of the country by the end of the 1980s: the price of the new stability was the increasing autonomy of, and the loss of political control over, the economy.

A very recent feature of Latin American culture is the revaluation of and renewed interest in political democracy and human rights by intellectuals and popular majorities. Paradoxically, this has contributed to the relative depoliticization of society because it has led to wide agreements between formerly antagonistic political forces and has refocused the interest of most social scientists. The years of bloody dictatorships in Brazil, Chile, Argentina, Uruguay, Paraguay and Bolivia, not to speak of the more or less permanent situation of repression in Central America, radically changed the perception of social scientists, many of them persecuted and exiled. Their focus of analysis switched from strategies for social change and development to problems of the political system, democracy and human rights.[11] In spite of the weaknesses of democratic institutions in Latin America, in spite of corruption, terrorism and human rights violations, the democratic system has recently emerged as the only legitimate framework for political action. Even in Central America, where authoritarianism, open or otherwise, has been endemic for many years, there has been a strong movement towards democracy in the 1990s.

Authoritarianism, legalistic lack of principle and masked racism

A cultural aspect which has survived from colonial days, at times in a moderate form, at other times in an exacerbated form, is authoritarianism. This is a trend which persists in the political field, in the administration of public and private organizations, in family life and, in general, in Latin American culture, which concedes an extraordinary importance to the role of and respect for authority. Its origin is clearly related to three centuries of colonial life in which a strong Indo-Iberian cultural pole was constituted which accentuated religious monopoly and political authoritarianism. As de Imaz has put it, 'for three centuries there existed a clear relationship between political authoritarianism and the legitimating role of the Inquisition.'[12]

Flores Galindo has documented how in the seventeenth century the persistent struggles of religious congregations against idolatry in the

central sierra of Peru had a connotation of political control: 'the relative precariousness of the military system forced an apparent hypertrophy of religious mechanisms, so that in that way, through fervour
or more frequently fear, control over men could be secured.'[13] In spite
of the democratizing influences of Enlightenment thought which
certainly achieved some partial moderation of the authoritarianism
of the Indo-Iberian cultural pole from independence onwards, its cultural force has not easily been extinguished in Latin American social-
political life.

In the particular case of Chile, various authors have highlighted
the historically crucial role of Portales' strong and authoritarian
government in the formation of the Chilean state.[14] Alfredo Jocelyn-
Holt differs from them in suggesting that it is not so much the state
or the figure of Portales as the domination of the landowning ruling
class and the submission of the people that have to be underlined:
what he calls 'the weight of the night'.[15] All the same, he also
acknowledges that as a result of this the nineteenth century left a
legacy of authoritarianism, which has not yet been overcome.[16] It was
Portales' conception that, due to a lack of republican virtues, democracy had to be postponed and unconditional obedience to a strong
authority had to be established. Laws and constitutions were not to
hinder the action of such an authority in favour of the public good.
This conception divided the country between the good (men of order)
and the bad (conspirators to whom the rigour of the law had to be
applied).[17] It is not surprising that General Pinochet's regime should
have frequently invoked it.

A feature that also comes from colonial times and has survived in
different ways until the present is a peculiar approach to principles,
laws and norms whereby they tend to be upheld in formal terms but
flouted in practice if they go against people's personal interests. The
origins of this tendency are multiple. On the one hand, it may have
to do with the plight of the Indians, who were forced to convert to
Catholicism under duress. In order to save their lives many of them
formally accepted the new religion but secretly continued to practise
their own, often using the same Catholic ceremony or liturgical cel-
ebration for their own purposes. On the other hand, a similar form
of pretending was also practised by the Spanish conquistadors whenever they were faced with royal decrees and laws, which in themselves might have been very just and good, but which, having been
drawn up too far away, could not be practically implemented without
causing damage to the conquistadors' interests. This was expressed
by the traditional formula 'se acata pero no se cumple', which in
respect of any such royal command roughly meant 'it is obeyed but

not implemented'. This happened invariably with respect to legislation intended to protect the Indians from the abuses of the conquistadors.

Almost without a doubt the king and his administrators knew that this was going on, but they too would turn a blind eye in the belief that the crown's own interest would be affected if they demanded total compliance with the royal edicts. Marcos García de la Huerta has suggested that this chain of complicity in the flouting of the law might also have reached the highest levels of the ecclesiastical hierarchy.[18] The interesting thing about these procedures is that the unwillingness to comply with the law in practice did not bring into question its validity or legitimacy, but on the contrary, respect for the norm had to be proclaimed. Principles are transgressed but in such a way that they are simultaneously recognized, thus keeping up the appearance of respect. This is crucial because in this way the principle of authority, so important in Latin America, as we have just seen, is not violated. In this way this feature accounts for both excessive legalism, the formal and ritualistic adherence to the norm, and readiness to ignore it in practice. Examples of this can be found everywhere in contemporary Latin America. It can be seen, for instance, in the way in which Latin American Catholics profess their obedience to the Pope's teachings about contraception but overwhelmingly make use of it, often with the complicity of local priests. It can also be seen in the wonderful declarations about human rights which appear in many regional constitutions while at the same time the governments making them systematically violate human rights in practice.

Another important feature is masked racism. The existence of racism in Latin America is well documented even though it is a relatively neglected area of social sciences and generally it is not perceived as an important social problem. It is clear, though, that from very early days there has been in Latin America an exaggerated valuation of 'whiteness' and a negative vision of Indians and blacks. For example, in the case of Peru, Flores Galindo has observed:

> In Peru nobody would define himself or herself as a racist. Nevertheless, racial categories not only tinge but also sometimes condition our social perceptions. They are present in the make-up of professional groups, in the messages transmitted by the media or in the terms of beauty contests . . . racism exists notwithstanding the fact that racial terms are suppressed in the procedures of public identification and do not have official circulation. Yet a masked and even denied phenomenon, does not cease to be real.[19]

Equally, in the case of Mexico, Raúl Béjar says that 'it is a commonplace to say that in this country there is no racial discrimination' yet it is possible to assert that 'prejudice has grown in the cultural history of Mexico' and that this affects 'especially the Indian or quasi Indian . . . blacks . . . and Chinese'.[20]

It is well known that various governments in Latin America attempted to 'improve the race' by means of 'whitening' policies which favoured European immigration. There also exists spatial segregation whereby Indian areas are the poorest and most abandoned, and the shantytowns in cities contain a higher proportion of people with darker skins, be they Indians, mestizos, mulattos or blacks. There is no equality of opportunity for them. Some surviving Indian groups constitute true internal colonies, geographically segregated, oppressed by mestizos, and subject to special laws and forms of administration. Nevertheless, the very fact of *mestizaje* and the fact that in many cases social class coincides with gradations in skin colour (the darker the skin the lower the class) leads frequently to a denial of racism.

This even has a base in the social sciences, which have often underlined the differences between the Spanish treatment of Indians and blacks and the British treatment of them. Gilberto Freyre, in his classic book *Casa Grande e Senzala* (*The Master and the Slaves*, 1946),[21] argued that the treatment of slaves in Brazil was softer than in North America, especially due to closer, even sexual, relationships between masters and slaves in the hacienda. Many historians and social analysts have subsequently noted that whereas in North America the white settlers imposed a separation between themselves and Indians or blacks, in Latin America a wide process of *mestizaje* took place, thus producing a continuum of racial gradations. From this the myth arose that in Latin America a 'racial democracy' existed and that racism was a problem of other countries.[22] This idea continues to be believed today and its prevalence is shown by the fact that, with the exception of some degrees in anthropology, there is a significant absence of courses and studies on Latin American race problems in social science degrees.

Exclusion and solidarity

One of the most decisive features of Latin American modernity is the wide extent of social marginality and the informal economy. In spite of the obvious progress of modernization processes and the dynamism of capitalism in the area, they have never been able to reach most of the population. A high proportion of the economically active population has no access to formal productive work during their lives and they therefore live in a context of exclusion and marginality, in casual petty trade or petty criminal activities. In some countries such as Peru, it is estimated that more than 50 per cent of the economically active population come into this category. About 25 per cent of the population of Latin America's major cities have no proper jobs, earn no regular income, and live in slums located on the periphery of big cities, in conditions of extreme poverty, thus constituting an underclass.

The emergence of urban underclasses is linked in Latin America to the process of urbanization which started in the 1930s and has accelerated since the 1960s. Between 1960 and 1990 the urban population in Latin America grew from 49.2 per cent to 71.5 per cent, and in the most urbanized countries such as Chile, Argentina and Uruguay it grew from 78.8 per cent to 85.9 per cent.[23] Unlike the process of urbanization in Europe, the urbanization process in Latin America is not the result of a dynamic expansion of internal industrialization which acts as a pole of attraction. The migration to the cities is rather the result of backward and poor conditions in the countryside. This means that in Latin American cities the tertiary sector of the economy is the one that grows faster, together with the so-called informal sector. But, on the whole, the economy is unable to absorb the new contingents of the economically active who look for a job each year. So there are enormous numbers of unemployed and underemployed people whose existence is usually concealed by statistics that consider as employed anyone who has worked for more than a few hours in the past month.

Another feature of Latin American modernity, which compounds the problems raised by marginality and poverty, is the fact that Latin America has never had a welfare state that was nearly as universal and efficient as the European one. In many countries of the area social security and unemployment benefits really do not exist or are so inadequate that nobody can survive on them. Furthermore, whatever welfare did once exist has been under constant threat since the 1980s, due to the neoliberal economic policies being followed throughout Latin America, which advocate cuts – sometimes very drastic ones – in public expenditure. Chile is a paradigmatic case because Pinochet's government made an overnight cut of roughly 30 per cent in the education and health budgets. The recovery from those cuts under the democratic regimes that followed has been painfully slow.

An important feature of Latin American modernity and identity can be derived from the last two traits: marginality and lack of social security make it imperative for many people suffering from poverty and social exclusion to organize a complex system of activities in order to survive. Hence the emergence of the informal economy, of private organizations such as work cooperatives and popular kitchens, but also a series of solidarity, reciprocity and mutual aid practices. This does not necessarily indicate the emergence of an alternative rationality to modern instrumental rationality, as many authors in the 1980s suggested;[24] on the contrary, the informal economy can even be considered as an expression of the same rationality in so far as it resorts to the only means that make a precarious survival possible in very difficult circumstances. There is no doubt that solidarity, reciprocity and mutual aid are important values, but they do not amount to a different rationality which can be said to be Latin America's alone. Besides, they cannot be considered as proper replacements for equality of opportunity, access to productive jobs and social security.

The phenomenon of exclusion as much as the phenomenon of solidarity has important effects on the processes of identity construction in vast sectors of the Latin American population. The former has clearly negative effects in that individuals get used to the idea that they are surrounded by a hostile and unfair world in which, however great the personal effort, positive results are never guaranteed. The link between personal action and result is broken; the external world appears as uncontrollable, and therefore everything that happens tends to be conceived in terms of fate or luck. When someone learns that his or her efforts are useless, a disposition may emerge which in social psychology has been called the 'learned hopelessness syndrome',[25] characterized by a fatalist conception of life, a lack of project and a passive attitude, all derived from a situation in which the individual has ceased to believe that his or her personal effort can change or influence the things that happen.

On the other hand, the experience of solidarity and communal participation in the resolution of problems may partially restore trust by showing the external world is not always hostile and threatening and that common actions can get positive results for all. These experiences return to individuals the sense that what happens is related to their own actions and that they have an important responsibility in the construction of their own destiny. Collective actions in solidarity restore a sense of individual value and relink individual effort to positive result. From learned hopelessness it is then possible to move to learned hope. The lack of equality of opportunity, access to jobs and social security for vast sections of Latin American society has made solidarity and popular collective organizations for survival an almost permanent feature of Latin American modernity and identity.

The religious factor

Finally, religion is a crucial dimension of Latin American identity.[26] There are at least three important religious sources in Latin America: the African, the Indian and the Christian. The complexity of the religious phenomenon and the variety of religious identities in Latin America are of such magnitude that I cannot hope to deal with them adequately in such a short space. This is why I have chosen to concentrate on religious identities of Christian origin, which are undoubtedly the most important ones since they cover the vast majority of the Latin American population.

As I showed in chapter 2, during the colonial time a religious identity was constructed in Latin America which had authoritarian and intolerant features, which opposed the scientific spirit and privileged external rites. The presence of this Catholic element in Latin American identity was very deep and persistent and in many ways still shows its strength in a number of respects. Paradoxically, at the very time this profoundly Catholic traditional identity was being constituted in Latin America, in Europe the beginning of modernity brought about a break in the unity or homogeneity of the religious factor: as a consequence, in the long term religious cultural identities began to decline, a process that has been called secularization. Given the centrality of Catholicism for the Latin American identity of the time it is not surprising that the process of secularization started much later and has been slower than in Europe. Nevertheless, its advance can be noticed in the progressive displacement of Catholicism as the central element of the region's cultural identity. From being the principal nucleus of all aspects of culture, Catholicism became a particular identity, one cultural element among many others of various kinds. In this sense secularization in Latin America has not meant the end of religion or religious sentiments, but rather the loss of the centrality of a narrow Catholic religious worldview and the arrival of pluralism.

This process can be seen over the last fifty years through many indicators such as the diminishing number of Catholics, the marked fall in religious practices and their frequency, the increasing prevalence of opinions in conflict with the traditional doctrine of the church and the diminishing number of priests. Just as an example, in Santiago, the Chilean capital, 89.9 per cent of individuals identified themselves as Catholics in 1950. By 1970 this figure had fallen to 81.7 per cent, by 1992 to 76.1 per cent and by 1997 to 72 per cent. Fewer than 25 per cent of Catholics go to mass every Sunday. About 70 per cent never go to confession; 63.1 per cent accept premarital sexual relations; 53.3 per cent accept cohabiting without the sacrament; 81.3 per cent favour the use of birth control devices; and 73 per cent are in favour of legalizing divorce.[27] The number of priests went down from 2,784 in 1969 to 2,165 in 1994, a fall of 22 per cent.[28]

The traditional Catholic identity in Latin America has been challenged not just by the process of secularization but also by the construction of new religious identities. In the 1960s there came first the movement of renovation and openness to the modern world which grew around Vatican Council II. Second, there emerged in the 1970s a more radical popular movement of left-wing political persuasion: the 'base communities' movement which was supported by a theology of liberation and which wanted a renewal of the church to put it at the service of justice and of the oppressed. This movement favoured a different church, committed to serving the poorest and most oppressed sectors of society, a church going back to a more genuine sense of community by means of the creation of small groups (base communities) of workers presided over by local leaders in shantytowns and poor sectors of the city. They wanted a church committed to social justice and human rights. Even the documents of the Latin American Council of Bishops, influenced by Vatican Council II, countenanced this position by arguing in favour of an 'option for the poor' (for instance, the 1968 Medellín document). In the face of a wave of dictatorships, this movement struggled for human rights and in certain countries like Chile and Brazil it represented the only articulate form of political resistance. Many of its members, including bishops and priests, were murdered in Chile, Brazil and Central America.

There are doubts today about the true extent achieved by this liberation theology movement. At its height in Santiago in 1985 there were about three hundred Christian base communities,[29] which might have represented about 10,000 people. In Brazil some estimates put the number of communities at between 80,000 and 100,000, thus involving between 2 and 4 million people.[30] Other estimates lower these figures to 30,000 communities with fewer than a million people. Berryman has argued that there has been an exaggeration about the number and influence of these base communities and that after years of work they existed in no more than 10 per cent of all Latin American parishes, thus involving a minority of Catholics. Even more remarkable is the ease with which they disappeared. Berryman questions whether they truly responded to the religious needs of the poor people or, rather, reflected the political radicalization of some priests and theologians who sought a fairer society and a more committed church. Even if this is so, the movement achieved quite a degree of publicity and its academic weight, represented by many important books, was always greater than its real popular impact. It did not survive because, to a large extent, the official church systematically repressed it and marginalized it, by persecuting its theologians and dismantling the base communities, as happened in São Paulo after the retirement of Cardinal Paulo Evaristo Arns.

In the third place, there emerged a Pentecostal movement in the 1980s and 1990s which was also rooted in the poorest sections of society, but it was politically more conservative and focused on personal conversion and a change of lifestyle. Its advance has been spectacular on all fronts, as much in the number of pastors and new members as in the number of churches and the frequency of religious practices. There is a grain of truth in what Caio Fabio d'Araujo, a Brazilian Presbyterian pastor, declared to the *New York Times*: 'the Catholic Church opted for the poor, but the poor opted for the Evangelicals.'[31] The Pentecostal identity has been in practice more successful and lasting than the more liberal Catholic identities. This is due partly to its great capacity for penetration among the poor, and partly because the more radical Catholic identities have been successfully resisted and dismantled by the Vatican and the hierarchy of bishops.

The biggest growth of Pentecostals has occurred in Brazil, Chile, Nicaragua, Guatemala and Costa Rica. While in Chile Pentecostals represented around 4 per cent in 1950, by 1992 they had risen to 11.2 per cent[32] and by 1997 to around 15 per cent. In Brazil, the number of Evangelicals is estimated at around 20 million out of 150 million inhabitants, that is to say around 14 or 15 per cent. In Central America, Evangelicals are estimated to number around 10 per cent of the population.[33] But big concentrations occur in Guatemala (30 per cent), Nicaragua (20 per cent) and Costa Rica (16 per cent).[34] In total Martin calculates that in Latin America there are 40 million evangelical believers.[35] Although these figures are lower than the numbers of Catholics, the Evangelicals outstrip the Catholics in their commitment and frequency of religious practice. In Santiago, more than 55 per cent of Evangelicals (as against 24.8 per cent of Catholics) consider themselves practising members of their churches.

The weekly frequency of attendance at services is also much greater than among the Catholics (62.7 per cent as against 23 per cent).[36] It is also a fact that in many countries the number of evangelical pastors is higher than or at least equal to the number of Catholic priests. In 1985 in Brazil there were 15,000 Protestant pastors as against 13,176 priests.[37]

Even within Protestantism the Pentecostal advance represents the emergence of a new identity, different from that of historical churches: it is more conservative in politics and in its rules about daily life, has a marked charismatic emphasis which accentuates the gifts from the Spirit, speaking in languages, healing, etc., has deep roots in the poorest layers of the population and has a great capability for the utilization of modern means of communication. Hollenweger sees it as a 'phenomenon typical of the popular classes' culture: it is an oral religion which expresses itself in symbols – singing, dance – and emotion, preconceptual, from which an explicit systematized theology cannot be expected.'[38]

Nevertheless, there are distinctive theological features. Pentecostal theology is closely linked to the experience of exclusion and marginality, to the experience of poverty, unemployment and disease. As Sepúlveda puts it, 'when a Pentecostal says: "this world offers nothing but damnation" s/he is not making a dogmatic affirmation but narrating or putting forward the theme of his/her own experience.' The insistence on the power of the Holy Spirit is a recognition of its 'multiple manifestations . . . from angelical languages to simple joy . . . the certainty of the closeness and live presence of a forgiving and welcoming God . . . it is a form of social and popular reappropriation of God's power in the face of the Catholic church's sacramental appropriation and the historical Protestantism's rationalistic appropriation.' The insistence on the healing by the Holy Spirit also has to do with the inaccessibility of medicine to the poorest strata.[39] Hence Pentecostalism shows an identity different from traditional religious identities in Latin America.

Pentecostal pastors have little theological education but are close to the people, seldom foreigners like so many Catholic priests, and endowed with a great pastoral zeal. In Brazil many of them are mulattos or black. They all dress in suit and tie. Their strength lies in transmitting a simple message of personal salvation. Yet the rules of daily life which converted members must follow are hard and demanding: they cannot go to the movies or drink alcohol or go to the beach or swimming pool. They cannot sell cigarettes or lottery tickets, or work in motels or stadiums, etc.[40] The end result of this is a different and frugal mode of life, a responsible work ethic, and mutual aid and fraternal support among brothers and sisters. The Pentecostal identity emphasizes a sense of belonging and also of opposition to 'the world'. In a context of injustice, oppression and poverty, 'the congregation was partly a substitute, for some also a model, for what could become a society with orderly personal relations.'[41]

Several explanations have been offered for the extraordinary success of Pentecostalism in Latin America. Many of them use the old Weberian scheme which sees Latin America as a region in transition from traditional society to modernity. Lalive, for instance, has argued that Pentecostalism offers a refuge to the poor by allowing them to recreate within the congregation a kind of traditional society which gives them security and strength to bear the excluding features of the new modern society in the making.[42] David Martin in his turn puts forward the thesis that Pentecostalism is the vanguard in the religious field of a vaster penetration of Anglo-Saxon values in Latin America. Although he does not say it in so many words, his work gives us to understand that South American underdevelopment is to a great extent the product of a Catholic-Iberian culture which has impeded the progress of modernity. The penetration of Anglo-Saxon culture and Pentecostalism in Latin America would allow its change towards modernity and development. The expansion of evangelical Christianity has signalled a break in a monolithic system whereby the Catholic religion was more significant in providing a sense of national identity than it was in its ability to bring about personal conversion.[43]

The Weberian thesis does not explain very well, however, why it is that Pentecostals and not historical Protestants have succeeded in attracting the poorest urban sectors. This suggests that as much in Brazil as in Chile there must have been internal factors within Pentecostalism with explanatory importance to account for their impact on the poor. As Sepúlveda has argued in the Chilean case, it is necessary to focus attention on Chilean Pentecostalism's capacity to translate the Protestant message into the forms of expression of the local popular culture.[44] The same can surely be said of Brazilian Pentecostalism.

The traditional Catholicism, confronted by the dual challenge of secularization and the new religious identities, both Catholic and Pentecostal, has responded with a turn towards the internal disciplining of liberation theologians, the dismantling of base communities and a return to more traditional postures, as much in the appointment of bishops as in doctrinal issues. In recent years the Vatican has sought to reorient in a more narrow and controlled manner the teachings of Vatican Council II. Beyond these responses, Berryman asks himself with some disappointment why it is that Catholics do not appear to recognize the success of Pentecostalism and do not feel the need to confront this challenge in a more active manner. He thinks that many Catholics, including the hierarchy, lack a clear conscience about the magnitude of the challenge, or perhaps do not want to face uncomfortable facts. It could also be that most Catholics feel confident that, whatever anybody may think, Catholicism is still everybody's cultural environment in Latin America, as it was in times of Christendom.[45]

This spontaneous, rather complacent answer of traditional Catholics has been backed by more rigorous and elaborated attempts to justify discursively the possibility that Catholicism might abandon its status of a particular identity to recover its position as a necessary substratum of Latin American cultural identity. The very essence of Latin American identity would then have an inevitable Catholic seal against which Evangelicals could not prevail. In other words, Protestantism would be inherently alien to Latin American cultural identity. In this way, there would be a justification for a necessary return to a situation of Christendom, which would be prefigured in the inner being of Latin American culture. Morandé's position, which I explored in chapter 6 and which conceives of popular religiosity as the reservoir of cultural identity in Latin America, belongs to this attempt. Yet even if the chances of this position prevailing or coming true are really negligible, it is still true to say that the impact of Christian religions, particularly Catholicism and Pentecostalism, upon Latin American culture is still very important.

Conclusion

Looking back at the Latin American trajectory to modernity, it is possible to affirm that it has been an important part of the process of identity construction: it cannot be put in opposition to an already-formed, essential and immovable cultural identity, nor does it entail the acquisition of an alien identity (Anglo-Saxon, for instance). Modernity as much as cultural identity are processes which are being historically constructed and which do not necessarily entail a radical disjunction, even if there may be tensions between them. The features of Latin American modernity which I have explored constitute, for better or worse, important elements of Latin American cultural identity today. But of course, nothing prevents their critical appraisal or their change in the future.

Nevertheless, there has been a manifest tendency among Latin American intellectuals to consider modernity as something external and in opposition to identity. The brief historical exploration carried out in chapters 2 to 7 about the ways in which modernity and identity have been constructed in practice, and theoretically presented by Latin American intellectuals, clearly shows the oscillation between the prominence given to one or the other in alternate periods – modernity in periods of expansion, identity in times of crisis. No doubt, as I suggested in the Introduction, part of the problem is due to the double failure of not distinguishing different trajectories to modernity and not considering cultural identity as historically constructed and changing.

Thus the polarity between modernity and identity has continued to be present in the Latin American cultural perspective while in practice modernity and cultural identity continue to be constructed in close connection with one another. At times of economic expansion, identity does not cease to have a presence. Equally, at times of crisis modernity does not cease to expand. During the alternating periods that I distinguished, identity and modernity were still being constructed even if they were not mentioned. In the depths of the 1930s Depression and of the 1980s 'lost decade', when identity problems were the main discussion issue, major modernizing transformations were begun. At the height of the postwar and neoliberal expansion periods, cultural identity acquired important new connotations. This dialectic between modernity and identity, never entirely resolved, is ultimately the major feature of Latin American culture.

Notes

Introduction

1 See Fernando Ainsa, *Identidad Cultural de Iberoamérica en su Narrativa* (Madrid: Gredos, 1986), pp. 439–57. In the case of this book, and all others where no English language edition is cited, I have translated any extracts myself.
2 For a brief account of modern European thought on Latin America see chapter 2.
3 See Mario Sambarino, *Identidad, tradición y autenticidad*, Centro de Estudios Latinoamericanos (Caracas: Rómulo Gallego, 1980), pp. 51–79.
4 See Darcy Ribeiro, *Las Américas y la Civilización* (Caracas: Biblioteca Ayacucho, 1968), p. 69.
5 See Sambarino, *Identidad, tradición y autenticidad*, p. 52.
6 Carlos Fuentes, *Valiente Mundo Nuevo: Épica, Utopía y Mito en la Novela Hispanoamericana* (Madrid: Narrativa Mondadori, 1990), pp. 12–13.
7 See Octavio Paz, *El Ogro Filantrópico* (Barcelona: Seix Barral, 1990), p. 64.
8 See Claudio Véliz, *The New World of the Gothic Fox: Culture and Economy in English and Spanish America* (Berkeley: University of California Press, 1994).
9 J. J. Brunner, *Cartografías de la Modernidad* (Santiago: Dolmen, 1994), p. 144. Cristián Parker has also spoken of a 'peripheral modernization' in Latin America. See *Otra Lógica en América Latina: Religión Popular y Modernización Capitalista* (Santiago: Fondo de Cultura Económica, 1993), ch. 3.

10   Kobena Mercer, 'Welcome to the Jungle: Identity and Diversity in Post-modern Politics', in J. Rutherford (ed.), *Identity, Community, Culture, Difference* (London: Lawrence and Wishart, 1990), p. 43.
11   See Guillermo Bonfil Batalla's excellent analysis of the Mexican case in 'El Patrimonio Cultural de México: un Laberinto de Significados', *Folklore Americano*, no 47 (Jan.–Jun. 1989), pp. 125–45.
12   See Ainsa, *Identidad Cultural de Iberoamérica*, pp. 23–4.

Chapter 1   Modernity and Identity

1   I. Kant, *Political Writings* (Cambridge: Cambridge University Press, 1992), p. 54.
2   G. W. F. Hegel, *Philosophy of Right*, trans. T. M. Knox (Oxford: Oxford University Press, 1980), p. 286.
3   See on this J. Habermas, *The Philosophical Discourse of Modernity* (Cambridge, Mass.: MIT Press, 1987), p. 83.
4   P. Wagner, *A Sociology of Modernity, Liberty and Discipline* (London: Routledge, 1994), p. 8.
5   A. Touraine, *Crítica de la Modernidad* (Buenos Aires: Fondo de Cultura Económica, 1994), p. 205.
6   Ibid., p. 13.
7   M. Weber, 'Science as a Vocation', in *From Max Weber*, ed. H. H. Gerth and C. Wright Mills (London: Routledge and Kegan Paul, 1970), p. 139.
8   Habermas, *The Philosophical Discourse of Modernity*, pp. 4–5.
9   Quoted in D. Frisby, *Fragments of Modernity* (Cambridge: Polity Press, 1985), p. 207.
10   Z. Bauman, 'The Fall of the Legislator', in T. Docherty (ed.), *Post-modernism, A Reader* (Hemel Hempstead: Harvester Wheatsheaf, 1993), pp. 128–9.
11   Enrique Dussel, 'Eurocentrism and Modernity (Introduction to the Frankfurt Lectures)', in J. Beverly and J. Oviedo, *The Postmodernism Debate in Latin America*, special issue of *Boundary 2* (Durham, N.C.: Duke University Press, 1993), p. 66.
12   Ibid., p. 67.
13   Marshall Berman, *All that is Solid Melts into Air* (London: Verso, 1982), pp. 16–17.
14   S. Hall, D. Held and T. McGrew, *Modernity and its Futures* (Cambridge: Polity Press and Open University, 1992), p. 2.
15   A. Giddens, *The Consequences of Modernity* (Cambridge: Polity Press, 1990), p. 1.
16   Ibid., p. 6.
17   Wagner, *A Sociology of Modernity*, p. 24.
18   See Berman, *All that is Solid*; Frisby, *Fragments of Modernity*; D. Frisby, 'Simmel and the Study of Modernity', in Frisby, *Simmel and Since, Essays on Georg Simmel's Social Theory* (London: Routledge,

1992); D. Harvey, *The Condition of Postmodernity* (Oxford: Blackwell, 1989).

19	Charles Baudelaire, *The Painter of Modern Life and Other Essays*, (London: Phaidon, 1964), p. 13.
20	Quoted by Frisby, *Simmel and Since*, p. 66.
21	Ibid., p. 67.
22	Harvey, *The Condition of Postmodernity*, pp. 10–12.
23	Ibid., p. 12.
24	N. García Canclini, *Culturas Híbridas, Estrategias para Entrar y Salir de la Modernidad* (Mexico: Grijalbo, 1989), pp. 31–2.
25	Wagner, *A Sociology of Modernity*, p. 37.
26	Ibid., p. 119.
27	See for example C. Offe, *Disorganized Capitalism* (Cambridge: Polity Press, 1987) and J. Urry and S. Lash, *The End of Organized Capitalism* (Cambridge: Polity Press, 1987).
28	Wagner, *A Sociology of Modernity*, p. 132.
29	Ibid., p. 167. Giddens's arguments can be found in *The Consequences of Modernity*.
30	The idea of various trajectories towards modernity has been developed by G. Therborn, *European Modernity and Beyond* (London: Sage, 1995) and by Wagner, *A Sociology of Modernity*.
31	This classification of trajectories differs from that proposed by Therborn, who proposes four routes: the European one, the new worlds one (including North America and South America), the colonial zone one (Africa and South Pacific) and the countries with externally induced modernization one (Japan) (*European Modernity and Beyond*, pp. 5–6). I differ from Therborn because in my view North America and South America cannot be located in the same trajectory.
32	The idea of a cultural transplant or of 'transplanted peoples' has been developed by Darcy Ribeiro in order to account for the settlement of European migrants who wanted to resume their style of life and culture in a different continent with more freedom and better prospects. See *Las Américas y la Civilización* (Caracas: Biblioteca Ayacucho, 1992), p. 377.
33	See on this Wagner, *A Sociology of Modernity*, p. 53.
34	Ibid., p. 4.
35	Ibid., p. 58.
36	Ibid., p. 73 and *passim*.
37	The term 'post-Fordism' comes from the 'regulation school' of Lipietz, Boyer and Aglietta (see note 2 to chapter 6 below), according to which the 'Fordist–Keynesian' regime of accumulation typical of postwar capitalism has been breaking up since the early 1970s, to be replaced by a more flexible regime of accumulation. The new 'post-Fordist' regime of accumulation seeks to overcome the rigidities of the Fordist regime and implies the emergence of entirely new sectors of production, new ways of providing financial services, new markets, relatively

high levels of 'structural' unemployment, the rapid destruction and reconstruction of skills, and the roll-back of trade union power.

38 See on this García Canclini, *Culturas Híbridas*, pp. 81–2.

39 I follow here the distinction between individual and qualitative identity propounded by E. Tugendhat, 'Identidad: personal, nacional y universal', *Persona y Sociedad* 10, no. 1 (Apr. 1996), pp. 29–40. See also his *Self-Consciousness and Self-Determination* (Cambridge, Mass.: MIT Press, 1986), pp. 254–62.

40 This seems to be Tugendhat's own position. It is true that in his first study of self-consciousness (*Self-Consciousness and Self-Determination*, pp. 219–23) Tugendhat insists on its social character by analysing the work of George Mead and maintaining that a relation of oneself to oneself must be understood as an intersubjective process that involves a relation to others. But then, in 'Identidad', Tugendhat, who is a philosopher, is reluctant to relate this fully to the concept of identity, in so far as he considers identity to be a very unclear and ambiguous term developed by social psychology.

41 William James, *The Principles of Psychology* (London: Macmillan, 1890), vol. I, p. 291.

42 Georg Simmel, *Sociología* (Madrid: Espasa Calpe, 1939), p. 363.

43 Georg Simmel, *La Filosofía del Dinero* (Madrid: Instituto de Estudios Políticos, 1976), p. 571.

44 Georg Simmel, *The Philosophy of Money* (London: Routledge, 1990), p. 322.

45 H. Gerth and C. Wright Mills, *Character and Social Structure* (New York: Harbinger Books, 1964), p. 80.

46 Ibid., p. 85.

47 David J. de Levita, *The Concept of Identity* (Paris: Mouton, 1965), p. 7.

48 E. Erikson, *Identity, Youth and Crisis* (London: Faber, 1968), p. 22.

49 Ibid., p. 24.

50 See Axel Honneth, *The Struggle for Recognition* (Cambridge: Polity Press, 1995), pp. 118–23.

51 See Charles Taylor, 'The Politics of Recognition', in *Multiculturalism*, ed. A Guttman (Princeton: Princeton University Press, 1994), p. 32. In this article Taylor develops the idea that identity is shaped by recognition or its absence in a way that complements Honneth's ideas.

52 Honneth, *The Struggle for Recognition*, pp. 132–5.

53 Ibid., p. 138.

54 Ibid., pp. 77–85.

55 See Carlos García-Gual, 'La visión de los otros en la antiguedad clásica', in M. León-Portilla et al. (eds), *De Palabra y Obra en el Nuevo Mundo* (Madrid: Siglo XXI, 1992), vol. I, pp. 7–19.

56 See Miguel León-Portilla, 'Imágenes de los otros en Mesoamérica antes del encuentro', in ibid., pp. 36–41.

57 Z. Bauman, interview with Helga Hirsch: 'Der Holocaust ist nich einmalig. Gesprach mit dem polnischen Soziologen Zygmunt Bauman'

(The Holocaust is not unique. Interview with the Polish sociologist Zygmunt Bauman), *Die Zeit*, 23 Apr. 1993, p. 68. I thank Jorge Iván Vergara for showing me and translating this quotation.

58 This idea is part of Anthony Giddens's structuration theory. See *The Constitution of Society* (Cambridge: Polity Press, 1984), esp. ch. 1.

59 C. Kluckhohn, *Culture and Behaviour* (New York: Free Press, 1962), p. 214.

60 See Renato Ortiz, *Um Outro Território, Ensaios sobre a mundializa-ção* (Sao Paulo: Olho d'Agua, n.d.), p. 70.

61 Maritza Montero, *Ideología, Alienación e Identidad Nacional, Una aproximación psicosocial al ser venezolano* (Caracas: Universidad Central de Venezuela, 1987), pp. 133–4.

62 D. M. Leite, *O Caráter Nacional Brasileiro* (Sao Paulo: Livraria Pioneira, 1969). Quoted in Ortiz, *Um Outro Território*, p. 71.

63 Hernán Godoy, *El Carácter Chileno* (Santiago: Editorial Universitaria, 1976), pp. 505–18.

64 B. Anderson, *Imagined Communities* (London: Verso, 1983), p. 15.

65 Ibid.

66 Ibid., pp. 18–19. Referring to one of those rites typical of nationhood, Anderson mentions for instance the importance of the tomb of the unknown soldier.

67 Hall, Held and McGrew, *Modernity and its Futures*, p. 293.

68 See E. Hobsbawm and T. Ranger, *The Invention of Tradition* (Cambridge: Cambridge University Press, 1988), p. 1.

69 See on this R. Johnson, 'Towards a Cultural Theory of the Nation: A British–Dutch Dialogue', in A. Galema et al. (eds), *Images of the Nation* (Amsterdam: Rodopi, 1993), p. 174.

70 It is notorious, for instance, how football as a widespread practice in many countries has become increasingly representative of a nation's identity, and yet practically no public version of national identity in the countries concerned takes account of this form of subjectivity.

71 See Giddens, *The Constitution of Society*, pp. 374–5.

72 See Johnson, 'Towards a Cultural Theory', pp. 194–204.

73 Ibid., pp. 191–4.

74 Ibid., p. 192.

75 Ibid., pp. 180–6.

76 Poststructuralism derives from and is a reaction against the Althusserian analyses of the subject and ideology. It is not surprising to find, therefore, that its representatives were originally disciples of Althusser: Michel Foucault in France, Paul Hirst, Barry Hindess, Ernesto Laclau and Chantal Mouffe in Britain.

77 On the relationship between narrative and identity in this perspective see Margaret R. Somers, 'The Narrative Constitution of Identity: A Relational and Network Approach', *Theory and Society* 23 (1994), pp. 605–49: 'we all *become* what we *are* ... by being situated or situate ourselves within social narratives which are rarely our own work' (p. 606).

78 Johnson, 'Towards a Cultural Theory', pp. 180–3.
79 S. Hall, 'Cultural Identity and Diaspora', in J. Rutherford (ed.), *Identity, Community, Culture, Difference* (London: Lawrence and Wishart, 1990), p. 223.
80 Johnson, 'Towards a Cultural Theory', p. 190.
81 García Canclini, *Culturas Híbridas*, p. 154.
82 Hall, 'Cultural Identity and Diaspora', p. 225.
83 J. Habermas, 'The Limits of Neo-Historicism', interview with J. M. Ferry, in J. Habermas, *Autonomy and Solidarity* (London: Verso, 1992), p. 243.
84 J. Habermas, 'Historical Consciousness and Post-Traditional Identity: The Federal Republic's Orientation to the West', in J. Habermas, *The New Conservatism* (Cambridge, Mass.: MIT Press, 1989), p. 263.
85 John B. Thompson, *The Media and Modernity: A Social Theory of the Media* (Cambridge: Polity Press, 1995), p. 207.
86 Ibid.
87 D. Kellner, 'Popular Culture and the Construction of Postmodern Identities', in S. Lash and J. Friedman (eds), *Modernity and Identity* (Oxford: Blackwell, 1992), p. 148.
88 Marie Gillespie, 'Soap Viewing, Gossip and Rumour amongst Punjabi Youth in Southall', in P. Drummond et al. (eds), *National Identity and Europe, the Television Revolution* (London: BFI, 1993), pp. 25–42.
89 See Alison Griffiths, 'Pobol y Cwm, the Construction of National and Cultural Industry in a Welsh Language Soap Opera' and Breda Luthar, 'Identity Management and Popular Representational Forms', in Drummond et al., *National Identity and Europe*, pp. 9–24 and 43–50.
90 See on this Thompson, *The Media and Modernity*, pp. 50–1, 198–9.
91 Ibid., pp. 213–19.
92 See Wagner, *A Sociology of Modernity*, p. 56.
93 Harvey, The Condition of Postmodernity, p. 33.

Chapter 2   The Colonial Stage, Modernity Denied

1 Jorge Gissi, 'Identidad, "Carácter Social" y Cultura Latinoamericana', *Estudios Sociales*, no. 33 (1982).
2 See E. Dussel, *El encubrimiento del otro, hacia el origen del mito de la modernidad* (Quito: Ediciones ABYA-YALA, 1994), p. 38.
3 Edmundo O'Gorman, *La Invención de América* (Mexico: FCE, 1984), pp. 135–6.
4 Ibid., p. 94.
5 Alberto Flores Galindo has said in respect of the Incas that 'the idea of an Andean human being inalterable in time and with a harmonious totality of common features, expresses . . . an imagined or desired history but not the reality of an overfragmented world.' See his *Buscando un Inca* (Lima: Editorial Horizonte, 1994), p. 16.

6   Fernando Ainsa, *Identidad cultural de Iberoamérica en su Narrativa* (Madrid: Gredos, 1986), p. 59.

7   De Imaz reckons that the only artefact which might be an American original contribution is the hammock! See J. L. de Imaz, *Sobre la Identidad Iberoamericana* (Buenos Aires: Editorial Sudamericana, 1984), p. 80.

8   Nathan Wachtel, *The Vision of the Vanquished: The Spanish Conquest of Peru through Indian Eyes 1530–1570* (Brighton: Harvester, 1977), p. 25.

9   See on this M. Picón-Salas, *A Cultural History of Spanish America* (Berkeley: University of California Press, 1971), pp. 7–12.

10 Quetzalcóatl was in Indian legend a former chief and god who left his kingdom and disappeared into the Atlantic, but not without promising that he would return one day to reclaim his kingdom.

11 Wachtel, *The Vision of the Vanquished*, p. 25.

12 T. Todorov, *La Conquista de América, el Problema del Otro* (Mexico: Siglo XXI, 1989), p. 137.

13 Wachtel, *The Vision of the Vanquished*, pp. 29, 30.

14 Ibid., ch. 2.

15 Olivia Harris, '"The Coming of the White People": Reflections on the Mythologization of History in Latin America', *Bulletin of Latin American Research* 14, no. 1 (1995), pp. 9–24.

16 See the work of W. Borah and S. Cook, *The Indian Population of Central Mexico 1531–1610* (Berkeley: University of California Press, 1960) and *Essays in Population History* (Berkeley: University of California Press, 1971–9).

17 Todorov, *La Conquista de América*, p. 144. See also Serge Gruzinski, *The Conquest of Mexico* (Cambridge: Polity Press, 1993), p. 81.

18 Ritchie Robertson, 'Introduction', in Urs Bitterli, *Cultures in Conflict* (Cambridge: Polity Press, 1989), p. 15.

19 See J. Bengoa, '500 Años Despues', *Nütram* 4, no. 1 (1988), pp. 8–18.

20 Referring to the extermination of the Tainos in the Hispaniola island in just fifty years, Urs Bitterli speaks of 'the first genocide perpetrated by Europeans'. See *Cultures in Conflict*, p. 80.

21 See on this Claudio Esteva Fábregat, *El mestizaje en Iberoamérica* (Madrid: Editorial Alhambra, 1988), p. 62.

22 In an incredibly racist remark, Hegel took this disruption of the reproductive processes to be the result of the Indians' stupidity and lack of imagination. See further below, note 67.

23 In Gunder Frank's view, Latin America became capitalist from the moment it was colonized because its economy was integrated into the world capitalist market. See A. G. Frank, *Capitalism and Underdevelopment in Latin America* (New York: Monthly Review Press, 1969), p. 239. The main problem of this thesis is that it defines capitalism exclusively in terms of market relations and forgets about relations of production. It is only the latter that essentially define capitalism. A feudal economy may export its produce without chang-

ing the nature of its productive system. For a development of these ideas see J. Larrain, *Theories of Development* (Cambridge: Polity Press, 1989), ch. 4.

24 The encomienda was a servile system whereby a group of Indians was allocated to a Spanish conquistador who had the right to exact tribute from them, in goods, money or personal services in his lands or mines during part of the year.

25 The number of Spanish women was never greater than 10 per cent of the Spanish conquerors. In Chile, for example, around 1583 there were about 50 Spanish women to 1,100 Spanish men. See Esteva Fábregat, *El mestizaje en Iberoamérica*, p. 38.

26 It was not rare to find Spanish men with twenty or thirty concubines, ibid., p. 40.

27 As early as the second half of the sixteenth century the 'mestizos' were more numerous than the Spanish. In 1810 in Chile the mestizos were three-fifths of the total population. Ibid., p. 41.

28 J. de Imaz, *Sobre la Identidad Iberoamericana*, pp. 83–4.

29 See David Brading, *The First America* (Cambridge: Cambridge University Press, 1991), p. 161.

30 Good examples are Gonzalo Fernandez de Oviedo's *Historia general y natural de la Indias* and Francisco López de Gómara's *Historia general de las Indias* and *Historia de la conquista de Mexico*. Both authors denigrated the Indians. For a good description of their views see Brading, *The First America*, ch. 2. On the perception of the Indians and the conquerors' discourse see also de Imaz, *Sobre la Identidad Iberoamericana*, pp. 70–7.

31 Stuart B. Schwartz, 'The Formation of a Colonial Identity in Brazil', in N. Canny and A. Pagden (eds), *Colonial Identity in the Atlantic World, 1500–1800* (Princeton: Princeton University Press, 1987), p. 26.

32 Ibid.

33 Bitterli, *Cultures in Conflict*, p. 75.

34 I use the term 'ideological' here in the sense of a concealing or masking device, derived from the critical tradition of the theory of ideology.

35 Quoted in Picón-Salas, *A Cultural History of Spanish America*, p. 20.

36 Todorov, *La Conquista de América*, p. 151.

37 Ibid., p. 157.

38 Bitterli, *Cultures in Conflict*, p. 27.

39 Todorov, *La Conquista de América*, p. 50.

40 Gruzinski provides no definition or conception of the term 'imaginary'. At points he tends to convey that it encompasses the system of representation, modes of expression and conceptions of time and space, in short, the whole of the mental structure of a people at a particular time in history. But in other places imaginary appears to be opposed to reality and in this sense it seems to refer to conceptions of the afterlife and the supernatural. I have taken the term in the first and more

inclusive meaning, although I suspect Gruzinski favours the second meaning.

41 Gruzinski, *The Conquest of Mexico*, pp. 1–5, 282–4.
42 Wachtel, *The Vision of the Vanquished*, p. 85.
43 Schwartz, 'The Formation of a Colonial Identity', p. 28.
44 Wachtel, *The Vision of the Vanquished*, p. 142.
45 A. Pagden, 'Identity Formation in Spanish America', in Canny and Pagden, *Colonial Identity in the Atlantic World*, p. 66.
46 Ibid., pp. 80–1.
47 Quoted in ibid., p. 82.
48 D. Hume, 'Of National Characters', in Hume, *Essays: Moral, Political, and Literary*, ed. T. H. Green and T. H. Grose (London: Longmans, Green, 1875).
49 Quoted by A. Gerbi, *The Dispute of the New World: The History of a Polemic 1750–1900* (Pittsburgh: University of Pittsburgh Press, 1973), p. 6. Taken from Georges-Louis Leclerc, Comte de Buffon, *Oeuvres complètes* (Paris: Delangle, 1824–8), vol. 15, pp. 443–6.
50 E. Cassirer, *The Philosophy of the Enlightenment* (Princeton: Princeton University Press, 1951), p. 77.
51 Ibid., p. 79.
52 Voltaire, *Essai sur les moeurs et l'esprit des nations*, in *Oeuvres complètes* (Paris: Garnier Frères, 1878), vol. 12, pp. 380, 381.
53 Ibid., p. 390.
54 Montesquieu, *The Spirit of the Laws* (Cambridge: Cambridge University Press, 1989), Book 17, ch. 2, p. 278.
55 Ibid., Book 15, ch. 5, p. 250.
56 Quoted by Gerbi, *The Dispute of the New World*, p. 55.
57 Ibid., p. 58.
58 Cassirer, *The Philosophy of the Enlightenment*, p. 79.
59 Quoted by Gerbi, *The Dispute of the New World*, p. 330.
60 Ibid.
61 Ibid., p. 331.
62 Ibid., pp. 331–2.
63 I. Kant, 'An Answer to the Question: "What is Enlightenment?"', in Kant, *Political Writings*, ed. H. Reiss (Cambridge: Cambridge University Press, 1992), p. 54.
64 T. R. Malthus, *An Essay on Population* (London: J. M. Dent, 1952), vol. 2, Book 3, ch. 4, p. 30.
65 Ibid., vol. 1, Book 2, ch. 13, p. 305.
66 T. R. Malthus, *Principles of Political Economy* (London: International Economic Circle, Tokyo and the London School of Economics and Political Science, 1936), Book 2, section 4, pp. 337–41.
67 G. W. F. Hegel, *Lectures on the Philosophy of World History* (Cambridge: Cambridge University Press, 1986), pp. 162–71.
68 Quoted by Gerbi, *The Dispute of the New World*, pp. 429–30.
69 Hegel, *Lectures on the Philosophy of World History*, p. 167.

70   F. W. Schelling, *Introduction à la philosophie de la mythologie* (Paris: Aubier, 1945), vol. 2, p. 279.
71   Ibid., pp. 292–3.
72   See M. Horkheimer, *Eclipse of Reason* (New York: Seabury Press, 1974).
73   Ibid., p. 19.
74   Ibid., p. 24.
75   The importance of the Counter-Reformation in the Spanish culture of the time and its effects on Latin America have been well analysed by Claudio Véliz, *The New World of the Gothic Fox: Culture and Economy in English and Spanish America* (Berkeley: University of California Press, 1994), ch. 3.
76   L. Zea, *América como Consciencia* (Mexico: Universidad Nacional Autónoma de México, 1972), p. 74.
77   See de Imaz, *Sobre la Identidad Iberoamericana*, p. 107.
78   New universities were created only in Spanish America because the Portuguese never allowed the same in Brazil, where they kept the educational monopoly which the University of Coimbra exercised. It is also worth mentioning that 'unlike Spanish America, no printing press operated in Brazil during the first three centuries of the colonial era.' All this made Brazil even more intellectualy dependent than Spanish America. See Schwartz, 'The Formation of a Colonial Identity', pp. 36–8.
79   Pagden has documented how 'as late as 1789, for instance, the courses in philosophy at Lima still rejected all forms of Cartesianism and accepted Copernicanism only as a hypothesis.' See Pagden, 'Identity Formation in Spanish America', p. 87.
80   Zea, *América como Consciencia*, p. 74.
81   de Imaz, *Sobre la Identidad Iberoamericana*, p. 121.
82   Flores Galindo, *Buscando un Inca*, p. 66.
83   Juan Sepúlveda, 'Crisis de la Independencia y ruptura de la homogeneidad religiosa en Chile', class notes from his course on The History of Churches in Chile, Comunidad Teológica Evangélica, Santiago, n.d.
84   See Wachtel, *The Vision of the Vanquished*, pp. 153–4 and de Imaz, *Sobre la Identidad Iberoamericana*, pp. 114, 127.
85   Bengoa, '500 Años Despues', p. 17.
86   Darcy Ribeiro, *Las Américas y la Civilización* (Caracas: Biblioteca Ayacucho, 1992), pp. 62–3.
87   Edward Sapir, 'Culture, Genuine and Spurious', *American Journal of Sociology* 29, no. 4 (Jan. 1924), pp. 401–29.
88   Arturo Uslar Pietri, *La creación del Nuevo Mundo* (Caracas: Grijalbo, 1991), p. 97.
89   Schwartz, 'The Formation of a Colonial Identity', p. 16.
90   I refer here to Giddens's distinction between discursive and practical consciousness with which I tried to illustrate the existence of identity at two poles of culture: the public discursive pole and the private pole.

Practical consciousness corresponds to the latter pole and consists of what actors know about their own reality but cannot express discursively. See A. Giddens, *The Constitution of Society* (Cambridge: Polity Press, 1984), pp. 374–5.

91 David Brading, *The First America*, p. 2.

92 Pagden, 'Identity Formation in Spanish America', pp. 84–5, 89.

93 Ribeiro, *Las Américas y la Civilización*, p. 69. Ribeiro's classification also includes a fourth category, 'emergent peoples', which does not apply to Latin America.

94 Ibid. pp. 85–91.

95 Ibid. pp. 187–98.

96 Ibid. pp. 377–83.

97 Brading, *The First America*, p. 3.

98 Of course, this does not mean that some modern ideas could not have some influence even within the Catholic Church itself. It is well known, for instance, that throughout the eighteenth century there were numerous theological disputes directly related to central themes of the Enlightenment and that this was particularly true within the Jesuit order. But on the whole, the thought of the most pro-modern Jesuits was clearly condemned by the General Congregations of the order itself. So, as Chiaramonte has argued, one can hardly speak of a 'Catholic Enlightenment'. See José Carlos Chiaramonte, 'Ilustración y Modernidad en el siglo XVIII Hispanoamericano', in R. Krebs and C. Gazmuri (eds), *La Revolución Francesa y Chile* (Santiago: Editorial Universitaria, 1990), pp. 83–109.

99 Carlos Cousiño, *Razón y Ofrenda, Ensayo en torno a los límites y perspectivas de la sociología en América Latina*, Cuadernos del Instituto de Sociología (Santiago: Pontificia Universidad Católica de Chile, 1990); and Pedro Morandé, *Cultura y Modernización en América Latina*, Cuadernos del Instituto de Sociología (Santiago: Universidad Católica de Chile, 1984).

100 Cousiño, *Razón y Ofrenda*, p. 115.

101 Ibid., p. 109.

102 J. A. Maravall, *La Cultura del Barroco* (Barcelona: Ariel, 1975), pp. 77, 192, 288.

103 Véliz, *The New World of the Gothic Fox*, p. 71.

104 It is surprising therefore that Véliz should consider Baroque as a modern phenomenon and that for him 'Baroque Spain was the avant-garde of modern monarchies and responded to the new problems of social and economic disruption in a modern manner . . .', ibid., p. 210. It can be accepted that baroque culture is modern only in the sense that it emerged within the modern epoch as a conservative response against its effects, but it does not share at all the essential characteristics of the modern project.

105 C. Parker, *Otra Lógica en América Latina: Religión Popular y Modernización Capitalista* (Santiago: Fondo de Cultura Económica, 1993), p. 354.

106 P. Wagner, *A Sociology of Modernity, Liberty and Discipline* (London: Routledge, 1994), p. 4.
107 Ibid., p. 24.
108 The anti-modern character of the Counter-Reformation is also recognized by N. García Canclini, *Culturas Híbridas: Estrategias para entrar y salir de la modernidad* (Mexico: Grijalbo, 1989), p. 65.

Chapter 3 Oligarchic Modernity

1 Alfredo Jocelyn-Holt, *La Independencia de Chile* (Madrid: Editorial MAPFRE, 1992), p. 120.
2 Tulio Halperin, *Historia Contemporanea de America Latina* (Mexico: Alianza Editorial, 1983), pp. 137–8.
3 See on this Néstor García Canclini, *Culturas Híbridas: Estrategias para entrar y salir de la modernidad* (Mexico: Grijalbo, 1989), p. 73.
4 J. L. de Imaz, *Sobre la Identidad Iberoamericana* (Buenos Aires: Editorial Sudamericana, 1984), p. 141.
5 See on this Pablo Gonzalez Casanova, *Internal Colonialism and National Development*, Studies in Comparative International Development, Rutgers University Monograph Series, vol. 1, no. 4 (New Brunswick: Rutgers University Press, 1965) and Dale L. Johnson, 'On Oppressed Classes', in James D. Cockcroft et al., *Dependence and Underdevelopment* (New York: Anchor Books, 1972).
6 Charles A. Hale, 'Political and Social Ideas in Latin America, 1870–1930', in L. Bethell (ed.), *The Cambridge History of Latin America*, vol. 4 (Cambridge: Cambridge University Press, 1986), p. 368.
7 See on this D. Bushnell and Neill Macaulay, *The Emergence of Latin America in the Nineteenth Century* (New York and Oxford: Oxford University Press, 1988), p. 12.
8 Simón Bolívar, 'Carta de Jamaica', in L. Zea (ed.), *Fuentes de la Cultura Latinoamericana* (Mexico: Fondo de Cultura Economica, 1993), vol. 1, p. 26.
9 Halperin, *Historia Contemporanea de America Latina*, p. 170.
10 Diego Portales, Letter to José M. Cea, March 1822, in Zea, *Fuentes de la Cultura Latinoamericana*, vol. 2, p. 175.
11 For instance, only 1.2 per cent of the Chilean population could vote in the 1864 parliamentary elections and only 2.8 per cent in the 1876 presidential elections. See on this, Alfredo Jocelyn-Holt, *El Peso de la Noche, nuestra frágil fortaleza histórica* (Buenos Aires: Ariel, 1997), p. 61 n 37.
12 J. S. Valenzuela, 'Hacia la formación de instituciones democráticas: prácticas electorales en Chile durante el siglo XIX', *Estudios Públicos*, no. 66 (1997).
13 See on this Cristobal Marín, 'Modernity and Mass Communication: The Latin American Case', Ph.D. thesis, University of Birmingham, 1999, pp. 174–7.

14 See Jean Franco, *Historia de la Literatura Hispanoamericana* (Barcelona: Editorial Ariel, 1980), pp. 45–52.

15 Ibid., p. 53.

16 Bolívar, 'Carta de Jamaica', p. 18.

17 Ibid., p. 22.

18 Simón Bolívar, 'Discurso de Angostura', in Zea, *Fuentes de la Cultura Latinoamericana*, vol. 1, p. 447.

19 Bolívar, 'Carta de Jamaica', p. 30.

20 Eugenio María de Hostos, 'El día de América', in Zea, *Fuentes de la Cultura Latinoamericana*, vol. 1, pp. 279–80.

21 Francisco Bilbao, 'Iniciativa de la América. Idea de un Congreso Federal de las Repúblicas', in Zea, *Fuentes de la Cultura Latinoamericana*, vol. 1, p. 56.

22 Gabino Barreda, 'Oración Cívica', delivered 16 Sept. 1867, in O. Terán (ed.), *América Latina: Positivismo y Nación* (Mexico: Editorial Katún, 1983), p. 26.

23 Quoted by Bernardo Subercaseaux, *Chile, ¿Un país moderno?* (Santiago: Grupo Editorial Zeta, 1996), p. 46.

24 Bilbao, 'Iniciativa de la América', p. 58.

25 See Hale, 'Political and Social Ideas', p. 370.

26 José Victorino Lastarria, *La América*, fragments in Zea, *Fuentes de la Cultura Latinoamericana*, vol. 2, pp. 505, 499.

27 Andrés Bello, 'Autonomía Cultural de América', in Zea, *Fuentes de la Cultura Latinoamericana*, vol. 1, pp. 192–4.

28 See on this Franco, *Historia de la Literatura Hispanoamericana*, pp. 70–6. See also Fernando Ainsa, *Identidad Cultural de Iberoamérica en su Narrativa* (Madrid: Gredos, 1986), p. 116.

29 Alfredo Jocelyn-Holt has shown how in the Chilean case the domination of a traditional elite and its culture was even more important than the state itself in the maintenance of the social order in the nineteenth century. See *El Peso de la Noche*, ch. 1.

30 See on this Manuel Vicuña, *El París Americano, la oligarquía chilena como actor urbano en el siglo XIX* (Santiago: Universidad Finis Terrae and Museo Histórico Nacional, 1996), pp. 35–57.

31 See on this Fernando Henrique Cardoso and Enzo Faletto, *Dependency and Development in Latin America* (Berkeley and Los Angeles: University of California Press, 1979), pp. 36–54.

32 This process was to continue for quite a while, until the middle of the twentieth century. In other words, the hacienda system proved to be extremely resilient.

33 Halperin, *Historia Contemporanea de America Latina*, pp. 211–15.

34 Cardoso and Faletto, *Dependency and Development*, p. 59.

35 Ibid., pp. 61–73.

36 Ibid., p. 70.

37 See on this Hale, 'Political and Social Ideas', pp. 377–80.

38 Halperin, *Historia Contemporanea de America Latina*, p. 258.

39 The term positivism is used today in many senses, but it generally refers to a conception of knowledge which privileges the scientific

method as the only valid means of knowing. For Comte the scientific method entailed observation, experiment and the search for the laws of phenomena; and came to replace religious and philosophical stages of knowledge. But Comte went further than these general premises to make of positive science a true religion of humankind. Many Latin American authors followed him even in this peculiar respect.

40 See on this Hale, 'Political and Social Ideas', pp. 384–5.
41 Ibid., pp. 387–91.
42 Domingo Faustino Sarmiento, *Facundo* (Buenos Aires: Editorial TOR, 1945), p. 58.
43 Ibid., pp. 19–20.
44 Domingo Faustino Sarmiento, *Conflicto y armonía de las razas en América*, quoted in Roberto Fernández, 'Nuestra América y el Occidente', in Zea, *Fuentes de la Cultura Latinoamericana*, vol. 1, p. 167. For a synthesis of Sarmiento's ideas see Leopoldo Zea, *Descubrimiento e Identidad Latinoamericana* (Mexico: UNAM, 1990), pp. 60–1.
45 Quoted by Bernardo Canal Feijóo, *Constitución y Revolución* (Mexico: Fondo de Cultura Económica, 1955), p. 18. It has to be borne in mind, though, that in his writings after 1853, Alberdi changed his mind and became a critic of Sarmiento and his opposition between civilization and barbarism.
46 Ibid., p. 178.
47 Quoted in Fernández, 'Nuestra América y el Occidente', p. 168.
48 Javier Prado, 'Estado Social del Perú', in Terán, *América Latina*, pp. 126–7.
49 José Gil Fortoul, 'La Raza', in Terán, *América Latina*, p. 104.
50 Ibid., p. 115.
51 J. Ingenieros, 'La Evolución Sociológica Argentina', in Terán, *América Latina*, p. 139.
52 See C.O. Bunge, *Nuestra América* (Madrid: Espasa Calpe, 1926).
53 Ibid., p. 133.
54 Ibid., p. 145.
55 Ibid., pp. 157, 166.
56 Quoted in Hale, 'Political and Social Ideas', p. 401.
57 See A. Arguedas, *Pueblo Enfermo*, in J. Siles Guevara, *La cien obras capitales de la literatura Boliviana* (La Paz: Editorial Los Amigos del Libro, 1975).
58 See on this Renato Ortiz, *Cultura Brasileira e Identidade Nacional* (Sao Paulo: Editora Brasiliense, 1985), pp. 13–27.
59 Domingo Faustino Sarmiento, 'Conclusiones' of *Conflicto y armonía de las razas en América*, in Zea, *Fuentes de la Cultura Latinoamericana*, vol. 1., p. 408.
60 From D. F. Sarmiento, *Argiropolis*, quoted in Zea, *Fuentes de la Cultura Latinoamericana*, vol. 1, p. 296.
61 Quoted in Canal Feijóo, *Constitución y Revolución*, p. 18.
62 Prado, 'Estado Social del Perú', p. 133.

63 Ingenieros, 'La Evolución Sociológica Argentina', pp. 151–2.
64 Quoted in E. Martinez Estrada, *Meditaciones Sarmientinas* (Santiago: Editorial Universitaria, 1968), pp. 134, 137.
65 Gil Fortoul, 'La Raza', p. 115.
66 See on this Marín, 'Modernity and Mass Communication', pp. 166–7.
67 See on this Franco, *Historia de la Literatura Hispanoamericana*, pp. 71–3.
68 Ibid., pp. 83–93.
69 See on this Ainsa, *Identidad Cultural de Iberoamérica*, p. 104.
70 See on this E. Bradford Burns, *The Poverty of Progress: Latin America in the Nineteenth Century* (Berkeley: University of California Press, 1980), pp. 25–31.
71 See on this Franco, *Historia de la Literatura Hispanoamericana*, pp. 105–15.
72 On modernism see António Cândido, 'Literatura y subdesarrollo' and Haroldo de Campos, 'Superación de los lenguajes exclusivos', in César Fernández Moreno (ed.), *América Latina en su literatura* (Mexico: Siglo XXI, 1992), pp. 323, 286–92. See also Arturo Uslar Pietri, 'El mestizaje creador', in J. Skirius (ed.), *El Ensayo Hispanoamericano del siglo XX* (Mexico: Fondo de Cultura Económica, 1981), M. T. Martínez Blanco, *Identidad Cultural de Hispanoamérica* (Madrid: Editorial de la Universidad Complutense, 1987) and Franco, *Historia de la Literatura Hispanoamericana*, ch. 6.
73 Alejo Carpentier, 'The Latin American Novel', *New Left Review*, no. 154 (Nov.–Dec. 1985), pp. 100–1.
74 Uslar Pietri, 'El mestizaje creador'.
75 See Octavio Paz, 'Traducción y Metáfora', in L. Litvak (ed.), *El Modernismo* (Madrid: Editorial Taurus, 1975).
76 Franco, *Historia de la Literatura Hispanoamericana*, p. 160.
77 See de Imaz, *Sobre la Identidad Iberoamericana*, pp. 224, 229.
78 L. Zea, *America Latina: Largo viaje hacia sí misma* (Caracas: Ediciones de la Facultad de Humanidades y Educación, Universidad Central de Venezuela, 1983), p. 18.
79 Augusto Salazar Bondy, 'Sentido y problema del pensamiento filosófico hispanoamericano', in Zea, *Fuentes de la Cultura Latinoamericana*, vol. 1, pp. 207–8.
80 See Subercaseaux, *Chile*, pp. 47–55. Subercaseaux argues this thesis for Chilean culture, but given the account of positivism in Latin America that I have just given, it can easily be extended to other countries in South America too.
81 In this I disagree with Subercaseaux, who seems to believe that the effects of the 'deficit of cultural depth' can be seen in a 'bland and grey identity', ibid., p. 49. The galvanizing effects of Chile's 1879 war against Peru and Bolivia on the Chilean national identity cannot be described in terms of blandness and greyness, even if one disagrees with the Chilean purposes in going to war.

82 This was particularly clear in the Chilean case, as Manuel Vicuña has demonstrated. See *El París Americano*, pp. 15–34.

Chapter 4   The End of Oligarchic Modernity

1   Karl Polanyi, *The Great Transformation* (Boston: Beacon Press, 1957), p. 29.
2   For a good account of the various forms of incorporation of the middle class see F. H. Cardoso and E. Faletto, *Dependency and Development in Latin America* (Berkeley: University of California Press, 1979).
3   See Renato Ortiz, *A Moderna Tradição Brasileira, Cultura Brasileira e Indústria Cultural* (Sao Paulo: Editora Brasiliense, 1988), p. 35.
4   On the realist novel see Ramón Xirau, 'Crisis del Realismo', in César Fernández Moreno (ed.), *América latina en su literatura* (Mexico: Siglo XXI, 1992), pp. 185–203 and Jean Franco, *Historia de la Literatura Hispanoamericana* (Barcelona: Editorial Ariel, 1980), ch. 7.
5   J. Martí, 'Nuestra América' (1891), in L. Zea (ed.), *Fuentes de la Cultura Latinoamericana* (Mexico: Fondo de Cultura Económica, 1993), p. 122.
6   Ibid., p. 124.
7   Ibid., p. 123.
8   Quoted by M. T. Martínez Blanco, *Identidad Cultural de Hispanoamérica* (Madrid: Editorial de la Universidad Complutense, 1987), p. 142. Taken from Rufino Blanco Fombona, *El Modernismo y los Poetas modernistas* (Madrid, 1929), pp. 28–30.
9   J. E. Rodó, *Ariel* (1900), in Zea, *Fuentes de la Cultura Latinoamericana*, p. 317.
10 Ibid., pp. 304–14.
11 Latin America for Vasconcelos is the new *par excellence* and the Latin Americans mestizos are neither European nor Indians. In 'El pensamiento Iberoamericano', an essay published in *Indología* (Barcelona, 1927), he argues that the Europeans and the Indians do not recognize the Latin Americans, nor do the Latin Americans recognize themselves in them. See J. Vasconcelos, 'El pensamiento Iberoamericano', in Zea, *Fuentes de la Cultura Latinoamericana*, p. 339.
12 J. Vasconcelos, *La Raza Cósmica* (Barcelona: S. A., 1927), p. 14.
13 Ibid., p. 15.
14 Pedro Heríquez Ureña, 'La Utopía de América. Patria de la Justicia' (La Plata, 1925), in Zea, *Fuentes de la Cultura Latinoamericana*, p. 387.
15 Ibid., p. 385.
16 João Cruz Costa, 'El Pensamiento Brasileño', *Cuadernos Americanos* 122, no. 3 (May–June 1962).
17 Renato Ortiz, *Cultura Brasileira e Identidade Nacional* (Sao Paulo: Editora Brasiliense, 1985), p. 26.

18 M. Gonzalez Prada, *Horas de Lucha* (Lima: Fondo de Cultura Económica, 1964), p. 204. *Gamonal* is one of the Latin American ways of referring to the landowner.

19 Ibid., pp. 204–5.

20 L. E. Valcárcel, *Del Ayllu al Imperio* (Lima: Editorial Garcilaso, 1925), p. 22.

21 L. E. Valcárcel, *Tempestad en los Andes* (Lima: Editorial Universo, 1972), p. 107.

22 Quoted by M. Francke Ballve, 'El Movimiento Indigenista en el Cuzco (1910–1930)', in C. I. Degregori et al., *Indigenismo, Clases Sociales y Problema Nacional* (Lima: Ediciones CELATS, n.d.), p. 166. From L. E. Valcárcel, 'Ideas en Marcha', *Wikuña*, no. 10 (Oct. 1929).

23 L. Zea, *Dependencia y Liberación en la Cultura Latinoamericana* (Mexico: Editorial Joaquín Mortiz, 1974), p. 59.

24 See Gonzalo Aguirre Beltrán, 'Un postulado de política indigenista', in A. Palerm (ed.), *Aguirre Beltrán: Obra Polémica* (Mexico: Centro de Investigaciones Superiores, Instituto Nacional de Antropología e Historia, 1976), p. 28.

25 Gonzalo Aguirre Beltrán, 'Informe ante el Presidente de la República', in Palerm, *Aguirre Beltrán*, pp. 161–72. Other articles collected in this book argue in the same direction.

26 Zea, *Dependencia y Liberación*, p. 68.

27 C. I. Degregori, 'Indigenismo, Clases Sociales y Problema Nacional', in Degregori et al., *Indigenismo, Clases Sociales*, pp. 37–9.

28 See J. C. Mariátegui, *Siete Ensayos de Interpretación de la Realidad Peruana* (Barcelona: Editorial Crítica, 1976), p. 28.

29 See *Report on the Americas* (New York: North American Congress on Latin America), vol. 24, no. 5 (Feb. 1991); esp. E. Galeano, 'The Blue Tiger and the Promised Land', L. G. Lumbreras, 'Misguided Development', and A. Quijano, 'Recovering Utopia'.

30 N. Mouzelis, *Politics in the Semi-periphery* (London: Macmillan, 1986), p. xvi.

31 See Carlos Cousiño and Eduardo Valenzuela, *Politización y monetarización en América Latina* (Santiago: Cuadernos del Instituto de Sociología de la Pontificia Universidad Católica de Chile, 1994), p. 116.

32 Cardoso and Faletto, *Dependency and Development*, p. 128.

33 See on this A. Villegas, *Cultura y Política en América Latina* (Mexico: Editorial Extemporáneos, 1977).

34 J. de Imaz, *Sobre la Identidad Iberoamericana* (Buenos Aires: Editorial Sudamericana, 1984), p. 298.

35 Quoted by L. Zea, *La Esencia de lo Americano* (Buenos Aires: Editorial Pleamar, 1971), p. 24. See also A. Gerbi, *The Dispute of the New World: The History of a Polemic 1750–1900* (Pittsburgh: University of Pittsburgh Press, 1973), p. 560.

36 Ortega y Gasset affirms: 'I repeat that I do not treat this question on the terrain of the telluric mysteries, today this is not treatable in this way. That is left for Count Keyserling.' See J. Ortega y Gasset, 'Med-

itación del Pueblo Joven', in *Obras Completas* (Madrid: Editorial Revista de Occidente, 1962), vol. 8, p. 399.

37 Ibid., pp. 399–400.
38 Ibid., pp. 404–5.
39 See Zea, *La Esencia de lo Americano*, pp. 23–4 and Gerbi, *The Dispute of the New World*, pp. 554–5.
40 Ortega y Gasset, 'Meditación del Pueblo Joven', p. 406.
41 See de Imaz, *Sobre la Identidad Iberoamericana*, pp. 315–17.
42 E. Martínez Estrada, *Radiografía de la Pampa* (Buenos Aires: Editorial Losada, 1946), vol. 1, p. 44.
43 Ibid., vol. 2, p. 184.
44 de Imaz, *Sobre la Identidad Iberoamericana*, pp. 322–4.
45 A. Arguedas, *Pueblo Enfermo*, in J. Siles Guevara, *Las cien obras capitales de la literatura Boliviana* (La Paz: Editorial Los Amigos del Libro, 1975), p. 72.
46 Ibid., p. 71.
47 O. Paz, *El Laberinto de la Soledad* (Mexico: Fondo de Cultura Económica, 1959), pp. 78–80.
48 This explanation in a sense coincides with Said's analysis of 'Orientalism'. The Western academic discourse on the 'Orient' somehow creates the very reality it appears to describe and it is therefore no wonder that many Arabs could frequently accept it. See E. Said, *Orientalism* (London: Penguin, 1985), p. 322: 'despite its failures, its lamentable jargon, its scarcely concealed racism, its paper-thin intellectual apparatus, Orientalism flourishes today in the forms I have tried to describe. Indeed, there is some reason for alarm in the fact that its influence has spread to "the Orient" itself: the pages of books and journals in Arabic . . . are filled with second-order analyses by Arabs of "the Arab mind", "Islam", and other myths.' It could be argued that something similar has occurred with the European discourse on Latin America.
49 See on this Fernando Ainsa, *Identidad Cultural de Iberoamérica en su narrativa* (Madrid: Gredos, 1986), pp. 127, 446–9.
50 Ibid., p. 139.
51 Ortiz, *Cultura Brasileira e Identidade Nacional*, p. 98; see also pp. 40–4, 90–106.
52 See J. Eyzaguirre, *Hispanoamérica del Dolor* (Madrid: Instituto de Estudios Políticos, 1947) and O. Lira, *Hispanidad y Mestizaje* (Santiago: Editorial Covadonga, 1985).
53 F. B. Pike, *Hispanismo, 1898–1936* (Notre Dame: University of Notre Dame Press, 1971), p. 1.
54 J. Vasconcelos, *La Raza Cósmica*, p. 7.
55 Quoted by Martínez Blanco, *Identidad Cultural de Hispanoamérica*, p. 124. Taken from J. de la Riva Agüero, *Carácter de la Literatura del Perú Independiente* (Lima, 1962), p. 267.
56 Eyzaguirre, *Hispanoamérica del Dolor*, pp. 17–18.
57 Ibid., p. 39.

58 J. Eyzaguirre, 'Por la Fidelidad a la Esperanza', in *Hispanoamérica del Dolor* (Santiago: Editorial Universitaria, 1969), pp. 21–2.
59 Eyzaguirre, *Hispanoamérica del Dolor*, p. 42.
60 Eyzaguirre, 'Por la Fidelidad a la Esperanza', p. 21.
61 Eyzaguirre, *Hispanoamérica del Dolor*, p. 79.
62 Eyzaguirre, 'Por la Fidelidad a la Esperanza', pp. 23–4.
63 Lira, *Hispanidad y Mestizaje*, pp. 13, 60.
64 Ibid., p. 40.
65 Ibid., p. 41.
66 Ibid., p. 42.
67 Ibid., p. 55.
68 Ibid., pp. 91–2.

Chapter 5   Postwar Expansion

1   E. Mandel, *Late Capitalism* (London: New Left Books, 1975), p. 63.
2   P. Wagner, *A Sociology of Modernity, Liberty and Discipline* (London: Routledge, 1994), p. 73.
3   N. García Canclini, *Culturas Híbridas: Estrategias para Entrar y Salir de la Modernidad* (Mexico: Grijalbo, 1989), pp. 81–2.
4   See Renato Ortiz, *A Moderna Tradição Brasileira, Cultura Brasileira e Indústria Cultural* (Sao Paulo: Editora Brasiliense, 1988), pp. 38–44.
5   See Cristobal Marín, 'Modernity and Mass Communication: The Latin American Case', Ph.D. thesis, University of Birmingham, 1999, p. 217.
6   J. B. Thompson, *The Media and Modernity* (Cambridge: Polity Press, 1995), p. 46. See also Thompson, *Ideology and Modern Culture* (Cambridge: Polity Press, 1990), pp. 12–20, 225–48.
7   On the impact of the mass media on the social and political life of Latin American societies see Marín, 'Modernity and Mass Communication', pp. 247–51.
8   See R. Gwynne, 'Industrialization and Urbanization', in D. Preston (ed.), *Latin American Development* (Harlow: Longman, 1996), pp. 228–9, 220.
9   For an analysis of modernization theories see J. Larrain, *Theories of Development* (Cambridge: Polity Press, 1989), pp. 85–102.
10 See on this Gino Germani, *Política y Sociedad en una Epoca de Transición* (Buenos Aires: Editorial Paidos, 1965), ch. 4.
11 Ibid., p. 72.
12 Ibid., p. 56. Germani's distinction is more general than Weber's because both elective and prescriptive actions can be either habitual or rational.
13 Ibid., p. 104.
14 See United Nations, Economic Commission for Latin America, *Development Problems in Latin America* (Austin: University of Texas Press, 1969), and *The Economic Development of Latin America and its Principal Problems* (New York: United Nations, 1950). See also R. Pre-

bisch, *Economic Development of Latin America and some of its Principal Problems* (New York: United Nations, 1950).

15 For an analysis of ECLA's ideas and policies see Larrain, *Theories of Development*, pp. 102–10.

16 See A. G. Frank, *Capitalism and Underdevelopment in Latin America* (New York: Monthly Review Press, 1969).

17 See F. H. Cardoso and E. Faletto, *Dependency and Development in Latin America* (Berkeley: University of California Press, 1979).

18 ISEB is the acronym for Instituto Superior de Estudos Brasileiros. On the cultural impact of ISEB authors see further below (note 20).

19 O. Sunkel, *Capitalismo Transnacional y Desintegración Nacional en América Latina* (Buenos Aires: Ediciones Nueva Visión, 1972), p. 81.

20 See on this Renato Ortiz, 'Alienação e Cultura: o ISEB', in *Cultura Brasileira e Identidade Nacional* (Sao Paulo: Editora Brasiliense, 1985), pp. 45–67.

21 I follow here the account given by M. T. Martínez Blanco, *Identidad Cultural de Hispanoamérica* (Madrid: Editorial de la Universidad Complutense, 1987), pp. 221–35.

22 Ernesto Mayz Vallenilla, *El problema de América* (Caracas: Universidad Católica de Venezuela, 1959).

23 Martínez Blanco, *Identidad Cultural de Hispanoamérica*, p. 222. See also a discussion on Mayz Vallenilla in Mario Sambarino, *Identidad, tradición y autenticidad*, Centro de Estudios Latinoamericanos (Caracas: Rómulo Gallego, 1980), pp. 284–97.

24 Quoted by Sambarino, *Identidad, tradición y autenticidad*, p. 291.

25 Alberto Caturelli, *América Bifronte* (Buenos Aires: Editorial Troquel, 1961).

26 Quoted by Martínez Blanco, *Identidad Cultural de Hispanoamérica*, p. 225. Taken from Alberto Caturelli, *América Bifronte*, p. 41.

27 Martínez Blanco, *Identidad Cultural de Hispanoamérica*, p. 224.

28 Ibid., p. 228.

29 H. A. Murena, *El pecado original de América* (Buenos Aires, 1954).

30 Ibid., pp. 115–16. Quoted by Martínez Blanco, *Identidad Cultural de Hispanoamérica*, p. 229.

31 Martinez Blanco, *Identidad Cultural de Hispanoamérica*, pp. 228–9.

32 Octavio Paz, *The Labyrinth of Solitude* (Mexico: Fondo de Cultura Económica, 1959), pp. 18–19.

33 Ibid., pp. 78–80.

34 Ibid., p. 151.

35 Ibid., p. 155.

36 Fernando Ainsa, *Identidad Cultural de Iberoamérica en su narrativa* (Madrid: Gredos, 1986), pp. 142–3.

37 Haroldo de Campos, 'Superación de los lenguajes exclusivos', in César Fernández Moreno (ed.), *América Latina en su literatura* (Mexico: Siglo XXI, 1992), pp. 290–1.

38 Ainsa, *Identidad Cultural de Iberoamérica*, p. 143.

39 Martínez Blanco, *Identidad Cultural de Hispanoamérica*, p. 244.

40 Ibid., p. 249.
41 Jean Franco, *Historia de la Literatura Hispanoamericana* (Barcelona: Editorial Ariel, 1980), pp. 385–8.
42 Roberto Fernández Retamar, 'Intercomunicación y nueva literatura', in Fernández Moreno, *América Latina en su literatura*, p. 323.
43 Juan José Saer, 'La literatura y los nuevos lenguajes', in Fernández Moreno, *América Latina en su literatura*, p. 305.
44 Quoted by Martínez Blanco, *Identidad Cultural de Hispanoamérica*, p. 240. Taken from Eligio García Márquez, *Son así* (Bogota, 1982), pp. 49–50.
45 Quoted by Martínez Blanco, *Identidad Cultural de Hispanoamérica*, p. 239. Taken from Mario Benedetti, *El escritor latinoamericano y la revolución posible* (Mexico: Nueva Imagen, 1980), pp. 94–5.
46 Quoted by Martínez Blanco, *Identidad Cultural de Hispanoamérica*, p. 238. Taken from a conference at the University of Montevideo, 11 Aug. 1966. Mario Vargas Llosa, *La Novela* (Buenos Aires: América Nueva, 1974), p. 37.

Chapter 6 Dictatorships and the Lost Decade

1 See on this E. Mandel, *The Second Slump* (London: Verso, 1978), ch. 1.
2 See A. Lipietz, *Towards a New Economic Order* (Cambridge: Polity Press, 1992); M. Aglietta, *A theory of Capitalist Regulation* (London: Verso, 1979); R. Boyer, *La théorie de la régulation: une analyse critique* (Paris, 1986).
3 In the case of the Chilean dictatorship it took the first four years (1973–7) for the harsh economic policies to begin to have some acceptable results, only for the economy to plunge again into a deep financial crisis in 1982. See on this T. Moulian, *Chile Actual, Anatomía de un Mito* (Santiago: LOM, 1997), pp. 201–12.
4 Renato Ortiz, *A Moderna Tradição Brasileira, Cultura Brasileira e Indústria Cultural* (Sao Paulo: Editora Brasiliense, 1988), pp. 114–15.
5 Ibid., p. 116.
6 See on this Cristóbal Marín, 'Modernity and Mass Communication: The Latin American Case', Ph.D. thesis, University of Birmingham, 1999, pp. 257–9.
7 Ortiz, *A Moderna Tradição Brasileira*, p. 145.
8 Telluric factors are those which come from an all-powerful and uncontrolled nature.
9 'Macondism' alludes to the fantastic frame of mind derived from the mythical town of Macondo in Gabriel García Márquez's *One Hundred Years of Solitude*. See on this José Joaquín Brunner, *Cartografías de la Modernidad* (Santiago: Dolmen, 1994), p. 167.
10 For instance, Fernando Ainsa has put forward the thesis that the Latin American identity has been best defined and expressed by its litera-

ture. See his *Identidad Cultural de Iberoamérica en su narrativa* (Madrid: Gredos, 1986), p. 23. See also the Introduction to this book.

11 Brunner, *Cartografías de la Modernidad*, p. 172.

12 Ainsa, *Identidad Cultural de Iberoamérica*, p. 502.

13 Seymour Menton, *La nueva novela histórica de la América Latina 1979–1992* (Mexico: Fondo de Cultura Económica, 1994), pp. 29–56.

14 Octavio Paz, *El ogro filantrópico* (Barcelona: Seix Barral, 1990), p. 44.

15 Carlos Fuentes, *Valiente mundo nuevo: épica, utopía y mito en la novela hispanoamericana* (Madrid: Narrativa Mondadori, 1990), pp. 12–13.

16 Ibid., p. 18.

17 Richard Morse, *El Espejo de Próspero, un estudio de la dialéctica del Nuevo Mundo* (Mexico: Siglo XXI, 1982), p. 178. According to Morse, 'literature is what best illustrates the fact that Ibero America, including its most modern or bourgeois sector, is not quite subjected to Western "disenchantment"' (p. 179).

18 Ibid., p. 168.

19 Ibid., p. 218.

20 Ibid., p. 200.

21 Fuentes, *Valiente mundo nuevo*, p. 14.

22 Paz, *El ogro filantrópico*, pp. 63–4.

23 See Alberto Methol Ferré, 'El resurgimiento católico latinoamericano', in Consejo Episcopal Latinoamericano (ed.), *Religión y Cultura* (Bogota: CELAM, 1981) and Pedro Morandé, *Cultura y Modernización en América Latina* (Santiago: Cuadernos del Instituto de Sociología, Universidad Católica de Chile, 1984), pp. 144–5.

24 A. Touraine, *Crítica de la Modernidad* (Buenos Aires: Fondo de Cultura Económica, 1994), p. 201.

25 Brunner, *Cartografías de la Modernidad*, p. 173.

26 García Canclini, *Culturas Híbridas,* p. 146.

27 C. Parker, *Otra Lógica en América Latina: Religión Popular y Modernización Capitalista* (Santiago: Fondo de Cultura Económica, 1993), pp. 73–96.

28 I take this terminology from G. Sunkel, 'Representations of the People in the Chilean Popular Press', Ph.D. thesis, University of Birmingham, 1988, p. 42. It can also be found in Parker, *Otra Lógica en América Latina*, p. 370.

29 Parker, *Otra Lógica en América Latina*, pp. 194–8.

30 Octavio Paz, *The Labyrinth of Solitude* (Mexico: Fondo de Cultura Económica, 1959), pp. 18–19.

31 P. Bifani, 'Lo propio y lo ajeno en interrelación palpitante', *Nueva Sociedad*, no. 99 (1989), pp. 105, 114.

32 M. Langon, '¿Qué tenemos que ver unos con otros?', *Nueva Sociedad*, no. 99 (1989), p. 138.

33 Ibid., p. 146.

34 Jorge Gissi, 'Identidad, "Carácter Social" y Cultura Latinoamericana', *Estudios Sociales*, no. 33 (1982).

35   E. Galeano, 'The Blue Tiger and the Promised Land', in *Report on the Americas* (New York: North American Congress on Latin America), vol. 24, no. 5 (Feb. 1991), p. 13.

36   Ibid., p. 14.

37   L. G. Lumbreras, 'Misguided Development', in *Report on the Americas*, p. 18.

38   Ibid., p. 22.

39   A. Quijano, 'Recovering Utopia', in *Report on the Americas*, p. 36.

40   Ibid., p. 38.

41   A. Quijano, *Modernidad, Identidad y Utopía en América Latina* (Lima: Ediciones Sociedad Política, 1988), p. 62.

42   'Ladino' is a synonym of 'mestizo' which etymologically derives from 'Latin': someone who speaks Latin or Spanish. This term is widely used in Central America, particularly Guatemala, but is hardly known in the Southern Cone. In Central America it has a more derogatory connotation than the term mestizo, which is more neutral. It designates someone who despises Indian values, whatever his or her origins. Gallardo's aggressiveness is shown in the very title of part 2 of his book: 'Fenomenología del ladino de mierda'. See H. Gallardo, *500 Años: Fenomenología del mestizo, violencia y resistencia* (Santiago: Producciones Gráficas Eduardo Inostroza, 1994).

43   Ibid., p. 114.

44   Ibid., pp. 122–3.

45   Ibid., p. 135.

46   Ibid., p. 148.

47   Daniel E. Matul, 'Estamos vivos. Reafirmación de la cultura maya', *Nueva Sociedad*, no. 99 (1989).

48   Véase Guillermo Bonfil Batalla, *México Profundo* (Mexico: Grijalbo, 1987).

49   Emilio Monsonyi, *Identidad nacional y culturas populares* (Caracas: Editorial La Enseñanza Viva, 1982).

50   Arturo Uslar Pietri, 'El mestizaje creador', in J. Skirius (ed.), *El Ensayo Hispanoamericano del siglo XX* (Mexico: Fondo de Cultura Económica, 1981).

51   Arturo Uslar Pietri, *La creación del Nuevo Mundo* (Caracas: Grijalbo, 1991), p. 44.

52   Ibid., p. 16.

53   Uslar Pietri, 'El mestizaje creador', p. 288.

54   Uslar Pietri, *La creación del Nuevo Mundo*, p. 177.

55   See Otto Morales Benítez, 'Mestización racial y cultural en la elaboración de un futuro común latinoamericano', in L. Zea (ed.), *Quinientos años de historia, sentido y proyección* (Mexico: Instituto Interamericano de Historia y F.C.E., 1991).

56   Gustavo Vega, 'Utopía mestiza o emancipación de la aculturación. Notas sobre la ideología de la mesticidad latinoamericana', *Cántaro* (Cuenca), no. 3 (1992).

57 See the document of the Latin American bishops' general conference, which took place in Puebla in 1979 (Santiago: Conferencia Episcopal de Chile, 1979), nos 412, 445.

58 It is important to note the influence that this tendency has on many bishops in Latin America, who in their turn continue to wield formidable political and cultural power in their countries.

59 Methol Ferré, 'El resurgimiento católico latinoamericano', pp. 68–71.

60 Juan Carlos Scannone, 'Nueva modernidad adveniente y cultura emergente en América Latina', *Stromata* 47, no. 1–2 (1991), p. 160. See also 'Modernidad, Posmodernidad y formas de racionalidad en América Latina', in D. Michelini et al. (eds), *Modernidad y Posmodernidad en América Latina* (Rio Cuarto: Ediciones del ICALA, 1991), pp. 27–8.

61 Scannone, 'Nueva modernidad adveniente', pp. 166–70.

62 P. Morandé, 'Latinoamericanos: Hijos de un Diálogo Ritual', *Creces*, no. 11–12 (1990), p. 10.

63 P. Morandé, 'La Síntesis Cultural Hispánica Indígena', *Teología y Vida* 32, no. 1–2 (1991), pp. 43–5.

64 That was the way, for instance, in which Malinche and another nineteen young women slaves were offered to Hernán Cortés. Malinche, an Indian woman given to Hernán Cortés as a wife by an Indian chief, learnt Spanish very quickly and became Cortés's translator, symbol of the union between the two cultures, but also suspected of being a traitor who switched sides and became powerful under Spanish protection.

65 Morandé, 'La Síntesis Cultural Hispánica Indígena', p. 48.

66 P. Morandé, *Cultura y Modernización en América Latina*, Cuadernos del Instituto de Sociología (Santiago: Universidad Católica de Chile, 1984), pp. 139–40.

67 Ibid., pp. 144–5.

68 Morandé, 'La Síntesis Cultural Hispánica Indígena', p. 51.

69 Even more, it is shared by a North American, E. Bradford Burns, who in a bitter critique of the elitism and partiality of the nineteenth-century Latin American historians says: 'The question was not whether to Europeanize but how, not whether to foster capitalism but how to expedite it. No consideration was given to the reality that the majority had no connection with Europe but rather had their own folk cultures and preferred communal arrangements to "competitive" ones . . . By ignoring those aspects and sectors of their society that resisted the European siren, the historians omitted the majority of the population from their pages. When they did notice the masses in their accounts, it was generally to deplore them as "backward" . . .' *The Poverty of Progress* (Berkeley: University of California Press, 1980), pp. 45, 48.

70 L. Zea, *América como Consciencia* (Mexico: Universidad Nacional Autónoma de México, 1972), p. 42.

71 Ibid., p. 43.
72 Morandé, *Cultura y Modernización en América Latina*, p. 129.
73 Ibid., pp. 161–2.
74 Parker, *Otra Lógica en América Latina*, p. 192.
75 Ibid., pp. 198, 199.
76 Ibid., pp. 192, 354, 370.
77 Ibid., p. 367.
78 Ibid., p. 380.
79 Ibid., p. 391.
80 Ibid., pp. 400–5.
81 It seems to me important to engage in a thorough critique of the essen-tialist theories presented above, in so far as many of them are still being debated in the Latin American cultural arena.
82 Marcos García de la Huerta, *Reflexiones Americanas, Ensayos de Intra-Historia* (Santiago: LOM Ediciones, 1999), p. 137.
83 See on this pp. 37–9 above.
84 Parker, *Otra Lógica en América Latina*, pp. 192, 354.
85 Ibid., pp. 396, 390.
86 Ibid., pp. 396, 388.
87 Ibid., p. 403.
88 Ibid., p. 357.
89 Ibid., p. 367.
90 C. Lévi-Strauss, *The Savage Mind* (London: Weidenfeld and Nicolson, 1974), pp. 9–16.
91 C. Lévi-Strauss, *Structural Anthropology* (Harmondsworth: Penguin, 1972), p. 230.
92 Parker, *Otra Lógica en América Latina*, p. 354.
93 I paraphrase here Marx's critique of Ravenstone and followers who were critics of capitalism. See K. Marx, *Theories of Surplus Value* (London: Lawrence and Wishart, 1972), vol. 3, p. 261.

Chapter 7   The Neoliberal Stage

1 This crucial point has been analysed by A. Giddens, *The Consequences of Modernity* (Cambridge: Polity Press, 1990), p. 16. On the impact of the media on the time-space relationship see J. B. Thompson, *The Media and Modernity* (Cambridge: Polity Press, 1995), pp. 30–7.
2 D. Harvey, *The Condition of Postmodernity* (Oxford: Blackwell, 1989), p. 240.
3 This point was first underlined by J. B. Thompson. See *Ideology and Modern Culture* (Cambridge: Polity Press, 1990), p. 4; see also pp. 12–20 and 225–48 and *The Media and Modernity*, p. 46.
4 See J. Habermas, *The Structural Transformation of the Public Sphere* (Cambridge: Polity Press, 1989).
5 Thompson, *The Media and Modernity*, pp. 125–34.
6 See on this ibid., p. 81.

7   Ibid., pp. 82–4.
8   Ibid., p. 208.
9   Giddens, *The Consequences of Modernity*, pp. 63–4.
10 S. Hall, 'The Question of Cultural Identity', in S. Hall, D. Held and T. McGrew, *Modernity and its Futures* (Cambridge: Polity Press and Open University, 1992), p. 299.
11 A. McGrew, 'A Global Society?', in Hall, Held and McGrew, *Modernity and its Futures*, p. 68.
12 Giddens, *The Consequences of Modernity*, pp. 70–8.
13 Ibid., p. 74.
14 See on this M. Waters, *Globalization* (London: Routledge, 1995), pp. 9–10.
15 S. Hall, 'The Local and the Global: Globalisation and Ethnicity', in A. King (ed.), *Culture, Globalization and the World-System* (London: Macmillan, 1991), p. 27.
16 Ibid., p. 28.
17 K. Robins, 'Tradition and Translation: National Culture in its Global Context', in J. Corner and S. Harvey (eds), *Enterprise and Heritage* (London: Routledge, 1991), p. 29.
18 Thompson, *The Media and Modernity*, p. 29.
19 For evidence of this see pp. 188–90 below.
20 See M. Horkheimer and T. Adorno, *Dialectic of Enlightenment* (London: Verso, 1979), pp. 120–67. See also T. Adorno, 'Culture Industry Reconsidered', *New German Critique*, no. 6 (1975).
21 K. Robins, 'Tradition and Translation', p. 31.
22 See on this McGrew, 'A Global Society?', pp. 74–6.
23 Thompson, *The Media and Modernity*, ch. 6.
24 A good proof of this is provided by the paradigmatic example of Chile, where in spite of high rates of growth for many years, the poorest 10 per cent of the population receives about 1.5 per cent of the national income while the richest 10 per cent of the population receives about 42 per cent. See Jacobo Chatán, *Deuda Externa, Neoliberalismo y Globalización: El saqueo de América Latina* (Santiago: Ediciones LOM, 1998), pp. 134–5.
25 Friedrich A. Hayek, 'The Principles of a Liberal Social order', in *Studies in Philosophy, Politics and Economics* (London: Routledge and Kegan Paul, 1978), p. 161.
26 A good case in point is Chile, where the Catholic hierarchy strongly opposed Pinochet's systematic violation of human rights, and created organizations to help, rescue and locate disappeared and tortured people. The situation was not the same in Brazil, Uruguay and Argentina, where the Catholic Church remained basically silent at the height of the repression.
27 According to Alfredo Jocelyn-Holt, in the Chilean case the weight of the traditional elite and its hierarchical order lasted throughout the nineteenth century and until the second decade of the twentieth century. Its legacy for the whole of the twentieth century is authori-

tarianism. See *El peso de la noche, nuestra frágil fortaleza histórica* (Buenos Aires: Ariel, 1997), pp. 27, 57.

28 It is well known that some bishops in Latin America concealed and did not want to publish some of the papal social encyclicals.

29 C. Véliz, *The New World of the Gothic Fox: Culture and Economy in English and Spanish America* (Berkeley: University of California Press, 1994), p. 11.

30 Ibid., ch. 1.

31 Ibid., p. 15.

32 Ibid., p. 32.

33 The Tridentine renovation of the Catholic Church refers to the new ecclesiastical discipline and rules established by the Council of Trent to prepare the Church for the fight against the Reformation.

34 Véliz, *The New World of the Gothic Fox*, p. 71.

35 Ibid., p. 86.

36 Ibid., p. 115.

37 Ibid., p. 180.

38 Ibid., p. 198.

39 Ibid., p. 219.

40 Ibid., pp. 229–30.

41 Ibid., ch. 9.

42 See for instance G. Germani, *Politica y Sociedad en una Epoca de Transición* (Buenos Aires: Editorial Paidos, 1965), p. 102.

43 Ibid., p. 104.

44 Nelly Richard, 'Cultural Peripheries: Latin America and Postmodernist De-centering', in J. Beverly and J. Oviedo (eds), *The Postmodernism Debate in Latin America*, special issue of *Boundary* 2 (Duke University Press, 1993), p. 160.

45 N. Richard, 'Postmodernism and Periphery', in T. Docherty (ed.), *Postmodernism, A Reader* (Hemel Hempstead: Harvester Wheatsheaf, 1993), pp. 467, 468.

46 Ibid., p. 468. The quoted text appears to come from R. Schwarz, 'Nacional por Sustracción', *Punto de Vista*, no. 28 (Buenos Aires); no date or page given.

47 See R. Schwarz, *Misplaced Ideas; Essays on Brazilian Culture* (London: Verso, 1992), p. 6.

48 Nelly Richard, 'Replay to Vidal', in Beverly and Oviedo, *The Postmodernism Debate*, p. 229.

49 Ibid.

50 Ibid.

51 José Joaquín Brunner, 'Notes on Modernity and Postmodernity in Latin American Culture', in Beverly and Oviedo, *The Postmodernism Debate*, p. 40.

52 Ibid., p. 42.

53 Norbert Lechner, 'A Disenchantment called Postmodernism', in Beverly and Oviedo, *The Postmodernism Debate*, p. 130.

54 Ibid., pp. 132–3.

55 Jesús Martín Barbero, 'Modernidad y posmodernidad en la periferia', *Escritos*, no. 13–14 (1996), p. 286.
56 It is perhaps worth mentioning that Alfonso de Toro has maintained the thesis that Jorge Luis Borges, the great Argentinian writer, inaugurated postmodernity with his book *Ficciones* (1939–44), not only in Latin America, but in general. See 'Postmodernidad y Latinoamérica (con un modelo para la narrativa postmoderna)', *Revista Iberoamericana* 57, no. 155–6 (1991), pp. 441–67.
57 Martin Hopenhayn, 'Postmodernism and Neoliberalism in Latin America', in Beverly and Oviedo, *The Postmodernism Debate*, pp. 101–9.
58 Ibid., p. 100.
59 Carlos Pérez, 'La no identidad latinoamericana: una visión peregrina', *Revista de Crítica Cultural*, no. 3 (Apr. 1991), p. 30.
60 Ibid., pp. 29–30.
61 Hernán Vidal, 'Postmodernism, Postleftism, Neo-Avant-Gardism: The Case of Chile's *Revista de Crítica Cultural*', in Beverly and Oviedo, *The Postmodernism Debate*, p. 205.
62 Pérez, 'La no identidad latinoamericana', p. 32.
63 See on this Cristóbal Marín, 'Modernity and Mass Communication: The Latin American Case', Ph.D. thesis, University of Birmingham, 1999, pp. 264–9.
64 Ibid., p. 293.
65 Carlos Catalán and María Dolores Souza, 'Calidad, Identidad y Televisión', paper presented to the Latin American Meeting on Television and Quality, Sao Paulo, 4–6 Aug. 1999, pp. 6–7.
66 Marín, 'Modernity and Mass Communication', p. 297.
67 Ibid., p. 295.
68 Alberto Fuguet and Sergio Gómez, *McOndo* (Barcelona: Mondadori, 1996), p. 15.
69 Ibid., pp. 16, 19.
70 See for instance Arturo Fontaine, 'Introducción al pensamiento de Friedrich A. Hayek', *Persona y Sociedad* 13, no. 2 (1999).

Chapter 8 Key Elements of Latin American Modernity and Identity

1 See M. Barrera, 'Las reformas económicas neoliberales y la representación de los sectores populares en Chile', *Estudios Sociales*, no. 88 (1996).
2 Habermas uses the concept of a 'refeudalization of the public sphere' in a different though related sense. He refers to the loss of the public space for rational critique and discussion of state affairs which had emerged at the beginning of modernity. This public space, due to state interventions and the commercialization of the media, was subsequently replaced by the manipulation of the masses as a new 'feudal'

means to avoid genuine discussion, thus legitimating public authority. See J. Habermas, *The Structural Transformation of the Public Sphere* (Cambridge: Polity Press, 1989), p. 164.

3 G. Germani, *Politica y Sociedad en una Epoca de Transición* (Buenos Aires: Editorial Paidos, 1965), p. 104.

4 Ibid., p. 112.

5 Renato Cristi, 'Estado nacional y pensamiento conservador en la obra madura de Mario Góngora', in R. Cristi and C. Ruiz, *El pensamiento conservador en Chile* (Santiago: Editorial Universitaria, 1992), p. 157.

6 See on this R. Levitas (ed.), *The Ideology of the New Right* (Cambridge: Polity Press, 1986) and S. Hall and M. Jacques (eds), *The Politics of Thatcherism* (London: Lawrence and Wishart, 1983).

7 J. J. Brunner, *El Espejo Trizado* (Santiago: FLACSO, 1988), p. 33.

8 Alfredo Jocelyn-Holt, *El peso de la noche, nuestra frágil fortaleza histórica* (Buenos Aires: Ariel, 1997), p. 55.

9 There have been various attempts to explain Latin American political instability. Two classic ones are Merle Kling, 'Hacia una teoría del poder y de la inestabilidad política en América Latina', in J. Petras and M. Zeitling (eds), *América Latina: ¿reforma o revolución?* (Buenos Aires: Tiempo Contemporaneo, 1970) and Samuel Huntington, *Political Order in Changing Societies* (New Haven: Yale University Press, 1968).

10 C. Cousiño and E. Valenzuela, *Politización y Monetarización en América Latina* (Santiago: Cuadernos del Instituto de Sociología de la Pontificia Universidad Católica de Chile, 1994), p. 17.

11 See on this Norbert Lechner, 'Las condiciones políticas de la ciencia política en Chile', paper presented to the seminar on the Theoretical Crisis of Latin American Social Sciences, CLACSO, XVI General Assembly, Santiago, 28–9 Nov. 1991.

12 J. L. de Imaz, *Sobre la Identidad Iberoamericana* (Buenos Aires: Editorial Sudamericana, 1984), p. 121.

13 A. Flores Galindo, *Buscando un Inca* (Lima: Editorial Horizonte, 1994), p. 66.

14 See for example A. Edwards, *La Fronda Aristocrática en Chile* (Santiago: Editorial Universitaria, 1987) and M. Góngora, *Ensayo histórico sobre la noción de Estado en Chile en los siglos XIX y XX* (Santiago: Ediciones La Ciudad, 1981).

15 This sentence refers to Portales' own metaphor in a letter to a friend where he tries to explain why Chile is governable. He says: 'The social order is maintained in Chile by the weight of the night and because we do not have in Chile cocky, skilful and subtle men: the almost universal tendency of the masses to rest is a guarantee of public tranquillity.' See Jocelyn-Holt, *El peso de la noche*, pp. 27, 148.

16 Ibid., p. 57.

17 See Góngora, *Ensayo histórico*, pp. 12–16.

18 See Marcos García de la Huerta, *Reflexiones Americanas, Ensayos de intra-historia* (Santiago: LOM Ediciones, 1999), p. 123.

19 See Flores Galindo, *Buscando un Inca*, p. 215.

20 See R. Béjar, *El Mexicano, aspectos culturales y psicosociales* (Mexico: UNAM, 1988), pp. 213–14.

21 G. Freyre, *The Master and the Slaves: A Study in the Development of Brazilian Civilization* (New York: Alfred Knopf, 1946).

22 See on this T. Cubitt, *Latin American Society* (Harlow: Longman, 1995), pp. 122–6.

23 Ibid., p. 151.

24 See for instance Aníbal Quijano, *Modernidad, Identidad y Utopía en América Latina* (Lima: Sociedad y Política/Ediciones, 1988), and Cristián Parker, *Otra Lógica en América Latina* (Santiago: Fondo de Cultura Económica, 1993). Both think that in Latin America there is a different rationality or logic.

25 See on this Maritza Montero, *Ideología, Alienación e Identidad Nacional* (Caracas: Universidad Central de Venezuela, 1987), pp. 29–41.

26 I am aware that some of the material in this section could have been developed within some of the historical stages that I distinguished. However, given its importance and in order to safeguard the guiding thread of its development I took the decision to concentrate it in this latter section.

27 Arzobispado de Santiago, *Mirada a la Realidad*, anexo al documento de trabajo para la primera asamblea presinodal (Nov. 1995), ch. 2.

28 Ibid., p. 42.

29 A. Pastor et al. (eds), *De Lonquén a los Andes, 20 años de iglesia católica chilena* (Santiago: Rehue, 1993), p. 66.

30 Phillip Berryman, *Religion in the Megacity: Catholic and Protestant Portraits from Latin America* (New York: Orbis Books, 1996), p. 66.

31 Ibid., p. 3.

32 Ibid., p. 45.

33 David Martin, 'Otro tipo de revolución cultural, el protestantismo radical en latinoamérica', *Estudios Públicos*, no. 44 (1991), p. 41.

34 David Martin, *Tongues of Fire: The Explosion of Protestantism in Latin America* (Oxford: Blackwell, 1990), pp. 50–1.

35 Martin, 'Otro tipo de revolución cultural', p. 41.

36 Arzobispado de Santiago, *Mirada a la Realidad*, pp. 93–4. It is true that the practising zeal of a religious group may respond more to the fact of its being a minority than to the nature of the religion itself. In Britain Catholics have relatively higher church attendance than Anglicans. Yet Catholics in Britain do not increase at the rate Pentecostals do in Latin America.

37 Martin, *Tongues of Fire*, p. 51.

38 Walter Hollenwerger, *El pentecostalismo, historia y doctrina* (Buenos Aires: La Aurora, 1976). Cited by José Míguez Bonino, *Rostros del Protestantismo Latinoamericano* (Buenos Aires: Nueva Creación, 1995), p. 61.

39   Juan Sepúlveda, 'Pentecostal Theology in the Context of the Struggle for Life', in D. Kirkpatrick (ed.), *Faith Born in the Struggle for Life* (Grand Rapids: Eerdmans, 1988), pp. 299ff.

40   It is necessary to take into account, though, that this puritanism in the Pentecostal style of life has little by little become more flexible under the impact of modernization processes.

41   Manuel Ossa, 'La Identidad Pentecostal', *Persona y Sociedad* 10, no. 1 (1996), p. 193.

42   Christian Lalive d'Epinay, *Religion, dynamique social et dépéndence* (Paris: Mouton, 1975), p. 86.

43   Martin, *Tongues of Fire*, p. 13

44   Juan Sepúlveda, 'Gospel and Culture in Latin American Protestantism: Towards a New Theological Appreciation of Syncretism', Ph.D. thesis, Department of Theology, University of Birmingham, 1996, pp. 95–7.

45   Berryman, *Religion in the Megacity*, ch. 14.

Glossary

APRA Alianza Popular Revolucionaria Americana (American revolutionary popular alliance), both a continental political movement created in Mexico in 1924, and the Peruvian Aprista Party, a populist party created in 1931 by Victor Raúl Haya de la Torre.

cabildos Local councils or meetings of local councils.

caciques Indian chieftains.

campesinos Peasants, particularly poor peasants or agricultural workers.

castas Category used in Latin America during the colonial time to refer to a variety of racial groups (up to sixteen) formed by the mixes between white Spaniards, Indians and blacks.

caudillo Military and political chieftain.

cholos Another name for mestizo in Peru. Also a scornful name given to an Indian who tries to climb socially.

Cinema Novo Expression used in Brazil in the 1960s to refer to a new kind of cinema that wanted to be socially and aesthetically subversive.

conquistador Spanish conqueror.

CORFO Corporación de Fomento de la Producción (Corporation for the Promotion of Production). Institution created in 1938 for the promotion of industrial production in Chile.

Creoles Criollos.

criollos Descendants of Spanish conquerors born in Latin America.

curacas In the Inca empire, local chiefs and nobility.

ECLA Economic Commission for Latin America. Regional United Nations organization created in 1948 to elaborate economic policies leading to economic development in Latin America.

encomenderos Spanish conquistadors who received an *encomienda* or *repartimiento de indios*, that is to say, a number of Indians to work for him under the encomienda system.

encomienda A corvée system under which a group of Indians was allocated to a Spanish conqueror who could extract tribute from them by making them work for free in his lands or mines.

fueros Old Spanish laws or codes given for a council.

gamonal Landowner in Peru.

gaucho Typical peasant worker in Argentina and Uruguay.

hacendado Owner of hacienda, large estate or farm.

hacienda Large estate or farm in which peasants were not entirely free and the hacendado had a great deal of power over all aspects of their lives.

huasipungueros Peasants working in haciendas in Ecuador.

Indianos Mestizos or Spanish conquerors coming from America to live in Spain.

Indigenismo Broad movement formed in the 1920s advocating a return to Indian values and defending the Indians from discrimination.

indigenista Individual belonging to Indigenismo, quality of someone belonging to Indigenismo.

inquilinos Peasants working in haciendas in Chile.

ISEB Instituto Superior de Estudos Brasileiros (High Institute of Brazilian Studies). This institute, formed in the 1960s, wanted to create an authentic national culture.

ladino Synonym of mestizo widely used in Central America with a derogatory connotation: someone who despises Indian values.

latifundia Traditional large estates or farms.

Macondismo Derived from Macondo, a mythical city in Gabriel García Márquez's *A Hundred Years of Solitude*; a metaphor for the magical and mysterious character of Latin America. Theoretical position which grants a special explanatory power to Latin American literature.

mamelucos Name given to mestizos in Brazil.

mestizaje Process of the mixing between Spanish and Indian.

mestizo Mix of Spanish and Indian.

mita A corvée system of labour used in mining or public works by the Inca empire and the Spanish conquerors.

mulattos Mix of black and white.

pampa The big plain in Argentina.

pardos One of the castas, mixed race.

pasadismo In C. I. Degregori's critique of Indigenismo, tendency to overrate the historical Indian and not to rate the present one.

pathos Greek for disposition or state of the soul, what is felt, suffered or experienced by an individual or a people.

Peninsulars Spaniards – people who come from the Iberian peninsula.

repartimiento Another name for encomienda; it comes from the Spanish *repartimiento de Indios* (distribution of Indians).

sierra (of Peru) Mountainous hinterland of Peru as opposed to the coast.

telenovelas Latin American soap operas.

yaravi Kind of Indian song.

Index

acculturation 147, 180
accumulation, regime of 133
  Fordist–Keynesian 80, 133–4
  post-Fordist flexible 19, 21, 134
Adorno, Theodor 17, 170
Africa 19, 46, 61, 76
Aguirre Beltrán, Gonzalo 99
Aguirre Cerda, Pedro 101
Ainsa, Fernando 2, 43, 129, 130,
    137, 208
Alberdi, Juan Bautista 83, 85, 86,
    90, 159, 180
Alegría, Ciro 2, 107
Alençar, José de 87
Alianza Popular Revolucionaria
    Americana (APRA) 104
alienation 126, 155, 160, 161, 165
Allende, Isabel 137
Altamirano, Ignacio 88
Anderson, Benedict 32, 34
Andrade, Mario de 94
Andrade, Oswald de 94
Archilochus 176
Argentina 2–4, 9, 65, 72, 74–6,
    79–80, 82, 83–5, 93, 95, 101,
    103–4, 118, 134, 135–7, 151,
    189, 194–5, 199

Arguedas, Alcides 84, 85, 95, 106
Aristotle 29
Asia 19–20, 117, 128
Asturias, Miguel Angel 107
Australia 19
authoritarianism 60–1, 82, 118,
    159, 175, 191, 195–6
Azevedo, Aluisio 87
Azuela, Mariano 95

Bacon, Francis 12
Barbero, Jesús Martín 185
Baroque 149–52, 177
  art 177
  hedgehog 177–9
  Spanish 178
Barreda, Gabino 77, 82
Barrera, Manuel 191
base communities 202–3, 205
Baudelaire, Charles 16
Bauman, Zygmunt 14, 30, 208
Béjar, Raúl 198
Bello, Andrés 77, 78
Benedetti, Mario 131, 137
Benedict, Ruth 31
Bengoa, José 62
Benítez Rojo, Antonio 138

Benjamin, Walter 14
Berlin, Isaiah 176
Berman, Marshall 14, 16
Berryman, Phillip 202–3, 205
Bifani, Patricia 143
Bilbao, Francisco 76, 77
Bitterli, Urs 49–50
Blanco Fombona, Rufino 95–6,
     109
Bolívar, Simón 73, 76
Bolivia 3–4, 8, 46–7, 65, 72–4, 94,
     102, 106, 134, 195
Bonfil Batalla, Guillermo 147
Bonfim, Manuel 97, 98
Brading, David 48, 64
Brazil 2–4, 8, 11, 23, 47, 49, 52,
     58, 64, 72, 79, 82, 84, 88,
     93–4, 97, 101, 103–4, 108,
     116–17, 125–6, 134–6, 169,
     174, 188–9, 195, 198, 202,
     203–5
Brunner, José Joaquín 137, 140,
     185, 193
Buarque de Holanda, Sérgio 108
Buffon, George-Louis, Comte de
     54, 55–7, 105
Bunge, Carlos Octavio 84
Burns, Bradford 178

caciques 47, 139
Canada 65, 124
capitalism 46, 79, 92–3, 104,
     114–15, 117, 123–5, 133–4,
     138–9, 157, 172, 175, 179,
     198
  disorganized 19
  organized 115, 117
Cardoso, Fernando Henrique 79,
     124
Carpentier, Alejo 88, 108, 130,
     131, 138
Casas, Bartolomé de las 47, 50–1,
     58–9
Cassirer, Ernst 54–6
castas 52, 72
Catholic Church 61, 80, 151, 177,
     193, 203–4

Catholic fundamentalism 142
Catholic substratum 151–2, 154,
     156–7, 160–2
Catholicism 10, 49, 61–2, 66–7,
     72, 161–2, 175, 196, 201, 206
Caturelli, Alberto 128
caudillo 139, 194
Central America 3, 8, 29, 33, 65,
     79, 81, 107, 194–5, 202–3
centre–periphery 121–3, 183
character
  Latin American 93, 104, 106,
     109
  national 31–2, 35, 54, 108
Chile 2–4, 9, 46–7, 53, 72–7,
     79–80, 82, 86, 90, 93, 101,
     104, 109, 123, 134–7, 151,
     175, 188–96, 199, 202–3, 205
China 58, 79
cholo 84
Christendom 60–1, 66–8, 80, 162,
     206
Christianity 48, 51–2, 62, 157,
     162, 205
Cinema Novo 127
civil society 152, 167, 191, 193
civilization and barbarism 83,
     86–8, 95
class
  bourgeoisie 64, 78, 80, 85, 93,
     98, 100, 102–3, 123, 193
  landowning ruling 93, 196
  middle 80, 92–4, 100–3
  ruling 9, 74, 78, 80–2, 89, 144,
     154, 174, 196
  struggle 165
  system 47, 120
  under- 199
  working 100–3, 120, 124
clientelism 100, 191
Colombia 73, 76, 79, 136, 150,
     189, 194
colonialism
  internal 72
  mental 126
Columbus, Christopher 43, 48,
     143, 148

community, imagined 3, 28, 32, 37
Comte, Auguste 82, 84
consciousness
  anti-imperialist 94
  discursive 35
  practical 35, 64
Conselheiro, Antonio 88
Constant, Benjamín 82
constructivism 37, 175–6
Contreras, Gonzalo 190
Corporación de Fomento de la Producción (CORFO) 101
Cortázar, Julio 130
Cortés, Hernán 44
Costa Rica 203
Council of Trent 67, 68, 177
Counter-Reformation 50, 60, 67–8, 138, 177–9
Cousiño, Carlos 66–7, 102, 178, 194
creole 58, 66
  see also criollo
criollo 1, 53, 64, 70–2, 75, 99, 109–10, 156, 161
  see also creole
Cristi, Renato 192
Cruz Costa, Joao 97
Cuba 72, 95
culture
  authentic 63, 126, 137–8, 155, 159, 187
  baroque 67, 68, 69, 182
  European 66, 128
  Hispanic 97
  inauthentic 139, 159
  Indo-Iberian 22, 65, 71, 82, 89, 158, 195–6
  industries 25, 136, 170
  liberal-positivist 97
  mass 116, 136, 169, 188
  mediazation of 166, 189
  popular 116, 135–6, 150, 156–7, 162, 205
  rational enlightened 142, 154–5
  symbolic dramatic 142, 155, 158, 182

Cunha, Euclides da 84–5, 87, 97
curaca 47

Darío, Rubén 2, 88–9, 95, 149
Darwinism, Social 84
decade, lost 7, 133, 135, 182, 207
deculturation 65, 143
Degregori, C. I. 99
democracy 138–9, 146, 159, 172, 174–6, 185–6, 188, 192, 194–6, 198
demonstration effect 119, 120, 180–1
dependency 122–6, 134
  theories of 123–4, 178
depoliticization 189, 190, 194, 195
depression of 1930 7, 8, 92–3, 105
Derrida, Jacques 159, 183
Descartes, René 12
development
  accelerated 5, 7, 187
  advanced 119
  capitalist 115, 122–4
  economic 17, 28, 102, 114–17, 120–6, 132, 134–5, 139, 158, 172, 176, 178, 180–1, 186, 192, 195, 205
  industrial 23, 122, 126, 188
  inward-oriented 101–2, 122
  Latin American 10
  national 104, 124–5, 127, 160
  neoliberal 187
  outward-oriented 93, 122
  sociology of 118
  stages of 129
  theories of 117, 129
Díaz, Eugenio 88
dictatorship 23, 134–9, 172, 174–5, 188–9, 194–5, 202
Diegues, Carlos 127
disenchantment of the world 13, 17, 139
Dominican Republic 95
Donoso, José 131, 137
Durkheim, Émile 13, 17
Dussel, Enrique 14, 43, 208

Echeverría, Esteban 78, 86
Economic Commission for Latin
    America (ECLA) 23, 101,
    121–3, 126
economy, informal 198, 200
Ecuador 65, 72, 150
El Salvador 107
emancipation
    mental 77–8, 83
    universal 182
    women's 75
    working class 125
empire
    Aztec 45, 47, 55, 66, 153
    British 20
    Inca 47, 55, 66, 153
encomienda 46–7, 61, 153–4
Engels, Friedrich 90
Enlightenment 4–5, 12, 17, 21–2,
    55, 57, 66, 68, 74–5, 86, 89,
    138, 151–2, 154, 156, 158–60,
    175, 182, 196
Ercilla, Alonso de 53
Erikson, Erik 27
Espinoza, Germán 138
essentialism 37, 38, 112, 127, 142,
    144, 157–8, 160, 162–4,
    178–9, 182, 186, 190
Estado Novo 108
    see also new state
ethic, Protestant 155
ethnocentrism 50, 52
ethos 3, 5, 61, 106, 127, 152,
    154–6, 163
Euripides 29
European Community 42
exclusion 135, 184, 199–200, 204
Eyzaguirre, Jaime 109, 110, 112

Faletto, Enzo 79, 124
Fallas, Carlos Luis 107
fascism 92, 104
Fernández de Lizardi, J. J. 75
Fernández Retamar, Roberto 131
Filho, Adonias 2
Flores Galindo, Alberto 61, 195,
    197

Fontaine, Arturo 190
Forn, Juan 190
Foucault, Michel 183
France 90, 143
Franco, Jean 89, 131
Frank, André Gunder 46, 123, 124
Frank, Waldo 105
Frankfurt School 17
Freire, Paulo 126
Freud, Sigmund 17
Freyre, Gilberto 108, 198
Frisby, David 16, 208
Fuentes, Carlos 5, 130–1, 138–9,
    141, 190, 208
Fuguet, Alberto 189–90
fusion effect 119–20, 181, 192

Galeano, Eduardo 145
Gallardo, Helio 146–7, 158
Gallegos, Rómulo 95
Galván, Manuel de Jesús 87
García, Alan 135
García Calderón, Francisco 84–5
García Canclini, Néstor 16, 38,
    116, 140
García-Gual, Carlos 29
García de la Huerta, Marcos 159,
    197
García Márquez, Gabriel 2, 130–1
gaucho 83, 87, 90, 106
Gerbi, Antonio 58, 105
Gerchunoff, Alberto 95
Germani, Gino 118–20, 181, 192
Giddens, Anthony 15, 19, 31, 34,
    168
Gil Fortoul, José 83–4, 86
Ginés de Sepúlveda, Juan 51
Gissi, Jorge 43, 143–4
globalization 19, 24, 33, 39, 41–2,
    168–71, 189
Gobineau, Arthur de 82, 84
Godoy, Hernán 32
Gómez, Sergio 189
Gonzalez Prada, Manuel 98, 109
gothic fox 177–80, 186
Great Britain 70–1, 74–5, 79, 90,
    174–5, 177, 192

Gruzinski, Serge 52
Guatemala 107, 203
Guimaraes Rosa, Joao 130
Güiraldes, Ricardo 95

Habermas, Jürgen 14, 39, 167,
    192, 208
hacienda 46, 72–4, 79, 81, 94–5,
    102, 198
Hale, Charles A. 73
Hall, Stuart 31, 34, 38
Halperin, Tulio 71, 79–80
Harris, Olivia 45
Harvey, David 16
Haya de la Torre, Víctor Raúl
    104
Hayek, F. A. 174–5, 190
Hegel, G. W. F. 12, 14, 57–8, 90,
    110, 128, 153, 159, 208
Henríquez, Camilo 75, 95–7
Henríquez Ureña, Pedro 95–7,
    109
Hernández, José 87
Hirszman, León 127
Hispanism 108–9, 112, 141–2,
    149, 154
Hollenweger, Walter 204
Honduras 107
Honneth, Axel 27–8
Hopenhayn, Martín 186
Horkheimer, Max 17, 59, 170
Hostos, Eugenio María de 76
human rights 135, 137, 152, 172,
    188, 194–5, 197, 202
Hume, David 54

Icaza, Jorge 95
identity
    agrarian 118
    as a project 39
    baroque 5, 176, 179, 180
    Brazilian 94, 108
    Catholic 201–2, 205
    class 41, 42, 78
    collective 9, 28, 30–4, 179
    colonial 60, 63, 65, 74, 76, 89
    crisis of 75–7, 95, 136, 141–2

cultural 3–7, 10, 24, 26, 31–5,
    38–9, 41, 61–2, 66, 81, 89,
    94, 107, 113, 141–2, 147–8,
    150–2, 155–6, 158–62, 165,
    179, 180, 182, 201, 206–7
    deep 143–4
    developmentalist 125, 187
    essentialist conceptions of 7,
        37–8
    ethnic 31, 42
    gender 42
    Hispanic 5, 49, 64, 143
    Indian 5, 147
    Latin American 1–11, 66, 76,
        97, 105, 107–9, 112–13,
        127–8, 137, 139, 141, 143,
        148–50, 153, 157, 160–2,
        176–9, 181, 189, 201, 206
    Mayan 147
    Meso-American 147
    mestizo 149–50, 158
    Mexican 147
    national 1–4, 9, 25, 33–7, 41–2,
        66, 78, 91, 108, 205
    Pentecostal 203–5
    personal 24, 26–8, 30–4, 39–42,
        189
    Portuguese 64
    qualitative 24
    religious 5, 66, 139, 151, 201–2,
        204–5
    sexual 42
    Venezuelan 148
    see also character, national
ideology 32, 153, 159
    liberal 81
    neoliberal 23, 172
    theory of 60
Imaz, José Luis de 61, 105, 195
immigration
    Chinese 79
    European 79, 85–6, 146, 198
    of inferior races 85
    Spanish 65
    white 85
imperialism 94, 104, 109, 124
    theory of 123

independence 4–9, 66, 70–5,
    77–80, 98, 109–13, 136, 139,
    151, 154–5, 159–61, 175, 177,
    194, 196
  wars of 1, 71, 75, 109
India 43, 46, 48, 143
Indiano 64, 149
Indians
  Aztecs 44, 46, 49
  Guaranies 72
  Mapuches 46, 72
  Pehuenches 83
  Quechuas 46, 72
Indigenismo 87, 94, 98–100, 104,
    109, 112, 141–2, 145, 148–9,
    151, 154
industrialization, import-
    substituting 93, 100, 124
Ingenieros, José 83, 84, 85, 159
Inquisition 60–1, 82, 177, 195
Instituto Superior de Estudos
    Brasileiros 125–6
Isaacs, Jorge 88
Isocrates 29

James, William 25
Japan 19, 20, 117
  Meiji rule 20–1
  Tokugawa rule 20
Jocelyn-Holt, Alfredo 70, 193, 196
Johnson, Richard 36–7

Kant, Immanuel 56
Kellner, Douglas 40
Keynes, John Maynard 173
Keyserling, Count 105
Kluckhohn, Clyde 31

ladino 146–7
  attitude 146–7
Lalive, Christian 205
Langon, Mauricio 143
Lastarria, José Victorino 77, 82
latifundia 46
  see also hacienda
Latorre, Mariano 95
Le Bon, Gustave 82, 84

learned hopelessness syndrome
    200
Lechner, Norbert 185
legalism 178, 197
Leite, D. M. 32
Letelier, Valentín 82
Lévi-Strauss, Claude 159, 164
Lezama Lima, José 130
liberalism 73–4, 80–2, 92, 174–5,
    192
liberation theology 151
Lillo, Baldomero 95
Linton, Ralph 31
Lira, Osvaldo 109, 111–12
literature, Latin American 137,
    150
  literary boom 123, 129–30
  magic realism 107, 130, 189
  mythical cities: Comala 2,
      130–1; El Valle 2; Macondo
      2, 130, 137; Rumí 2, 107;
      Santa María 2, 130
  new historical novel 137
  novel 2, 123, 129, 131–2
  real marvellous 108, 130
López de Avellaneda, Gertrudis 87
Lumbreras, Luis Guillermo 145
Lyotard, Jean François 182

McGrew, Antony 171
Machiavelli, Niccolo 12
Macondismo 137
Magariños, Alejandro 87
Malthus, Thomas 57
mameluco 85
Mansilla, Lucio 87
Maravall, J. A. 67
Marcuse, Herbert 17
marginality, social 72, 198–9, 204
Mariátegui, J. C. 99–100
Marín, Cristóbal 189
market forces 134–5, 172–3
Mármol, José 87
Martí, José 2, 95, 98, 131
Martin, David 203, 205
Martínez Blanco, M. T. 130
Martínez Estrada, Exequiel 106

Martins, Carlos Estevan 126
Marx, Karl 13, 17, 24, 90
Marxism 124, 126, 142, 145
Matto de Turner, Clorinda 87
Matul, Daniel Eduardo 147
Mayz Vallenilla, Ernesto 127
Mead, Margaret 28, 31
media 131, 135–6, 166–7, 169–71,
    188, 190–1, 193, 197
  electronic 39, 116, 169
Melgar, Mariano 75
Menton, Seymour 137–8
Mera, Juan León 87–8
Mercer, Kobena 8, 208
mestizaje 47, 76, 84, 89, 93–4,
    96–9, 108–9, 112, 142,
    148–50, 186, 198
  cultural 142, 148–51, 158
metanarratives 182, 184
Methol Ferré, Alberto 139–40,
    151–2, 159, 162
Mexico 2–4, 8, 23, 45–7, 53, 55,
    57, 65–6, 71, 74–5, 79–80, 82,
    88, 94–5, 98–9, 102, 104, 109,
    117, 135–6, 147, 174, 189,
    198
Miranda, Francisco de 76
mita 98
Mitre, Bartolomé 88
Moctezuma 44
mode of production 46–7, 145
  capitalist 13, 46, 123–4
  community-based 145
  servile 46
  slave 47
modernism 86, 88, 89, 94, 149
  Brazilian 94
  French 88
  Hispanic 94
modernity
  African 20
  baroque 66, 69, 156
  crisis of 18, 21, 92
  enlightened 4, 66–7, 69, 140,
    156, 159, 182
  European 4, 6, 14, 21–3
  late 33, 39–40, 166, 192

Latin American 5–6, 20, 136–7,
    139–40, 185, 191, 193–4,
    198–9, 201, 206
  liberal 18
  oligarchic 7, 22, 92
  organized 18, 21
  pseudo- 5, 139–40
modernization 18–20, 22, 66,
    70–1, 73, 81, 85–6, 89, 100,
    113–14, 116–18, 120–2,
    125–6, 129, 131–2, 135, 137,
    139–41, 155, 158, 161, 164–5,
    171–2, 176, 178, 180, 185–6,
    189, 198
  as opposed to modernity 185
  capitalist 124
  neoliberal 8, 23, 148, 186–7
  oligarchic 73
  populist 22, 92
  theories 5, 7, 23, 117–18,
    120–3, 160, 180–1
  Western 136
Monteagudo, Bernardo 76
Montero, Maritza 32
Montesinos, Antonio de 50
Montesquieu, Charles-Louis de
    Secondat Baron de 55, 60
Morales, Otto 150
Morandé, Pedro 66, 139–41,
    151–62, 165, 176, 178,
    206
More, Thomas 145
Morse, Richard 138–9, 141
Mosonyi, Emilio 148
Mouzelis, Nicos 100
movements, social 28, 42
  anti-racist 42
  feminist 42
  homosexual 42
Murena, H. A. 128–9
myth 158–9, 164, 198

nationalism 41, 115
nation-state 33, 41, 168
Nazism 92
neo-Indigenismo 142, 144, 146,
    151, 157

neoliberalism 135, 145, 157,
171–5, 181, 186–7, 189–90,
191, 199
Neruda, Pablo 2
Neves, Tancredo 188
New Right 192
new state 104
see also Estado Novo
Nicaragua 95, 203
Nietzsche, Friedrich 17
nordomanía 96, 147
Nyerere, Julius 102

O'Gorman, Edmundo 43
Onetti, Juan Carlos 2, 130
Ortega y Gasset, José 105
Ortiz, Renato 31, 108, 135
other
absent 40, 166–7
European 3
external 48
internal 48
Latin American 3, 4, 182
significant 26–7, 40, 107

Pagden, Antony 53, 64
pampa 78, 83, 87, 95, 106
Paraguay 57, 72, 195
Parker, Cristián 68, 140, 142,
156–7, 162–5
Pauw, Cornelius de 56–7
Paz, Octavio 5, 89, 106, 128–9,
138–9, 141, 143, 146–7, 153,
208
Pentecostalism 10, 151, 161,
203–6
peoples
new 63, 65
transplanted 65
without history 58, 128
witness 65, 66
world-historical 58
Pérez, Carlos 186–7
Peron, Juan Domingo 104
Peronism 104
Peru 3–4, 8, 45–7, 55, 57, 61,
65–6, 71–4, 79–80, 83–4, 93,

98, 104, 134–5, 194, 196–7,
199
Philip II 51
Pike, F. B. 109
Pinochet, Augusto 175, 188, 196,
199
pluralism 185, 201
Polanyi, Karl 92
Popular Front 101
populism 99, 101–2, 104, 113,
126
Portales, Diego 73, 196
Portugal 22, 46, 57, 64, 97
positivism 4, 81–2, 84, 86, 89, 93,
97
Posse, Abel 138
postmodernism 16–17, 19, 181–7
poverty 136, 141, 159, 174,
199–200, 204–5
Prado, Javier 83–5, 159
Prebisch, Raul 121
productive forces 13, 116
Programa de las Naciones Unidas
para el Desarrollo (PNUD)
141
protectionism 117
Protestantism 204, 206
Puerto Rico 72, 76

Quetzalcóatl 44
Quijano, Aníbal 146
Quiroga, Horacio 95

race
cosmic 96, 99
integral 96
racism 60, 81–2, 88, 89, 110, 146,
149, 163, 195, 197–8
radio 2, 9, 116–17, 135, 167,
189
rationality
Enlightened 152, 157
instrumental 17, 141, 146, 152,
154–7, 163, 200
sapiential 152, 163–4
rationalization 13, 17, 138, 155
Reagan, Ronald 135

reason
  instrumental 13, 59–60, 66, 69,
    142, 146, 148, 156, 159, 160,
    163–4, 182
  historical 146
  objective 59, 60
  subjective 59, 60
  technological 17
recession 133, 134
Reformation 138
regulation school 133
religion, popular 9, 142, 156, 162
religiosity, popular 5, 140, 152,
    154–6, 160–1, 206
repartimiento 98
Requirement 49–50
resentment 106–7
resistance 22, 28, 41, 44, 48, 62,
    71, 118, 137, 143–4, 171,
    176, 178–9, 184, 187, 202
revolution
  Bolivian 102
  bourgeois 100
  Cuban 116, 124, 131–2
  Hispano-American 77
  industrial 21, 93, 100, 178,
    180
  Latin American 132
  liberal 139
  literary 131
  Mexican 95, 102, 104
  neoliberal 190
  Russian 7, 92
  scientific 139
  socialist 124
  Spanish cultural 179
Ribeiro, Darcy 3, 62–3, 65, 126,
    208
Richard, Nelly 183–4, 187
Riva Agüero, José de la 109
Rivera, Eustasio 95
Roa Bastos, Augusto 130, 131
Rocha, Glauber 127
Rodó, José Enrique 95–6, 98, 109,
    146–7
Rodrigues, Nina 84–5, 97
Romero, Sílvio 84, 97

Rousseau, Jean Jacques 159
Rulfo, Juan 2, 130

Sábato, Ernesto 130
Sahagun, Bernardino de 29
Salas, Manuel de 77
Salazar Bondy, Augusto 90
Sambarino, Mario 3, 208
Samper, José María 76
San Miguel, Jerónimo de 50
Sapir, Edward 63
Sarmiento, Domingo Faustino
    82–3, 85–6, 95, 146, 159,
    180
Scannone, Juan Carlos 151–2,
    163–4
Schelling, F. W. von 58–9
Schwarts, Stuart 49, 64
Schwarz, Roberto 183
secularization 67, 151, 155–6, 161,
    201–2, 205
Sepúlveda, Juan 61, 204–5
Service, Elman 3
Sierra, Justo 82, 88, 196
Sigüenza y Góngora 53
Simmel, Georg 16, 25
slavery 29, 47, 49, 56, 58, 60–1,
    72, 82
  black 47, 58, 72
  Indian 49, 61
Slovenia 40
soap opera 2, 40, 136
  see also telenovela
social question 18, 20–2, 93, 94
socialism 99, 102, 104, 115,
    124–5, 134, 136, 145, 155,
    158, 172, 178
society, traditional 68, 118–19
solidarity 145–6, 152, 157, 163,
    198, 200–1
Soriano, Eduardo 137
Soviet Union 41, 115–16, 169
Spain 4, 22, 46, 48, 57, 60–2, 64,
    68, 70–1, 76–7, 109, 111,
    138–9, 153–4, 176–7
Spencer, Herbert 82, 84
structuralism 178

struggle for recognition 27, 28
    self-confidence 14, 27
    self-esteem 27, 143, 184
    self-respect 27
Suárez y Romero, Anselmo 87
Subercaseaux, Bernardo 90
Sunkel, Osvaldo 125

Taine, Hippolite 82
Tanzania 102
Taylor, Charles 27
telenovela 2, 136
    see also soap opera
television 23, 40, 116–17, 135,
    167–70, 188–9
Thatcher, Margaret 174–5
theology of liberation 202
Thompson, John 39–40, 117,
    167–8, 171
Todorov, Tzvetan 44–5, 50–1
Touraine, Alain 13, 140, 208
traditionalism 175, 191–3
    ideological 119, 192
trajectory to modernity 1, 6, 19,
    191, 207
    African 20
    Asiatic 23, 117, 174
    European 21, 74
    Latin American 22, 24, 174, 206
    North American 20

Ugarte, Manuel 95, 98
underdevelopment 123–4, 127,
    159, 205
United States 20, 31, 71, 76, 82–3,
    86, 94–7, 109, 115–16, 143,
    169, 177, 192–3
urbanization 141, 199

Uruguay 3–4, 9, 65, 80, 95, 134,
    137, 151, 195, 199
Uslar Pietri, Arturo 64, 88, 131,
    149, 150
utilitarianism 139

Valcárcel, Luis Eduardo 98–9
Valenzuela, Eduardo 102, 194
Vallejo, César 2
Vargas, Getulio 104, 108
Vargas Llosa, Mario 130–2, 138,
    190
Vasconcelos, José 95–9, 109,
    146–7
Vatican II Council 202, 205
Vega, Garcilaso de la 150
Vega, Gustavo 150
Véliz, Claudio 5, 68, 176–81, 186,
    208
Venezuela 2–4, 8, 73, 76, 79, 81,
    83, 94–5, 136, 149, 194
Vidal, Hernán 187
Vieira, Alvaro 126
Villaverde, Cirilo 88
Villegas, A. 104
Voltaire 55

Wachtel, Nathan 44–5, 52
Wagner, Peter 13, 15–16, 18–19,
    21, 68–9, 115, 208
Weber, Max 13, 17, 208
welfare state 18, 21, 23, 93, 103,
    116–17, 172–3, 199

Yugoslavia 30, 41

Zea, Leopoldo 60–1, 99, 105,
    155